CURRENT ISSUES IN CRIMINAL JUSTICE
(VOL. 6)

# INNOVATIVE TRENDS AND SPECIALIZED STRATEGIES IN COMMUNITY-BASED CORRECTIONS

GARLAND REFERENCE LIBRARY
OF SOCIAL SCIENCE
(VOL. 864)

# CURRENT ISSUES IN CRIMINAL JUSTICE

GENERAL EDITORS, FRANK P. WILLIAMS III AND MARILYN D. MCSHANE

STRANGER VIOLENCE
*A Theoretical Inquiry*
by Marc Riedel

CRIMES OF STYLE
*Urban Graffiti and the Politics
of Criminality*
by Jeff Ferrell

UNDERSTANDING
CORPORATE CRIMINALITY
edited by Michael B.
Blankenship

POLITICAL CRIME IN
CONTEMPORARY
AMERICA
*A Critical Approach*
edited by Kenneth D.
Tunnell

THE MANAGEMENT OF
CORRECTIONAL
INSTITUTIONS
by Marilyn D. McShane and
Frank P. Williams III

INNOVATIVE TRENDS AND
SPECIALIZED STRATE-
GIES IN COMMUNITY-
BASED CORRECTIONS
edited by Charles B. Fields

THE WINDS OF INJUSTICE
*American Indians and the
U.S. Government*
by Laurence Armand French

ALTERED STATES OF MIND
*Critical Observations of the
Drug War*
edited by Peter Kraska

CONTROLLING STATE CRIME
*An Introduction*
edited by Jeffrey Ian Ross

MEDIA, PROCESS, AND THE
SOCIAL CONSTRUCTION
OF CRIME
*Studies in Newsmaking
Criminology*
edited by Gregg Barak

# INNOVATIVE TRENDS AND SPECIALIZED STRATEGIES IN COMMUNITY-BASED CORRECTIONS

*Edited by*
Charles B. Fields

GARLAND PUBLISHING, Inc.
*New York & London / 1994*

**Library of Congress Cataloging-in-Publication Data**

Innovative trends and specialized strategies in community-based
corrections / edited by Charles B. Fields.
p. cm. — (Current issues in criminal justice ; vol. 6)
(Garland reference library of social science ; vol. 864)
Includes bibliographical references and index.
ISBN 0-8153-0986-4 (alk. paper)
1. Community-based corrections—United States—Evaluation.
2. Community-based corrections—United States—Management.
I. Fields, Charles B.  II. Series.  III. Series: Garland reference library of
social science. Current issues in criminal justice ; v. 6
HV9304.I56  1994
365'.6—dc20                                                          93-39859

Printed on acid-free, 250-year-life paper
Manufactured in the United States of America

# Contents

# Series Foreword

In a recent attempt at an innovative correctional strategy, seven young skinheads sat in a circle with survivors of the Holocaust, a black minister, and members of a campus coalition on cultural diversity. Having pled guilty to weapons and conspiracy charges, the self-proclaimed racists began a punishment carefully crafted into three days of discussion, a visit to a Holocaust museum, a movie on World War II concentration camps, and a meeting with inmates at the state prison. Part sensitivity training, part Scared Straight, customized punishments such as these are built on the popular belief that some things do work for some people. Across the country, offenders today are taking part in specially tailored programs, such as juvenile light opera, inner city cavalry, and coroner's autopsy tours. Although costly and only available on a limited basis, the success of programs that carefully match offenders and punishments has been supported in current evaluation research.

In reality, however, community corrections is not an "alternative" approach for a carefully selected few. It is and has been for years the mainstay of corrections. It is also the battleground of treatment and punishment methodologies. More than any other aspect of corrections, it directly involves the public and depends on its goodwill and support. The articles collected in this edition give us ideas for making the many complex relationships in this arena work and provide some reasons why they may have been less successful in the past.

If any aspect of community corrections is considered an alternative, it is perhaps intensive supervision which may, because of budget and space constraints, truly represent attempts to divert more serious offenders from incarceration.

The articles presented in this work give us insight into the controversies that currently surround its use. The reader is guided toward an understanding not only with the technical aspects of the operation of supervision but the more elusive philosophical questions as well.

In keeping with the tradition of this series, Charles Fields and his knowledgeable contributors have put together an interesting and highly readable book containing everything one needs to know about a particular aspect of crime and criminal justice today, in this case, community corrections. The challenges of community corrections are clear; it is our choice whether to meet them with enthusiasm and innovation or anguish in our past failures.

Frank P. Williams, III
Marilyn D. McShane

# Acknowledgments

I wish to acknowledge the support of several individuals who assisted in developing, organizing, and completing this edition. My colleagues at Appalachian State, especially Joel Thompson, encouraged the project and provided needed support at all stages. Richter Moore, mentor and friend, deserves a special note of thanks.

Frank Williams and Marilyn McShane, series editors of Current Issues in Criminal Justice and cherished friends, were instrumental in getting this book to press. Their comments, constructive criticisms, and suggestions for deletions and additions were extraordinarily helpful at all stages of this project. Phyllis Korper and Chuck Bartelt of Garland Publishing also deserve much of the credit.

Many thanks also to the chapter authors, who endured my seemingly endless procrastination and badgering: they were most patient.

Finally, I wish to dedicate this book to my wife, Penny Anne Robinette, whose love and friendship continue to sustain me. *Carpe diem, quam minimum credula postero!*

# Introduction

Throughout the country, probation as well as parole, the traditional community-based alternatives to incarceration, are in a state of transition. From probation being hailed as the "brightest hope for corrections" by the 1973 National Advisory Commission, through the "nothing works" sentiment averred by Robert Martinson and others, to the recent resurgence in the use of probation, a number of innovative and successful community-based strategies have emerged.

This renewed interest, coupled with the serious prison crowding situation, has led many jurisdictions to experiment with a range of seemingly innovative community treatment programs. Although the practice of processing and supervising offenders within the community is not new, recent applications in this area utilize a number of novel approaches that have only recently gained widespread acceptance.

The articles included in this collection comprise, in this editor's opinion, examples of some of the more unique and innovative programs in community-based corrections today. While not meant to be exhaustive, they nevertheless provide the reader with an overview of some of the most important and interesting practices currently in operation. They reflect a "renewed interest" in providing viable and acceptable alternatives to traditional incarceration.

# Intensive Supervision:
## Examining and Evaluating Policies and Practices

In the past ten years, intensive probation programs have gained widespread acceptance around the country, both as innovative solutions to prison overcrowding and as promising "tough" supervision for more serious and chronic offenders. But has it lived up to these promises? In the first chapter in this section, "Intensive Supervision: Why Bother?" Todd Clear and Anthony Braga address the historical problems of evaluating intensive supervision. They suggest that if we are to "bother" with the concept, we must redefine and clarify our goals. They conclude with a discussion of five principles that might aid us toward these ends.

The next two chapters deal with intensive supervision in Idaho and Texas, respectively. Classification and arbitrary overrides of probation classification instruments can sometimes contribute to client/offender litigation and judicial intervention. Jerry Beyer, in a study of an Idaho intensive supervision program (ISP) addresses specifically the decision to place selected offenders or deny participation in an ISP. Mark Jones and Terry Wells provide an excellent descriptive chapter on one of the oldest and most innovative intensive probation programs in existence—the Texas ISP.

In the final chapter in this section, Ed Latessa and Jill Gordon explore the issue of program effectiveness by examining various provisions of intensive supervision in Cuyahoga County, Ohio. Included in their analysis is an identification of the type of offenders being placed in the program, their likelihood of failure, and the identification of factors related to program outcome.

## Targeting Special Offender Populations

As acceptance of probation and other community-based alternatives continues, many feel that special offender populations could, in fact, benefit greatly from these programs. Christine Curtis, Darlanne Hoctor, and Susan Pennell in

"Intensive Supervision for Drug-Involved Probationers," report on an innovative approach to the treatment of drug offenders. Probationers in Recovery (PIR) is an intensive probation program in San Diego County (CA), and preliminary results suggest that this program may be successful in balancing the surveillance and treatment components for certain high-risk drug offenders.

The second chapter in this section, "Drug Abuse Treatment and Community Corrections: Findings from the Kentucky Substance Abuse Program," by Gerry Vito, focuses on a program designed to make substance abuse treatment available to probation and parole officers and their clientele. After four years of operation, the results of the KSAP evaluation demonstrate the effectiveness of the program for certain types of offenders.

In "Community Corrections for Spouse Abusers," Sue Mahan and Lori Osta report on an experimental program in one Florida jurisdiction developed in response to changes in the Florida criminal law with regard to spouse abuse. The PAVE (Providing Alternatives to Violence Through Education) program was instituted in 1991, and preliminary evaluation results demonstrate its effectiveness in providing short-term crisis intervention and skills training as immediate alternatives to spousal violence.

Electronic monitoring of offenders and court-ordered home detention have increased greatly over the past few years. In the final chapter in this section, Sudipto Roy provides a concise, although preliminary, examination of the EMHDP (Electronic Monitoring Home Detention Program) instituted in 1990 as a diversionary alternative for juvenile offenders in Lake County, Indiana.

## New Models for Community Supervision

A growing trend in community-based corrections is to combine a sense of punishment with increased control in probation. Reactions by offenders have resulted in increased numbers of absconders and revocations coupled with growing noncompliance with conditions of probation. The chapter by Faye Taxman and James Byrne examines the response of the Maricopa County, Arizona, probation department to this increase in absconders. Their study found that early identification by supervising probation officers, combined with proactive location and apprehension strategies, may result in lower rates of absconding.

The goal of vocational networks is to provide training and employment to offenders in the community by providing ways to network various community resources. Tom Tomlinson's chapter, "Reintegrating the Criminal Offender Through Community-Based Vocational Networks," describes four such networks. Funded by the Illinois State Board of Education, these four projects were developed to determine the most effective strategies in providing these services to offenders in the state. The projects indicate different degrees of success, but all have achieved the goal of securing employment for some types of offenders.

As more and more juvenile offenders come in contact with the justice system, they bring with them a variety of social and behavioral problems, including an increase in dysfunctional family structures. "The Probation Mentor Home Program: An Evaluation," by Chinita Heard, reports on an innovative community-based program for nonviolent juvenile offenders age ten to seventeen in Allen County, Indiana. Designed to place these offenders in a structured, stable foster home environment for a period of six months, the program's primary goal is to reintegrate them into their original homes.

The final chapter, by Dave Camp, deals with diversion centers in Georgia; specifically their staffing patterns and needs. One of the fastest-growing diversionary alternatives in the state, these centers provide judges with a cross between traditional probation and incarceration. Based on interviews with diversion center personnel, the results of the study indicate that they are a very diverse group with varied educational, career, and personal backgrounds who share a number of common jobs. An interesting historical review of the literature is included in the chapter.

# PART ONE

# Intensive Supervision: Examining and Evaluating Policies and Practices

# CHAPTER ONE

# Intensive Supervision: Why Bother?

*Todd R. Clear*
*Anthony A. Braga*

The question for anyone who wants to start an intensive supervision program (ISP) is very simple: "Why bother?" This may sound like a curious way to open a discussion of intensive supervision, but, as we shall see, the most pressing question about ISPs is also the most basic: "Why?"

Ten years ago, the Georgia Intensive Probation Supervision program was brand new and unevaluated. It was also widely hailed as an extremely innovative approach to Georgia's chronic problem of prison crowding, a problem not unlike that in most states around the United States. Georgia's highly acclaimed program eventually spawned innumerable copies around the country, partly because it was such a visible way of reasserting the field of community supervision, and partly because it promised something everybody wanted—a solution to prison crowding that left the community safe.

In the last ten years, the intensive supervision movement of the 1980s has been subjected to widespread evaluation. At least fifty papers, research reports, and monographs have been published evaluating ISPs. The results, as summarized below in one report, are not anything to celebrate:

- The ISPs did not alleviate prison crowding and may have actually increased it in some states.

- They cost considerably more than most advocates have realized, particularly if agencies incarcerate for technical violations and infractions.
- They were no more effective than routine supervision in reducing recidivism.  (Petersilia, Peterson, and Turner, 1992: 6)

So the question many people now ask is: "Has intensive supervision failed?" Like many questions about criminal justice policy, this one does not easily lend itself to a simple answer. To respond beyond mere glibness requires first an analysis of the nature of the popularity of ISPs, and then an evaluation of the role they have played in correctional policy.

## Getting Tough in the Community

The first thing to recognize when considering the recent rush toward ISPs is that the intention of these programs has been unabashedly to "get tough" with offenders. Perhaps this was an inevitable result of the envy most community supervision administrators felt when they considered how correctional budgets were allocated. In the 1980s, prison systems grew in size and in political influence. Even though community corrections agencies absorbed a greater increase in offenders than the prisons during the 1980s, it was the prison budgets that grew: increasing by about two-thirds in *real dollars* during the decade, while non-prison correctional budgets for traditional programs (probation and parole) remained stagnant (Austin, 1990).

The reason for the popularity of prisons lies in their imagery. A prison is an undeniable intrusion into a criminal's freedom. It restricts his movement, isolates him from family and friends, and represents a certain form of harshness that cannot be evaded. It is not coincidental that the growth of the prison occurred while citizens seemed to be calling for "tough" measures to deal with crime. The clarion call for harshness with offenders took two forms. First, there was a desire to increase the proportion of convicted felons sentenced to prison; thus, most states passed laws making certain offenses and offenders ineligible for probation. Second, there was a desire to increase prison terms; many sentencing codes were revised to lengthen maximum terms in prisons.

By comparison to prison, community supervision must have seemed puny to most citizens. Certainly, the national "get tough" movement in which we find ourselves has not been hospitable to the idea of community corrections. The political message has been that leniency is the "enemy" of all citizens; no better illustration of leniency could be found than to allow a convicted felon to continue to live in the community. To this public perception must be added the realities of modern probation, particularly in urban settings. Neglect in funding meant caseloads routinely in excess of 150 probationers, often as high as 300 or more (Cunniff and Shilton, 1991). Under these conditions, it was unusually good if an offender was seen even monthly, in office visits lasting fifteen minutes or less. No one pretended that such approaches were meaningful as crime control or service delivery.

But correctional administrators had a secret. They knew that time spent on community supervision need not be "easy" time, and they set about to design "tough" community supervision that would be palatable to a concerned public. One reason ISPs have been popular is because they appeal to both conservatives and liberals. For liberals, ISPs claim to divert prisoners from incarceration without appearing soft on crime; for conservatives, they claim to allow an increase in control over offenders without additional cost to corrections (Byrne, 1990a). These are hefty promises, indeed, for any program to live up to.

Critics have expressed some concern over ISPs becoming the next in a long line of failed panaceas (Byrne, 1990a). If ISPs promise more than they can deliver, then undoubtedly they will be viewed as failures when their shortcomings are realized (Clear and Hardyman, 1990). But perhaps equally important, we need to recognize that intermediate sanctions in general, and ISPs in particular, represent the latest of the correctional "bait and switch" tactics. In fact, it has been estimated that less than 5 percent of the total correctional population was under intensive supervision in 1989 (Byrne, 1990b). The public hears much about the impact (cost, diversion, recidivism) of these new intermediate sanctions, but everyone ignores the fact that it is "business as usual" for the vast majority of offenders supervised in community settings.

The elements of "tough" supervision are, by now, well known. The main component is heavy surveillance, in which offenders are put under various forms of scrutiny that are as close to the total control of the prison as possible. Thus, a person can be seen on a frequent but irregular schedule—the "rules" of control systems show that frequent, irregular monitoring provides superior control to other types of systems, even constant monitoring (Weinberg, 1975). The supervision schedule and supporting technologies can call for a myriad of controlling actions:

- Surprise (unannounced) visits by the probation officer to the offender's home at varying hours during the day or night.
- Routine visits by the officer to the offender's workplace.
- Regular urine tests to determine degree of drug use.
- Weekend or evening curfew.
- Electronically monitored house arrest.
- Mandatory attendance at school or employment.
- Mandatory involvement in treatment programs outside of probation.
- Regular reports to the probation officer.
- Routine inspection of pay stubs and other financial matters.
- "Collateral" contacts by the probation officer with friends, family, and neighbors.
- Restrictions on life choices: recreation, associations, living arrangements, etc.

This is, by any standard, a considerable list of inconveniences, restrictions, and limitations. But the annoyances of a "tough" supervision do not end there, for a number of punitive requirements can also be imposed:

- Monthly fees for supervision.
- Restitution.
- Court costs.
- Attorney fees.

- Fines.
- Payments to victim compensation funds.

The point of these lists is to demonstrate that community supervision need not be puny or lenient. Every ISP incorporates some or all of these restrictions, and nearly every ISP can revoke supervision for failure to abide by whatever restrictions are imposed. This fact is eloquently attested to by the numerous studies that have shown more ISP clients fail due to inability to live by its restrictions than by falling back into criminal ways. In Houston, four times as many ISP clients (21 percent) were imprisoned for technical violations when compared to regular supervision probationers (4 percent) (Petersilia, Peterson, and Turner, 1992), and in New Jersey's ISP, 30 percent failed due to rules violations, compared to 10 percent who failed due to a rearrest (Byrne, Lurigio, and Baird, 1989).

Cynics would still believe that, regardless of the type of restrictive "toughness," prison *has* to be a worse experience than community supervision can ever be. Not so—and offenders have voted with their feet to prove it. There are documented instances in which the restrictions of these programs are perceived by offenders to be so onerous that, when offered a chance to be in them, offenders choose incarceration instead. In Oregon, 25 percent of offenders eligible for ISP diversion chose the certainty of prison instead of the punitive conditions of intensive supervision (Petersilia, Peterson, and Turner, 1992). Apparently, these offenders would rather be incarcerated (knowing they would serve minimal time due to overcrowding) than be subject to ISP constraints.

## Who Is on ISP?

That these new programs have been "tough" is not subject to debate. What can be debated is the nature of the offenders placed in the programs—how tough are they?

ISPs draw from two different pools of clients. All the programs claim they are diverting people from prison, one way or another, but this is often a misrepresentation of ISP admission practices. In fact, the standard ISP draws its clients from among the most difficult offenders who are already under community supervision or are bound for such supervision. Instead of diverting from prison, the program is used to deal with offenders currently (or about to be) placed in the community for whom the traditional supervision is deemed inadequately intense.

As we shall see, this creates considerable problems for the "main payoff" of these programs—the claim that they save money. But it also creates supervision problems. This is due, in part, to the disorganized nature of the lives of the most difficult probation clients. They are not dangerous offenders. Indeed, almost all ISPs report extremely low rates of serious crime by program clients. Even the drug ISPs that Turner and Petersilia (1992) judged "failures" reported serious felony arrest rates of between 10 and 11 percent. But they are certainly persistent misbehavers. The most troublesome probation clients are often those who suffer from drug dependency, limited intellectual capacity, inability to exert self-control, or chronic disregard for authority. Looking back at the extraordinarily bothersome set of regulations such people must face, is it any surprise they so often fail to survive the rules? Even a saint might struggle to comply.

The problem is even more dramatic for the few programs that actually divert the prison-bound offender. This is so because the prison-bound offender who is eligible for ISP is typically, in fact, a *less* serious offender than the probation enhancement ISP counterpart. Diversion is being accomplished by combing through the ranks of the incarcerated to find those who are the least risky and least serious offenders. Due to sentencing disparity and ambiguity about sentencing goals, there are always examples of the petty type of offender to place in these programs.

ISP programs typically claim to work with "high risk" or "dangerous" offenders. However, the ISP client is not the predatory criminal we are led to believe. Target group selection rules often exclude offenders with a long criminal history or a violent current offense (Clear and Hardyman, 1990). These exclusionary criteria restrict the target group to one that is not likely to have "high risk" or "dangerous" clients. In fact, some clients who are ineligible for ISP may be eligible for regular supervision (Clear and Hardyman, 1990). Hence, ISP clients are often not a considerably higher threat to the community than regular probationers.

The presence of a long list of "tough" requirements for these less problematic offenders raises a different kind of logical problem: why the heavy emphasis on control? Since their arrival on ISP represents a replacement for a jail or prison term, one can understand onerous restrictions on their freedom. Yet, on the other hand, they represent such an unremarkable risk to the community that it is hard to justify the intensity of control resources they receive, compared to other offenders. Put in another way, the "best" risk offenders are diverted from prison and watched closely under ISP rules to see if there is evidence of misconduct of any kind. The "worst" risks are released to regular parole supervision, where they may receive little or no effective control. It does seem a backwards application of resources, all to make up for the fact that some people are going to institutions who could well be kept under community supervision.

## Why, Then, Doesn't ISP Save Money?

The ingredients of the ISP, then, are these: very strict strategies of supervision applied to either persistent probation nuisances or petty offenders bound for prison. This is why they cannot save money. With the persistent probation offender, the closer one watches, the more one is likely to see behavior that raises official hackles. This is also true for the prison-bound offender, though here, as we shall see, there is at least a chance to emerge with a few pennies saved, if the program is run correctly.

But the most common variety of ISP—the so-called "probation enhancement" program—is almost a guarantee to cost more money than it saves. After all, these programs *start out* costing up to ten times more money per client than "regular" probation. Then, because they are so "tough," these "probation enhancements" result in more technical violations, subsequent court appearances, and incarcerations. No wonder this results in expenditures twice that of ordinary probation *and* increases the prison crowding problem (Petersilia, Peterson, and Turner, 1992).

Most ISPs claim to reduce costs because they divert offenders from prison. But do intensive supervision programs that provide a diversionary impact actually save money? The answer is no. In Oregon's diversion program, evaluators discovered that ISP costs were 75 percent of prison costs to begin with (Petersilia, Peterson, and Turner, 1992). Since then, half of the ISP clients recidivated and were incarcerated, while almost half of the prisoners served short prison terms (Petersilia, Peterson, and Turner, 1992). As a result, the overall costs of the two sanctions are comparable.

Tonry (1990) identifies two problems with diversionary ISPs. First, there are problems with the use of ISP for offenders who were not prison bound. Half of the offenders of Georgia's ISP, for instance, got there by an amended sentence, suggesting a questionable true diversionary effect. Some have argued that New Jersey's ISP, which takes offenders directly from prison, has inadvertently resulted in some probation cases being sent to prison so they will be eligible for the program. Second, high revocation rates due to close surveillance undercut the ISP's ability to reduce prison populations. In Georgia, only half of ISP offenders successfully complete the program (Petersilia, 1987); in New Jersey, close to 50 percent return to prison, usually for a technical violation (Pearson and Harper, 1990). When high revocation rates are combined with the use of ISP for offenders who were not prison bound, it becomes apparent that the net effect of ISPs may be to increase prison populations (Tonry, 1990).

Since an ISP's cost effectiveness is directly related to its diversionary impact, the available evaluation research indicates that these programs have had only a limited effect on prison populations. Some critics (see Tonry, 1990) suggest that these programs have not diverted offenders from prison at all, due to net widening effects. If this is true, then addition of an ISP will not result in an overall cost saving for the department launching the program (see Byrne, 1990b; US GAO, 1990). In fact, it is possible for these programs to increase the total overall cost for the department.

## Why Should Probation and Parole Be Responsible for Solving the Prison Crowding Crisis?

We often discuss the problem of institutional over-crowding, but neglect to mention the crowding problems of community corrections. Between 1980 and 1989, the total corrections population rose from 1,842,121 to 4,059,433 (an increase of 120 percent) (Dillingham and Greenfield, 1991). Corrections did not expand resources to an equivalent degree during this period. In 1988, 306 jails and the entire prison system in ten jurisdictions were under court order to limit the number of inmates held due to overcrowded conditions (Bureau of Justice Statistics, 1991). In the past decade, the prison population has more than doubled, while prison capacity has not increased at the same rate.

The typical response to alleviate some of the pressure caused by today's correctional crowding problem has been to increase the use of community corrections (i.e., probation and parole). However, probation and parole populations grew at an even faster rate than prison populations, while resources did not proportionately increase. Probation receives less than one-third of correctional resources, while almost two-thirds of convicted adult offenders are sentenced to probation (Byrne, Lurigio, and Baird, 1989). In addition, an increasing number of new admissions to prison are probation and parole failures. Given these overcrowded conditions, how can probation and parole be expected to absorb the overflow of prison crowding?

Various factors are linked to institutional and community corrections crowding; however, shifts in judicial decision making and legislation are often discussed as having the greatest impact. Irwin and Austin (1987) argue that the nation's population and crime rates have remained relatively constant over the past ten years, while correctional populations have skyrocketed. The increase in incarcerations is more the result of "harsher" sentencing legislation and sentencing than rates of crime. If the primary cause of the crowding problem is legislative change, then why should community corrections be responsible for the crowding crisis?

To hold probation and parole responsible for alleviating institutional crowding is both a penological non sequitur and a strategic error. It is a penological non sequitur because the probation and parole systems *feed* the correctional populations. In some states, as many as one-third of the new entries into prison populations are revocations from community supervision—it is unlikely that the construction of "tougher" supervision practices will have any effect other than exacerbating this problem. Besides, the forces that drive population stem from government agencies over which community supervision has virtually no influence.

As a strategic error, using community supervision to "solve" crowding is an immense displacement of its goals. Community supervision "works" when it is designed to deal with the individual characteristics of offenders on its caseload (Gendreau and Ross, 1987). To shift the emphasis away from offender case management toward system workload management may have the deleterious effect of damaging the very tasks community supervision does best.

## What If We Decided That We Didn't Have To Get Tough for Its Own Sake?

Most ISPs are designed to reduce recidivism of the offender in the community through the use of increased surveillance and control. But does increased surveillance ("getting tough") actually reduce recidivism? The results from an experiment comparing regular probation and ISP in California do not support that claim (Petersilia and Turner, 1990). The ISP groups had two to three times the surveillance intensity of the regular probation group, yet there was no difference in arrest rates (Petersilia and Turner, 1990). If the increased monitoring affects arrest rates, then there should have been a lower arrest rate for the ISP participants. Higher surveillance levels for the experimental groups did not result in a reduction in recidivism. Generally, experimental and control groups were not significantly different in percentage of offenders employed or percentage of offenders in counseling, either.

If "getting tough" is not effective in recidivism reduction, then what can be done to improve these programs? Byrne (1990b) suggests that if the emphasis of these programs on treatment was increased, then there might be a reduction in recidivism rates. The results of the Massachusetts ISP evaluation seem to support this proposition. "It appears that the effect of the surveillance component (i.e., contacts) of the Massachusetts ISP program was indirect, through its effect on the offender change measures (in employment, substance abuse, and marital/ family problems)" (Byrne, 1990b: 7). This finding suggests that there is an interaction between surveillance and treatment, and if we want to reduce recidivism, there should be an emphasis on treatment as supported by surveillance.

## Why Bother?

Traditionally, we talk about effectiveness using evaluation outcomes, i.e., we talk about the cost, diversionary impact, and recidivism reduction effects of ISPs. As we have seen, an examination of ISP performance using these outcome measures reveals dismal results. Moreover, our policy analysis suggests ISP is unlikely to improve its performance in these goals. Thus we return to the original question: "Why bother?"

Some have suggested (see von Hirsch, 1990; von Hirsch, in press; Petersilia and Turner, 1990) that we may now need to think in terms of the effectiveness of ISPs simply as a punishment (or "just deserts"). From this perspective, an ISP would be viewed as successful if it provides a level of punishment consistent with the stated sentence of the judge (e.g., in terms of limitations on movement, hours of community services, contact levels, required drug tests, etc.). An ISP could be an effective intermediate punishment that is commensurate with the seriousness of certain acts. Indeed, there is a need in society for a penalty on the punishment continuum somewhere between traditional probation and incarceration. To refocus ISPs as a punishment for crimes of middle-range seriousness might be an important way to salvage the value of these programs.

However, the concept of punishment limits the ability of community supervision to intervene in the lives of offenders (Clear and O'Leary, 1984). This approach is only concerned with punishing the offender for a crime and is not directly interested in preventing or limiting the risk of future crimes. Yet, as we have seen, one of the few potential benefits of an ISP can be achieved through its role of changing behavior, and to refocus ISPs in a way that rejects that objective seems unsound.

This brief discussion of ISPs as "punishment" suggests that if we are to "bother" with ISP, then we must clarify our goals. Let us suggest a few principles that might guide these efforts:

1. *If ISPs are to alleviate the prison crowding problem, then these programs must be targeted at prison-bound offenders.* A considerable amount of non-prison-bound offenders are placed in ISPs who neither deserve the punishment nor need the control these programs provide. If the goal is to reduce the prison population through diversion of offenders, then it is crucial that the correct target population be selected. Otherwise, the goal of population reduction will not be achieved. Yet, if these programs are even to alleviate prison crowding, then once an offender is accepted into them, every effort must be made to *avoid* revocation and return to prison.

2. *If the primary goals of an ISP are crime control and community protection, then there must be a focus on high-risk cases.* As prior evaluators have suggested, an ISP "success would be viewed as the identification and quick revocation of persons who are committing crimes" (Petersilia and Turner, 1991: 657). Available evaluation research indicates that ISPs are effective in detecting subsequent technical violations and offender recidivism. When dealing with high-risk offenders, increased arrest rates could be viewed as indicators of program prosperity, not failure. Since ISPs emphasize surveillance

and control of the offender in the community, it makes sense that programs should be evaluated based on crime control criteria (higher arrests, etc). Obviously, these programs will not save money or reduce prison populations.

3. *Intensive supervision can be valuable as a method for improving informal social control over offenders.* Some have argued that ISPs can be effective in changing the behavior of offenders by increased informal social control (see Whitehead and Lindquist, 1992; Byrne, 1990a). Informal social controls are a consequence of interactions with family, peers, employment, and the community. These areas are traditional targets for probation officer intervention (Byrne, 1990a). An ISP's higher contacts between probation officer and probationer can develop these relationships and attachments. As a result, these offenders could become more deeply integrated into the community and, in the long run, commit less crime.

4. *ISPs must avoid toughness just to be "tough" because to do so must inevitably backfire.* The primary objective of the Texas drug ISP was to reduce the state's prison crowding problem, but the focus of the program consisted of increased offender control and surveillance. The "toughness" of the program structure made it difficult for participants to comply with the increased contacts. Between 70 and 80 percent of ISP parolees tested positive for drug use at least once (Turner and Petersilia, 1992). After one year, 30 percent of ISP participants were returned to prison, as compared to 18 percent of those on routine parole (Turner and Petersilia, 1992). As a result, the program did not result in any prison population reduction and it cost nearly twice as much as routine parole. The experience of the Texas program mirrors that of many others around the country. If the objective of the program is to keep prison populations down, then ISP methods must create conditions that make this more possible, not impossible.

The veneer of "toughness" is not much more than a guarantee of program failure for most clients.

We believe that two types of limits on "toughness" are potentially very useful. First, the ISP agency must be circumspect in the types of conditions it sets for its clients. Any condition that is merely "tough," but not directly related to the aims of community safety or punishment *for that particular client* is an invitation for the client to fail in a way that achieves no legitimate program goal. Therefore, ISPs should have *fewer*, not more conditions. Second, there should be limits on the amount of prison or jail time that is imposed for ISP failures. "Program" failures—technical violators—should never serve more than three to six months for their violations. ISP clients who are rearrested should serve only the sentence for their new crime, once they are convicted.

5. *We must investigate the value of the intrusiveness of any coercive treatments.* Treatment attempts to achieve a permanent change in the thinking, feeling, or behavior patterns of offenders so they will no longer commit crimes (Clear, 1991). What ISPs do in the community, by strictly enforcing treatment provisions, is by definition intrusive. In addition, they are punitive because they limit the freedom of offenders by making them experience treatment. Future research on ISP will help us sort out whether the treatment aims are more effectively achieved from the punitive aims. Yet, regardless of this question, we already know that offenders will be inconvenienced by bothersome mandatory conditions as part of their sentence. By limiting their freedom, we are controlling their behavior in the community. The intrusiveness of these treatments can be ranked and made proportional in order to target different levels of risk and crime seriousness (see Clear and O'Leary, 1984). This approach will aid in solving the net-widening dilemma and increase the prospects of ISPs changing offender behavior.

# REFERENCES

Austin, James (1990). "America's Growing Correctional–Industrial Complex." *NCCD Focus.*

Bureau of Justice Statistics (1991). *Sourcebook of Criminal Justice Statistics 1990.* Washington, DC: Bureau of Justice Statistics.

Byrne, James M. (1990a). "The Future of Intensive Probation Supervision and the 'New' Intermediate Sanctions." *Crime and Delinquency* 36 (1): 6–41.

—— (1990b). "Assessing What Works in the Adult Community Corrections System." Paper presented at the annual meeting of the Academy of Criminal Justice Sciences, Denver, CO (March).

Byrne, James M., Arthur Lurigio, and S. Christopher Baird (1989). "The Effectiveness of the 'New' Intensive Supervision Programs." *Research in Corrections* 5: 1–70.

Clear, Todd R. (1991). "Juvenile Intensive Probation Supervision: Theory and Rationale." In *Intensive Interventions with High-Risk Youths,* edited by Troy L. Armstrong. Monsey, NY: Willow Tree Press.

Clear, Todd R., and Patricia Hardyman (1990). "The New Intensive Supervision Movement." *Crime and Delinquency* 36 (1): 42–60.

Clear, Todd R., and Vincent O'Leary (1984). *Controlling the Offender in the Community.* Lexington, MA: Lexington Books.

Cunniff, Mark A., and Mary K. Shilton (1991). *Variations of Felony Probation Persons Under Supervision in 32 Urban and Suburban Counties.* Washington, DC: Bureau of Justice Statistics.

Dillingham, Steven D., and Lawrence A. Greenfield (1991). "An Overview of National Corrections Statistics." *Federal Probation* 55 (2): 27–34.

Gendreau, Paul, and Robert R. Ross (1987). "Revivification of Rehabilitation: Evidence from the 1980s." *Justice Quarterly* 4 (3): 349–408.

Irwin, John, and James Austin (1987). *It's About Time: Solving America's Prison Crowding Problem.* San Francisco, CA: National Council on Crime and Delinquency.

Pearson, Frank S., and Alice Harper (1990). "Contingent Intermediate Sentences: New Jersey's Intensive Supervision Program." *Crime and Delinquency* 36 (1): 75–86.

Petersilia, Joan (1987). "Georgia's Intensive Probation: Will the Model Work Elsewhere?" In *Intermediate Punishments: Intensive Supervision, Home Confinement, and Electronic Surveillance,* edited by Belinda McCarthy. Monsey, NY: Willow Tree Press.

Petersilia, Joan, and Susan Turner (1990). "Comparing Intensive and Regular Supervision for High-Risk Probationers: Early Results from an Experiment in California." *Crime and Delinquency* 36 (1): 87–111.

Petersilia, Joan, and Susan Turner (1991). "An Evaluation of Intensive Probation in California." *Journal of Criminal Law and Criminology* 82 (3): 611–658.

Petersilia, Joan, Joyce Peterson, and Susan Turner (1992) (working draft). *Intensive Probation and Parole: Research Findings and Policy Implications.* Santa Monica, CA: Rand Corporation.

Tonry, Michael (1990). "Stated and Latent Features of ISP." *Crime and Delinquency* 36 (1): 174–191.

Turner, Susan, and Joan Petersilia (1992). "Focusing on High-Risk Parolees: An Experiment to Reduce Commitments to the Texas Department of Corrections." *Journal of Research in Crime and Delinquency* 29 (1): 34–61.

U.S. General Accounting Office (1990). "Intermediate Sanctions: Their Impacts on Prison Crowding, Costs, and Recidivism Are Still Unclear." Washington, DC: U. S. General Accounting Office.

von Hirsch, Andrew (1990). "The Politics of Just Deserts." *Canadian Journal of Criminology* 32 (2): 397–413.

——— (in press). "Scaling Intermediate Punishments: Morris–Tonry Proposals." In *Smart Sentencing: The Emergence of Intermediate Sanctions,* edited by James Byrne, Arthur Lurigio, and Joan Petersilia. Newbury Park, CA: Sage.

Weinberg, Gerald M. (1975). *An Introduction to General Systems Thinking.* New York: John Wiley and Sons.

# CHAPTER TWO

# Assignment to Intensive Supervision: An Assessment of Offender Classification and Subjective Override in the State of Idaho

*J. Arthur Beyer*

In recent years, jail and prison overcrowding has been identified as one of the most pressing issues facing the criminal justice system (Gettinger, 1984; Skovron, 1988; Klofas, 1991). Ostensibly, the problem stems from continuing public concern over what is taken to be high rates of crime. In response, the public has demanded that more resources be devoted to law enforcement and more stringent sanctions be assessed against criminal offenders; governmental reaction to these demands has resulted in burgeoning jail and prison populations (Clear and Hardyman, 1990; Colson and Van Ness, 1988; Petersilia, 1986; Krajik and Gettinger, 1982; Silberman, 1980).[1]

During the eight-year period from 1978 to 1986, jail populations increased by 73 percent, with only a 16 percent increase in rated jail capacity (Mancini, 1988). On any given day in 1985, 3 million, or one of every fifty-eight adults in the United States, were either incarcerated or under some form of community supervision; by 1989, one of every forty-five U.S. adults were under correctional supervision and the total correctional population had increased to more than 4 million adults (Bureau of Justice Statistics, *Probation and Parole, 1989*, 1990).

A report released by The Sentencing Project in Washington, D.C., in January of 1991 acknowledged the United States as having achieved yet another world leadership position, that of having the highest rate of incarceration. According to the report, the United States assumed this singular position with an incarceration rate of 426 per 100,000, followed by South Africa (333 per 100,000), and the Soviet Union (268 per 100,000). Interestingly, the rate of incarceration in the United States for black males is 3,109 per 100,000, compared with 729 per 100,000 in South Africa (Mauer, 1991).

## Introduction

The increase in prison and jail population in many jurisdictions has resulted in judicial intervention requiring local governments to reduce inmate populations and/or improve conditions of confinement (Krantz, 1981; Welsh et al., 1991). To relieve prison overcrowding, criminal justice administrators have been challenged with the task of developing innovative methods for dealing with those individuals who are placed under correctional custody. An approach to managing the correctional system overload which has received extensive attention is known as the intensive supervision program (ISP); the level of contemporary interest in ISPs is reflected in the January 1990 issue of *Crime and Delinquency*, which is devoted entirely to adoption and operation of ISPs.

ISPs can assume a number of forms of jail or prison "relief valves" by providing either for diversion or early release (or some combination of these actions). ISP placement of offenders under some level of community supervision is accomplished either by the courts placing convicted adult felons on probation, or through early release and parole from prison.

There are fundamental similarities between ISPs in that they are all designed to extract a high degree of accountability from the individual being supervised. Accountability is reinforced through "intense" contact with the client, which may vary in intensity from one contact per week to daily face-to-face contacts; in some programs and jurisdictions, contact may be made without notice at any time of the day or night. Finally, programs may be designed to address either high- or low-risk offender-clients, based on the offender population that elected officials and correctional managers decide to focus on. ISPs commonly include provisions for mandatory participation in rehabilitative efforts, and in some cases entail the imposition of remote location constraints such as electronic monitoring, house arrest, and similar conditions of off-site supervision.

The concept of community-based intensive supervision of convicted offenders has received wide attention for several years. California should perhaps be credited with introducing the idea of ISPs into modern-day criminological practice. In the 1960s, that state introduced a program designed to reduce the rates of recidivism[2] experienced by high-risk parolees; general interest in the program declined, however, when a formal evaluation indicated that recidivism rates for ISP parolees was not significantly affected by participation in the program (University of California, School of Criminology, 1967).

Some ten years after the California experience, the state of Washington, taking a similar approach to managing low-risk probationers, implemented an ISP as a diversion from incarceration. It "was initiated in June 1976 to provide . . . [an] alternative to lengthy incarceration for low-risk felons" (Fallen et al., 1981). Since these initial efforts in California and Washington, interest in ISP programs has grown steadily. By June 1986 some twenty-nine states had adopted various forms of the ISP, and four others were awaiting legislative approval or funding for similar programs (Byrne, 1986). By 1990, more than forty states had adopted ISPs, and support for these programs continued to increase (Lurigio, 1990).

A basic premise of all correctional programs, including ISPs, is the placement of offenders in the least restrictive environment possible consistent with the requirements of legislative intent, public safety, and judicial edict. This premise is reflected in the various sanctions[3] and approaches available to the criminal justice system decision makers when they address and target high-risk or low-risk offenders.

A formal decision regarding the systematic placement of offenders is essentially a public policy decision which "requires not only good information about what is at stake but also conclusions about how to weight these considerations when they come into conflict" (Kelman, 1987). In this regard, it has been argued that the selective placement of offenders in ISPs in communities does not adversely affect the public safety to any serious extent (Fallen et al., 1981). According to a number of empirical studies, the correctional goals of deterrence, retribution, restitution, and rehabilitation can be achieved at least as effectively through community supervision as through incarceration (Krajik and Gettinger, 1982).

At the operational level, a decision to reduce jail and prison populations by the selective release of offenders into the community is theoretically based on the careful application of some criteria which accurately assess the potential risk that offenders present to society. Offenders are thus classified as presenting either an acceptable level of risk for community supervision or as presenting an unacceptable risk requiring incarceration.

## Predictions of Risk

Virtually all professions are required to make predictions. Whether they are called economic forecasts, revenue projections, medical prognoses, demographic projections, or simply "ball park," predictions are a common feature of governmental operations. Prediction is an inherent part of rational decision making, which implies an appropriate choice between alternatives entailing differing predicted outcomes. The decision made may not represent the perfect solution to a problem, but given the information available, it is the optimal choice. Given the twin objectives of the criminal justice system to both ascribe the minimal necessary restriction of liberty required to "correct" misconduct *and* reduce the incidence of criminal behavior of community supervised offenders, it is necessary to limit both false positive (overestimation of risk) and false negative (underestimation of risk) predictions by optimizing the decision to incarcerate or release offenders.

Probation and parole classification instruments produce predictions of the risk that an offender presents to the community and reflect an identification of the form of correction the offender needs to make a successful return to liberty. The effectiveness of these instruments in producing accurate predictions, however, is in some question; "critics claim that predictions are too inaccurate to serve as the basis for limiting the liberty of any individual" (Morris and Miller, 1987). A Rand Corporation study involving parolees, cited by Henry Steadman, found that "the best statistical prediction of violent reconviction achieved only a 71 percent accuracy, as compared with the chance probability (the 'base rate' of the behavior) of 68 percent" (Steadman, 1987).

In response to the critics' argument, proponents assert that if the instrument is both reliable and valid, predictions of risk for individuals "do permit identification of *groups* of offenders who pose sharply different levels of risk" (Toborg and Bellassi, 1987: 104), and we can accordingly make a "probabilistic statement about future behavior" of group members (Miller, 1987).

Predictions are of three types: *clinical*, which are based on expert diagnosis and evaluation; *anamnestic*, which are based solely on an individual's prior behavior; and *statistical* (or actuarial), which are based on individual behavior patterns in comparison with similar behavior patterns of others (p. 40).

> Statistical predictions are the preferred method of prediction because they can be tested and are open to scientific challenge. They are easier to understand and use. Indeed, psychological theory has not been found as effective as statistical theory in selecting what is relevant to and important in predicting behavior. There have been no demonstrations that the addition of an individualized clinical element in predictions can improve upon actuarial predictions of group behavior. (Morris and Miller, 1987: 3)

In spite of the assertion that statistical methods of prediction are far superior to clinical prediction, certain issues that affect the adequacy of the prediction must be addressed; specifically, the base rate problem, the cross-validation problem, the validity problem, and the reliability of the predictors. The base rate problem deals with the relative frequency of occurrence of a phenomenon within a given population; "in order to be operationally useful, a device must demonstrate predictive power better than that which would result from simple use of the base rate alone" (Gottfredson and Gottfredson, 1982). The cross-validation problem, which is derived from the characteristics of the sample that are tested, is resolved by developing the prediction instrument with one random sample and then applying the device to a second similar random sample. The validity and reliability problems are inextricably linked and are best dealt with together.

Validity deals with operationalization of variables; that is, are the actual variables employed truly reflective of the criteria used for determining the threat or danger that an offender presents to another individual or the community. Reliability is "whether a particular technique, applied repeatedly to the same object, would yield the same result each time" (Babbie, 1989). For example, if we repeatedly place a weight on a scale and the scale gives the same reading of fifty grams each time, we can say that the scale is reliable; what we would not know is how valid the measurement is; that is, is the measure of fifty grams consistently higher or lower than the "true" weight of the object in question.

The development of predictors that are both reliable and valid represents a substantial challenge to criminal justice decision processes. Sentencing, for example, in some important sense represents a process of evaluating and weighing criteria which are theoretical predictors of the threat an offender presents to the community. Through the application of such weighted criteria, offenders can be classified as unacceptable risks and fit for incarceration or as acceptable risks and fit for probation and release to a community corrections program.

## Classification

The primary objective of criminal justice classification is the protection of the public. The classification of offenders is a principal management technique employed by judicial and correctional administrators to allocate resources efficiently for the placement and supervision of offenders (Beyer, 1987). The most ambitious offender classification study was conducted by the Wisconsin Bureau of Community Corrections over the period 1975–1979; the resulting instrument has become a national standard and is the basis of the National Institute of Justice Classification Model.

> Although the factors analyzed explained only 58 percent of the variance in criminal behavior, the results proved sufficient to classify clients in less precise rankings. . . . Utilizing these rankings and comparing them to predicted scores indicated that, overall, 72 percent of the cases were "placed" correctly. (Baird et al., 1984)

In the opinion of some researchers, the two-scale (risk/need) Wisconsin Classification Model has been shown to be an effective management tool for predicting levels of intervention necessary for community supervised clients (Baird et al., 1984; Baird, 1981). The risk scale measures the client's tendency to engage in further criminal activity, and the need scale represents a measurement of problems and deficits suffered by the client which are thought to predispose individuals to criminal behavior.

The Idaho Department of Corrections (ID-DOC) adopted the Wisconsin model[4] for the classification of probation and parole clients. The instrument was modified to reflect the values and demographics of the state of Idaho, yet it appears that there has been no research to validate the modified instrument.

Idaho's failure to evaluate the predictive strength of the *new* instrument gives rise to the problem of cross-validation between jurisdictions (Wisconsin and Idaho). It is not known if the classification variables are predictive for Idaho; accordingly, arbitrary modification and weighing of values may well invalidate the instrument for use in Idaho. If predictive criteria are to be used, it is necessary to demonstrate that "they help to discriminate between the groups of persons" (Gottfredson and Gottfredson, 1982: 93) who do not reoffend while participating in the ISP from those who do.

## The Idaho Intensive Supervision Program

In the judicial district used for this study, an ISP team consisting of one supervisor and two probation/parole officers monitors the activities of twenty-five clients on a 24–hour basis; no electronic devices are employed. The caseload is limited to a maximum of twenty-five clients; on any given day there may be between three and five clients awaiting assignment to the ISP.

Under the Idaho program, during the first two months of participation, a supervising officer makes face-to-face contact with the client a minimum of seven times per week. In addition, weekly collateral contacts with the employer and service providers are made to verify both employment and therapeutic progress.

As part of the ISP supervision process, the client is provided with a schedule of assigned activities for each 24-hour day. The schedule is designed to inform both the client and the officer where the client is located at any given time; the officer is therefore able to make unannounced visits in an attempt to reinforce positive behavior (compliance) and to detect negative behavior (noncompliance). During the final four months, contact may be decreased to four face-to-face contacts per week, with other conditions subject to modification as deemed appropriate by the supervising officer and approved by the supervisor.

Inasmuch as the ISP is less costly than housing high-risk offenders in a secure facility, it is an attractive alternative to incarceration. However, it is substantially more expensive than regular supervision wherein a single officer may supervise 100 or more clients. Given the additional expense of supervising an offender in an ISP, it is necessary for the correctional manager to identify those offenders who would risk what freedom is afforded while participating on probation or parole. By placing those offenders who present the greatest perceived risk to the community in an ISP, the community is afforded protection from the offender, and the "intensive" contact can have both a therapeutic affect and a preventive effect.

From a practical or "political" perspective, it is further necessary to identify those offenders who present an unacceptable "psychological threat" to the community either by virtue of the type of offense they committed (e.g., sexual molestation of a child), or due to media coverage of a "celebrated case" (e.g., organized crime figure). By use of a subjective override, the correctional manager is able to place those lower-risk offenders on the more restrictive ISP. Approaching the placement of potential ISP clients from this combination of objective and subjective perspectives, the managers of the corrections system seek to use their resources in a politically responsive manner which promotes both public safety and the wise use of available resources.

Two specific evaluative questions guide the analysis to follow. First, does the Idaho classification instrument, as used in the judicial district under study, reliably predict risk of reoffending and violation of conditions of release among offenders assigned to the ISP? Second, do those offenders assigned to the ISP as overrides constitute an actual psychological threat to the community or a political threat to the criminal justice system?

In theory, clients assigned to a high-risk ISP, such as is practiced in Idaho, present a greater risk to the public than do regular supervision clients. By virtue of the intent of the classification instrument, a supervision level of "maximum" based on a risk score reflects a substantial threat to the community on the part of the offender. A valid assumption is that the greater the classified risk, the greater the likelihood of failure.

It should be noted, however, classification at a maximum level of supervision might indicate an extraordinary *need* on the part of the client for help with problems. Similarly, some offenders are products of overrides as indicated above. Notwithstanding these exceptions:

> The null hypothesis is that classification levels for ISP supervision are not predictive of the threat or danger an offender presents to the community and thus there will be no difference in success/failure rates based on classification levels.

# Methodology

Between the time the ISP was adopted in Idaho in December 1984 and November 1987, 223 clients entered the program in the judicial district under study. According to ID-DOC data, 125 clients had completed the program, 25 were still participating, 46 had absconded supervision, 21 had received technical violations for failure to adhere to the assessed conditions or for use of alcohol or drugs, and 6 had committed new felonies.[5] For this study, all those clients still participating in the program and all clients for whom data were incomplete (i.e., risk/needs or other data unavailable) were excluded. A final sample of 159 probationers and parolees who were initially classified at the maximum (N=101), medium (N=54), or minimum (N=4) supervision levels proved available for use. No distinctions are made in the study with regard to gender (male=154, female=5), ethnicity (anglo=118, hispanic=41), or release status (probation=110, parole=49).

With the exception of the cross-validation issues addressed earlier, the Idaho classification instrument satisfies professional standards of assessment established by the American Correctional Association (ACA, 1981). One area in which Idaho, operating under very restricted resource conditions, has departed from the Wisconsin model is the assessment of fifteen points for "aggressive offenses" within the previous five years. The Wisconsin Division of Corrections, in the interest of community protection, instituted this practice to assure that any offender meeting this criterion would be placed under maximum supervision. Owing to resource constraints due to increased case loads and a fixed number of personnel, cutoff scores for levels of supervision were raised in June 1987 to restrict the number of clients being supervised at a maximum level (Table 1).

In this sample, risk scores range from 1 to 33, with a mean of 20.786, a median of 22, and a standard deviation of 7.344. Need scores have a range from 10 to 57, with a mean value of 33.151, a median of 34, and a standard deviation of 8.447. The median and mean values place a substantial number of offenders at medium or minimum supervision levels.

In practice, the risk/need classification process yields two scores, 0 to 37 for risk, and 5 to 61 for need. Offender supervision levels are based on the highest of the two scores; if a client scored at a minimum risk level but at a maximum need level, then an overall supervision level of maximum may be assigned.

Table 1: Idaho Supervision Cutoff Scores

| Level | Prior to June 1987 | | After June 1987 | |
|---|---|---|---|---|
| | Risk | Need | Risk | Need |
| Maximum | 21–37 | 29–61 | 24–37 | 34–61 |
| Medium | 11–20 | 14–28 | 13–23 | 19–33 |
| Minimum | 0–10 | 5–13 | 0–12 | 5–18 |

To analyze the data, it was necessary to standardize risk and need scores to percentiles of the total possible value in each category. By using percentiles, it was possible to develop a comparable score for risk and need ratings. The *composite* score for an offender represents the sum of the risk and need percentile scores.

## Classification Overrides

A policy standard of the Idaho Department of Corrections requires any client supervised on the ISP to be classified as a maximum supervision client. It is apparent in reviewing the composite classification levels presented in Table 2 that fifty-eight offenders (medium [N=54], minimum [N=4]) in the ISP sample required that the classification level be overridden from medium or minimum levels to a maximum supervision level to permit participation in the ISP.

Table 2: Risk/Need and Composite Classification

|        | Raw Risk | | Raw Need | | Composite | |
| Level  | N | % | N | % | N | % |
| --- | --- | --- | --- | --- | --- | --- |
| Maximum | 61 | 38.4 | 81 | 50.9 | 101 | 63.5 |
| Medium  | 73 | 45.9 | 73 | 45.9 | 54 | 34.0 |
| Minimum | 25 | 15.7 | 5 | 3.1 | 4 | 2.5 |

In this study, 69 percent (N=40) of the clients who received an override satisfactorily completed the program, as compared with 45.6 percent (N=46) of those offenders initially classified as maximum who satisfactorily completed the program. Slightly less than one-third (31 percent, N=18) of the override offenders failed, whereas more than one-half (54.5 percent, N=55) of those legitimately classified as maximum failed to complete the program.

Based on the experience of this sample, it appears that subjective assignment of low-risk, low-need clients to an ISP is not an efficient use of resources. The two-thirds success rate of override offenders can arise from a number of possibilities. One possibility is that "creaming" is occurring to produce a high rate of program success. Another possibility is that the presence of a bias favoring extreme concern for public criticism of soft treatment of specific offenders or those thought to enjoy special favor on the part of the decision maker who has the authority to override classification scores is in operation. The override has an obvious negative impact on a select population of low- to medium-risk offenders inasmuch as the offender assigned to an ISP is denied the degree of freedom given those of equal scores and assigned to regular supervision.

A final explanation is that the administrator has identified an important offense or source of potential concern of the community in which the offender is being supervised that is not addressed by the objective aspects of the classification instrument. Given that a primary goal of the criminal justice system is the protection of the public, the response of the administrator could well be in keeping with the values of political responsiveness and public safety.

## Analysis

To test the null hypothesis that the risk/need scores obtained by the assessment tool utilized by the state of Idaho are not predictors of success/failure for clients participating in the ISP in the Idaho judicial district under study, a series of contingency tables for chi-square testing of the relationship between success/failure and classification levels and crime were constructed.

We note in Table 3 that the Chi-square value is significant at less than the .02 level. We are able to reject that portion of the null that holds that there will be no difference in success/failure rates based on classification level. We are also able to see that a positive association does exist between the classification level of the offender and success or failure in the ISP; the probability of program failure increases with classification level. Our confidence in rejecting the null hypothesis is reinforced with the strongest measure of association, Gamma, which provides a statistic of .4448. Kendall's Tau B, which is a more conservative measure of association than Gamma, also shows a weak positive association between assigned classification levels and success or failure in the program.

Table 3: Offender Status by Composite Classification (Crosstabulation)

|  | Minimum | Medium | Maximum | Row Total |
|---|---|---|---|---|
| Success in Program | 3 (3.5%)[*] (75.0%)[**] (1.9%)[***] | 37 (43.0%) (68.5%) (23.0%) | 46 (53.5%) (45.5%) (28.9%) | 86 (54.1%) |
| Failure in Program | 1 (1.4%) (25.0%) (0.6%) | 17 (23.3%) (31.5%) (10.7%) | 55 (75.3%) (54.5%) (34.6%) | 73 (45.9%) |
| Column Total | 4 (2.5%) | 54 (34.0%) | 101 (63.5%) | 159 (100%) |

[*] Row Percent $X^2$—8.21 (2 DF) p = .017
[**] Column Percent
[***] Total Percent Gamma .445 Kendall's Tau B .224

Crosstabulation of program success by override, reported in Table 4, strongly suggests that the results of the cell frequencies are not by chance, but rather that there is an association between the overrides and success in the program. As we observed earlier, there is a positive association between classification level and success in the ISP.

Computation of the odds ratio[6] indicates that assignment to the ISP through normal channels (override not required) will result in program failure a little more than $2^1/2$ times as frequently as those who receive overrides.

It can be noted in Table 4 that of the fifty-eight clients who received overrides, only eighteen (31 percent) failed the program; if it is possible to identify and target the groups to which the 31 percent belong, it may be possible to formalize policy which addresses the risk and or need of the offender group. In an attempt to identify the group or groups to which the 31 percent belong, a new series of contingency tables was constructed. By controlling for crime, age, and override, we are able to discern, at least at a rudimentary level, the frequency and intensity of override failure.

Table 4: Completion/Override

|  | Override | | No Override | | Row Total | |
|---|---|---|---|---|---|---|
| Completed Program | 40 | (46.5%)[*] | 46 | (53.5%) | 86 | (54.1%) |
|  |  | (69.0%)[**] |  | (45.5%) |  |  |
|  |  | (25.2%)[***] |  | (28.9%) |  |  |
| Violated Program | 18 | (24.7%) | 55 | (75.3%) | 73 | (45.9%) |
|  |  | (31.0%) |  | (54.5%) |  |  |
|  |  | (11.3%) |  | (34.6%) |  |  |
| Column Total | 58 | (36.5%) | 101 | (63.5%) | 159 | (100%) |

[*]Row Percent          $X^2$—7.22 (1 DF) p=.007
[**]Column Percent
[***]Total Percent       Gamma .123          Kendal's Tau B .226

Although the substance abuse related crimes are currently targeted for strict enforcement and ISP participation, as are the sexual offense crimes, the data indicate that both types of crime present low rates of failure in the sample studied. Conversely, those convicted of burglary or theft had failure rates of 50.9 percent and 72.4 percent, respectively, thus indicating a higher rate of failure than those targeted for intensive enforcement.

From Table 5 it can be noted that the burglary offenders constitute seventeen of fifty-three burglary offenders who are being supervised on ISP as a result of classification overrides; almost one-half (8) of those overrides failed on the ISP. Of the burglary failures, seven were in the age group through age twenty-five. It is interesting to note that the override burglary failures constitutes 27 percent of the total burglary failure rate. Any policy considerations based on the burglary clients would be pure conjecture.

Table 5: Type of Crime Controlled for Failure, Age, and Override

| Offense | N | (%) | Override Total | Failure | Override by Age < 25 | 26–30 | 31–35 | > 35 |
|---|---|---|---|---|---|---|---|---|
| Arson | 1 | (.6%) | 0 | | | | | |
| Assault/Battery | 11 | (6.9%) | 4 | | | | | |
| Burglary | 53 | (33.3%) | 17 | 8 | 7 | | 1 | |
| Controlled Substances | 10 | (6.3%) | 3 | | | | | |
| DUI | 6 | (3.8%) | 3 | | | | | |
| Forgery | 21 | (13.2%) | 5 | 1 | | 1 | | |
| Insufficient funds/ checks | 4 | (2.5%) | | | | | 1 | |
| Lewd Conduct w/child | 12 | (7.5%) | 8 | 1 | | | | 1 |
| Manslaughter | 3 | (1.9%) | 3 | | | | | |
| Robbery | 6 | (3.8%) | 2 | 2 | 1 | 1 | | |
| Statutory Rape | 3 | (1.9%) | 1 | | | | | |
| Theft | 29 | (18.2%) | 9 | 6 | 4 | 1 | 1 | |
| Totals | | 159 | 58 | 18 | 12 | 3 | 2 | 1 |

The next area that piques interest is robbery. Of the six cases assigned to the ISP, two clients failed. Four of the six offenders assigned to ISP were classified through the override mechanisms. The two failures were override clients, both of whom were thirty years of age or less. Whether founded on fact or not, robbery is a crime which creates fear in the community; as a public administrator charged with offender placement, an offender thirty years of age or less, charged with robbery, would be considered as a prime candidate for the ISP.

The crime of theft also draws concern. We know that theft represents only 18.2 percent of the sample, but accounts for 13.2 percent of all violations; an internal violation rate of 72.4 percent. Nine of the offenders convicted of theft were placed in the ISP through overrides, and six of those offenders violated the conditions of release from incarceration; four of those who violated were age twenty-five or less, the other two were between the ages of twenty-six and thirty-five. Based on the limited data reviewed here, a thief in the nineteen to twenty-five age group would be a prime candidate for ISP participation.

## Conclusion

The administrative function of addressing subjective values is an inherent part of protecting society by use of special programs. The intensive supervision program is one such intervention tool. By providing intervention in a timely manner through the ISP, both client risk and client need can effectively and efficiently be addressed.

It is the composite scale which objectively determines the level of supervision. In this sample, it was necessary to override 36.5 percent of the participants to establish their eligibility for the program. There is a 45.9 percent rate of failure in the program. With an override factor of 36.5 percent and only 31 percent of those who had an override failing, it does appear that something is being done correctly. However, with an override factor of this strength, grave concerns develop with regard to the validity of the classification instrument for use in the ISP. The instrument used to assign supervision levels of intervention does not appear to be valid for the intensive supervision program, although it appears that the classification instrument works quite well in general.

Regardless, we are able to reject the null hypothesis that classification levels for ISP supervision are not predictive of the threat or danger an offender presents to the community and thus there will be no difference in success/failure rates based on classification levels or based on offense at the .0166 and .0068 levels, respectively.

Further research is necessary to establish a valid predictor of risk/need for assignment of clients to special programs. Subjective, arbitrary, or capricious decision making tends to expose agencies to judicial litigation, the cost of which must be borne by the taxpayers. It is the responsibility of agency administrators to identify quantitative as well as qualitative decision-making tools.

## NOTES

1. The Federal Bureau of Investigation's annual report, *Crime in the United States,* shows an almost linear increase in crime since 1960 when there were 1.9 offenses per 100 population increasing to 5.5 offenses per 100 population in 1985. With regard to evidence of a hardening of public attitudes on violent crime, a Gallup report has shown a steady increase in those persons favoring the death penalty for convicted murderers: 72 percent of the respondents in the survey favored capital punishment in 1985 as compared with 40 percent in 1967 (Gallup, 1985: 4).

2. Insofar as there is no universally agreed-upon definition of recidivism (Silberman, 1980), I am defining failure (recidivism) as any illegal action which results in the revocation of probation or parole. Revocation or failure presumes that the client has presented an unacceptable risk to the public for continued community supervision without additional sanctions or intervention. Success, therefore, is defined as positive completion of the ISP.

3.  The sanctions and approaches range from application of capital punishment to unsupervised probation depending on the severity of the offense, prior criminal history of the offender, the status of the offender, community values, and political pressures.

4.  The Idaho instrument, which was adapted from the Wisconsin model, used the Wisconsin scores as a base to establish values which reflect regional intuitive perceptions of risk and need. The Wisconsin scale has established an interrater reliability score of 87 percent (N=449 raters). Items scored include: prior felony convictions, periods of probation or parole and any revocations, age at first adjudication, history of alcohol or drug abuse, enhancement for selected offenses, educational and vocational levels or skills, employment history, financial status, relationships with significant others, living arrangements, and psychological and physical health.

5.  These figures reflect the official data. It is likely that the technical violations are somewhat lower and the rate of felony violation is slightly higher. The practice of transferring an offender from the ISP caseload to that of the ISP supervisor pending adjudication of felony proceedings is necessary to allow additional clients an opportunity to participate. The ISP caseload has a maximum limit of twenty-five clients, all of whom are actively supervised by a team of two officers and one supervisor. The supervisor may have a caseload of up to ten clients; these clients are not necessarily actively supervised and may have pending legal action.

6.  Odds ratio = AD/BC = $(40 \times 55)/(18 \times 46) = 2.657{:}1$

# REFERENCES

American Correctional Association (1981). *Standards for Adult Probation and Parole Field Services*. College Park, MD: Author.

Babbie, Earl (1989). *The Practice of Social Science*, 5th ed. Belmont, CA: Wadsworth.

Baird, S. Christopher (1981). "Probation and Parole Classification: The Wisconsin Model." *Corrections Today* (May–June): 36–41.

Baird, S. Christopher, Richard Heinz, and Brian J. Bemus (1984). "The Wisconsin Case Classification/Staff Deployment Project: A Two-

Year Follow-up Report." In *Classification,* American Correctional Association Monographs, 1 (4). College Park, MD: American Correctional Association.

Beyer, J. Arthur (1987). "Prison Classification and Assessment." In *Understanding, Assessing and Counseling the Criminal Justice Client,* edited by Anthony Walsh. Pacific Grove, CA: Brooks/Cole.

Byrne, James M. (1986). "The Control Controversy: A Preliminary Examination of Intensive Probation Programs in the United States." *Federal Probation* 50(2): 4–16.

—— (1985). "The Control Controversy: A Preliminary Examination of Intensive Probation Programs in the United States." Paper presented at the annual meeting of the Academy of Criminal Justice Sciences, Las Vegas, NV (April).

Clear, Todd R., and Patricia L. Hardyman (1990). "The New Intensive Supervision Movement." In *Crime and Delinquency* 36 (1): 42–60.

Colson, Charles, and Daniel W. Van Ness (1988). "Alternatives to Incarceration." In *Journal of State Government* (March–April): 59–64.

Fallen, David L., et al. (1981). *Intensive Parole Supervision.* Olympia, WA: Department of Social and Health Services, Analysis and Information Services Division, Office of Research.

Gallop (1985). "Support for the Death Penalty Highest in Half-Century." *Gallop Report* (January–February): 4.

Gettinger, Stephen (1984). "Assessing Criminal Justice Needs." National Institute of Justice, *Research in Brief* (NCJ-9407) (June).

Gottfredson, Stephen D., and Don M. Gottfredson (1982). "Risk Assessment: An Evaluation of Statistical Classification Methods." In *Classification as a Management Tool: Theories and Models for Decision-Makers.* College Park, MD: American Correctional Association.

*The "Intensive" Supervision Caseload: A Preliminary Evaluation* (1967). University of California, School of Criminology.

Kelman, Steven (1987). *Making Public Policy.* New York: Basic Books.

Klofas, John M. (1991). "Disaggregating Jail Use: Variety and Change in Local Corrections over a Ten-Year Period." In *American Jails,* edited by Joel A. Thompson and G. Larry Mays. Chicago: Nelson-Hall.

Krajik, Kevin, and Steve Gettinger (1982). *Overcrowded Time.* New York: Edna McConnell Clark Foundation.

Krantz, Sheldon (1981). *The Law of Corrections and Prisoner's Rights*, 2nd ed. St Paul, MN: West.

Lurigio, Arthur J. (1990). "Introduction." *Crime and Delinquency* 36(1): 3–5.

Mancini, Norma (1988). *Our Crowded Jails: A National Plight*. U.S. Department of Justice, Bureau of Justice Statistics (NCJ-111846). (June).

Mauer, Marc (1991). *Americans Behind Bars: A Comparison of International Rates of Incarceration*. Washington, D.C.: Sentencing Project.

Miller, Marc (1987). "Legal and Ethical Limits on the Use of Predictions of Dangerousness in the Criminal Law." In *The Prediction of Criminal Violence*, edited by Fernand N. Dutile and Cleon H. Foust. Springfield, IL: C. C. Thomas.

Morris, Norval, and Marc Miller (1987). "Predictions of Dangerousness in the Criminal Law." National Institute of Justice, *Research in Brief* (March).

National Institute of Corrections (1981). *Prison Classification: A Model Systems Approach*. Washington, DC: Author.

Petersilia, Joan (1986). *Georgia's Intensive Probation: Will the Model Work Elsewhere?* Santa Monica, CA: Rand Corporation.

*Probation and Parole, 1989* (1990). Bureau of Justice Statistics Bulletin. U.S. Department of Justice.

Silberman, Charles E. (1980). *Criminal Violence, Criminal Justice*. New York: Random House.

Skovron, Sandra Evans (1988). "Prison Crowding: The Dimensions of the Problem and Strategies of Population Control." In *Controversial Issues in Crime and Justice*, edited by Joseph E. Scott and Travis Hirschi. Beverly Hills, CA: Sage.

Steadman, Henry J. (1987). "How Well Can We Predict Violence for Adults? A Review of the Literature and Some Commentary." In *The Prediction of Criminal Violence*, edited by Fernand N. Dutile and Cleon H. Foust. Springfield, IL: C. C. Thomas.

*Time to Build? The Realities of Prison Construction* (1984). New York: Edna McConnell Clark Foundation.

Toborg, Mary A., and John P. Bellassi (1987). "Attempts to Predict Pretrial Violence: Research Findings and Legislative Responses." In *The Prediction of Criminal Violence*, edited by Fernand N. Dutile and Cleon H. Faust. Springfield, IL: C. C. Thomas.

Welsh, Wayne N., Matthew C. Leone, Patrick T. Kinkade, and Henry N. Pontell (1991). "The Politics of Jail Overcrowding: Public Attitudes and Official Policies." In *American Jails*, edited by Joel A. Thompson and G. Larry Mays. Chicago: Nelson-Hall.

# CHAPTER THREE

# Intensive Probation in Texas

*G. Mark Jones*
*Terry L. Wells*

In the early 1980s, Texas joined the ranks of states employing a complicated array of intermediate sanctions to deal with prison crowding. Boot camps, residential halfway houses, electronic monitoring, house arrest, community service, and shock probation were some of the programs instituted in reaction to prison crowding. This chapter discusses one of the older intermediate sanctioning mechanisms, intensive supervision probation. The stated goal of the Texas intensive supervision program (ISP), like that of many other states, is to serve as a suitable community-based sanction for felony offenders who otherwise would have received a prison sentence. By suitable, we mean that the sanction is sufficiently restrictive so that close surveillance can be kept on the offenders. The hope among policy makers is that intensive supervision serves as a crime prevention mechanism. Also, theoretically at least, the cost-benefits of an ISP are preferable to that of a prison sentence. Though some judges and probation personnel lend rehabilitative assistance to offenders, rehabilitation is not the driving force in the Texas ISP.

In addition to problems concerning prison crowding, Texas's situation was further complicated by the highly publicized and well-chronicled *Ruiz v. Estelle* litigation which drastically changed the structure and operation of Texas prisons. A lengthy list of inmate lawsuits, centering to a large degree on living conditions within the prisons, has been a persistent headache for administrators in Texas prisons.[1] However, living conditions in Texas prisons have improved, so much so that unaffectionate references to the "Winn (a TDC Unit) Hotel" and "Texas Day Care" abound. Inmates are serving less time in prison because of crowding, and at least one empirical work (Crouch et al., 1991) suggests that Texas imprisonment has lost some of its punitive effectiveness.

Inmate lawsuits have also been a persistent problem for numerous Texas counties. Complaints of inmates who have filed lawsuits against individual counties is traceable in large part to the overcrowding problem. In turn, some counties experiencing overcrowding problems in their jails have filed suit against the Texas Department of Criminal Justice (TDCJ). Harris County (Houston) has had an especially protracted and bitter feud with the state of Texas. Complaints stem from inmates being forced to sleep on the floor due to the extended waiting period for transfer to TDCJ facilities. The wait is so long that many inmates are being paroled from the county jail before serving any time in a state facility. The issues and particulars of the suit are numerous and complex, but it can safely be said that all legal claims could be quickly settled if crowding problems in state and county facilities were resolved.

This discussion of the Texas ISP is divided into three sections. The first section briefly examines punishment in Texas from a historical viewpoint. In most evaluations and discussions of intermediate sanctions, this topic is neglected completely or receives cursory attention. Attention to this area is merited because it may provide etiological explanations for a program's creation. It also provides some explanation for the philosophical underpinnings of a particular program. For example, ever since John Augustus began administering probation-type services in Massachusetts during the 1840s, that state has placed heavy emphasis on assistance and rehabilitation in its community-based corrections programs. Consequently, Massachusetts instituted its intensive probation program not as a punitive prison alternative, but as a tool to more closely supervise and meet the needs of offenders. In contrast, some states, like Georgia, Florida, and as we shall demonstrate, Texas, have a history of acting punitively toward their offender populations.

The Georgia, Florida, and Texas programs have instituted intermediate sanctions as measures which punish offenders to the satisfaction of their retributive citizenry.

This chapter also reviews the academic literature on the Texas ISP, as well as related empirical and theoretical literature on intensive probation overall. It then discusses where the Texas program is now. This section includes discussions of the components and characteristics of the Texas ISP, how the model operates, the number of persons involved with the program, plus the strengths and weaknesses of the Texas ISP.

The chapter concludes with a look at the future of the Texas ISP. The question, "Will the ISP survive?" is answered in the affirmative. The chapter discusses the implications of its continued existence from sociological and justice administration viewpoints.

## The Historical Roots and Creation of the Texas ISP

Texas is, and always has been, a punitive state. Like citizens from most southern states, the majority of Texans have always supported the death penalty. Texas consistently ranks at or near the top in numbers of death row inmates and executions. During the period 1930–1989, Texas officially carried out 330 executions, second in the nation to Georgia, which had 380. Of the ninety-three executions carried out in the United States between 1977 and 1987, twenty-six (28 percent) occurred in Texas. As of December 31, 1989, Texas led the nation with 304 inmates under death sentence (BJS, 1991).

Texas and other southern states also rely on imprisonment to a greater extent than many other states. In a 1990 comparison of the fifty states, Texas was among the top twenty in the number of adults per 100,000 population who are in prison (BJS, 1992).[2]

More significantly, Texas ranks much higher in terms of total correctional control. This measure is based on the total correctional population, as a percentage of the total state adult resident population, who are under some form of correctional control, be it prison, jail, probation, or parole. Texas is second, exceeded only by Georgia, in the total percentage of adults under supervision. At the end of 1989, 3.87 percent of Texas's adult resident population was under some form of correctional control (BJS, 1991).

The outlook for the rehabilitative ideal is bleak in Texas. According to recent editions of the *Texas Crime Poll* (Farnworth and West, 1991; Hume et al., 1990), Texans believe that the primary value of prison lies in deterrence, followed by punishment, then incapacitation, and lastly rehabilitation. In spite of the cost of constructing, staffing, and maintaining prisons, the consensus among Texans is that building more prisons is a better way of dealing with crowding problems than rehabilitative or community-based alternatives.

Possible explanations for this punitive outlook are numerous. A detailed examination of those explanations is beyond the scope and range of this paper. Plus, no explanation would satisfy everyone. It to safe to conclude though, that Texas, in both past and present times, has dealt with its offender population more severely than most other states. The attitudes of Texans toward the administration of justice are reflected in the history of its prison system.[3] Prior to the 1970s, Texas prisons were based on the model of the old southern plantation. Most Texas prisons were located in rural areas of eastern Texas, and were governed by the ideals of paternalism, an unquestioning submission to authority, a strong work ethic, and the classical notion that all offenders could be helped if they would only help themselves. The plantation-type setup relied on slave overseers to help maintain order. Accordingly, Texas prison officials delegated a great deal of authority to a select group of inmates. These "building tenders," or BTs, were typically the strongest and most experienced (in terms of prison life) inmates, and they had license and the responsibility to maintain order in cell blocks. BT's would not hesitate to use force to insure compliance, and allegations of extreme abuse are detailed in several historical and qualitative studies of Texas prisons (Crouch and Marquart, 1989; Martin and Ekland-Olson, 1987).

During the 1960s, under the charismatic leadership of George Beto, the Texas Department of Corrections (TDC) received worldwide praise for its efficiency, stability, and low rate of inmate violence. To most other states prisons were regarded as a perpetual headache. In contrast, Texas's prisons became a source of pride, indeed a secular "sacred cow," to its populace, policy makers, and the employees who worked in them. Academic researchers and penologists from around the world praised both Beto and the TDC system.

But TDC's situation began to change in the early 1970s. Prisoners' rights movements around the country had gained momentum. The Attica prison riot of 1971 brought increased public scrutiny on life behind prison walls. American courts, especially at the federal level, lended a more sympathetic ear to inmate litigation. Texas could not shield itself from these outside developments. The tide began to turn in favor of inmate rights shortly before Beto's retirement in 1972. Lawyers and prison reform advocates both within and outside Texas joined the inmates fight against the TDC establishment.

All of these changes culminated in a suit filed against TDC and Beto's successor, W. J. Estelle, by an inmate named David Ruiz. *Ruiz v. Estelle*, according to Crouch and Marquart (1989), became the most comprehensive civil action suit in correctional law history. The *Ruiz* decision ultimately resulted in the improvement of living conditions, removal of the building tender system, and greater ethnic diversity among staff members. Overall, Texas prisons, like those of most other states, became increasingly formalized and bureaucratized.

The attitudes of prison reformers and William W. Justice, the federal judge who presided over *Ruiz*, did not mirror those of most TDC employees, nor the Texas populace. Most court-imposed reform measures were met with extreme resistance by TDC officials, employees, and Texas policy makers. In addition, Texans, like most other Americans, adopted even more retributive attitudes toward criminal offenders during the late 1970s and early 1980s than they had before. But the state of Texas was faced with some hard realities. Under *Ruiz*, a population cap of 95 percent total capacity governed TDC. Even without the population cap, Texas could not afford to build and staff enough prisons to incarcerate its growing offender population. Alternatives had to be developed.

Following the lead of states experiencing similar problems, especially Georgia, Texas policy makers adopted prison "alternatives" in the early 1980s. One of those alternatives was intensive probation. The Texas legislature initially appropriated $2.5 million for fiscal 1982 and $3 million for fiscal 1983 with the intention of diverting at least 1,000 prison-bound offenders into ISPs (Williams et al., 1982). The legislative mandate stated that the Texas Adult Probation Commission should "provide alternatives to incarceration by providing financial aid to judicial districts for the establishment and improvement of probation services and community-based correctional programs and facilities other than jails or prisons" (Fields, 1984: 3).

The Texas legislature has made intermediate sanctions attractive by providing funding to counties that create intermediate sanction programs. Texas House Bill 2335, passed in 1989, is best known because it consolidated state probation agencies, parole agencies, and prison institutions under one department, the Texas Department of Criminal Justice. The bill also empowered a state agency called the Community Justice Assistance Division (CJAD) "to fund innovative correctional programs operated by counties through the sheriff's office, in addition to programs under the aegis of the judicially operated probation/community supervision and corrections departments" (Reynolds, 1989: 9). As a result, several large Texas counties, including Harris (Houston), Travis (Austin), and Tarrant (Fort Worth) have also joined the prison alternative movement.

## The ISP Concept

The first experiments in ISP were in the 1970s. The Law Enforcement Assistance Association sponsored several ISPs, primarily to find out if closer supervision and smaller caseloads correlated with success. They did not, and the programs were phased out. But they were brought back in the early 1980s as a desperation measure to help eliminate prison and jail crowding.

There is little empirical literature concerning intensive supervision programs in Texas. A few counties, such as Bexar

(San Antonio), had their ISPs evaluated during the early 1980s (Williams et al., 1982). However, the first substantive empirical evaluation of the Texas ISP came from Fields (1984), who conducted a two-year assessment of the program. Fields's examination of the program focused on two issues. First, he wanted to see if the offenders being supervised were indeed prison-bound or if they would have exited the justice system through a less stringent sanction had they appeared in court before the creation of the ISP. Second, Fields wanted to determine whether the ISP was actually diverting offenders from prison.

Fields's analysis consisted of two procedures. First, he compared ISP offenders with regular probationers under maximum supervision.[4] Secondly, ISP clients were compared to a sample of offenders who were sent to prison. Fields concluded that the ISP was satisfying the legislative mandate by supervising high-risk offenders. However, he was unable to conclude whether or not the ISP was actually making an impact on prison diversion.

Since the study by Fields, there have been no empirical evaluations of the Texas ISP other than in-house evaluations produced by probation administrators. Similar to evaluations conducted on ISPs in Georgia and New Jersey, these reports are usually disseminated to policy makers with the primary intention of justifying the continuation and/or expansion of the programs. The Texas Adult Probation Commission audited the ISP in 1987 and concluded that the program was "effective and met the intent of the legislature by diverting felony offenders from the Texas Department of Corrections" (Adult Probation Department, 1988: 3).

The literature on ISPs in general can best be divided into two main groups, evaluative and theoretical/philosophical, though there is some overlap between the two. Agency-sponsored evaluations include works such as Coyle's (1990) and Erwin's (1990). Such evaluations are often simple descriptions and project a very positive image of a particular agency's ISP. Coyle's (1990) report on New Jersey's intermediate sanctions typifies many of the evaluations on ISPs. Like Texas, New Jersey initiated its intensive supervision program to affordably alleviate a prison crowding program. In his report, Coyle calls the New Jersey ISP a success. He writes:

> New Jersey currently spends $5,722 per participant for ISP supervision, however, the offender contributes $3,315 to taxes thus putting the net cost of supervision at $2,407 per participant. This cost represents a considerable savings when compared to traditional incarceration. . . . The Intensive Supervision Program in New Jersey has demonstrated its ability to be a viable, cost-effective intermediate sanction for certain groups of offenders. The program should be expanded to permit inmates currently eligible under existing program criteria to be considered and, upon review, admitted to the program. (Coyle, 1990: 23–24)

But Coyle's criteria for success does not address the most important question: is the ISP diverting offenders from prison? The answer to this question is better found in the admission criteria and procedures that the program employs. His report as well as other discussions of the New Jersey program well outline the criteria for admission to the program. After viewing the Georgia ISP model, which, because of its admission criteria, left great potential for net-widening,[5] New Jersey officials instituted a procedure to guard against this possibility.

In order to be admitted to the New Jersey intensive supervision program, an offender must first receive a prison sentence. While incarcerated, an offender may apply for admission to the ISP. The offender must show evidence, both in the application and in an open hearing, that he/she stands a good chance of succeeding on an ISP. Employment prospects, ties to the community, the availability of a "sponsor" who will monitor the activities of the offender; these and other factors are taken into account when deciding whether or not an offender is admitted to the program. Coyle reports that only 20 percent of those who apply for admission are accepted. Pearson and Harper (1990) acknowledge the ISP's faults and successes in New Jersey. Their work concludes with suggestions on improving the ISP. Calling the human element a major success ingredient, one important suggestion is to avoid the temptation to let advances in electronic monitoring substitute for face-to-face contact. Recidivism rates will suffer otherwise.

The Rand studies in Oregon (Petersilia and Turner, 1990A) and California (Petersilia and Turner, 1990B) give mixed reviews on ISP effectiveness. The results of a randomized field experiment in Marion County, Oregon, are not encouraging. Petersilia and Turner conclude that the Oregon model perpetuated "revolving door justice, with ISP and prison participants moving between the community and incarceration every few months" (Petersilia and Turner, 1990A: vii). Because of this revolving door justice, the authors also state that the ISP is only 25 percent more cost-effective than prison.

After evaluating intensive supervision programs in three California counties (which had loosely adopted the Georgia ISP model), Petersilia and Turner state that strict supervision does not correlate with lower recidivism. The authors also conclude that ISP clients have more technical violations than regular probationers, and that intensive supervision, because of its high violation rate, does not meet cost expectations. Interestingly, they find a negative correlation between recidivism and participation in counseling, employment, restitution, and community service. In effect, their conclusions echo those of Pearson and Harper in New Jersey: *Do not forget the human element.*

Some of the better work in the theoretical and philosophical area comes from Gordon (1990) and Morris and Tonry (1990). Excepting the Massachusetts program, Gordon views ISPs primarily as another net-widening device. Morris and Tonry argue that ISPs should be included in a continuum of intermediate sanctioning mechanisms. They view ISPs and other intermediate sanctions not so much as prison alternatives, but as long-needed bridges between regular probation and prison. In a similar vein, Nidorf (1991) claims that calling ISPs a failure because of high recidivism rates misses the point. He refers to ISPs as primarily a probation enhancement mechanism. According to Nidorf, one of the purposes of ISPs is to have a better way of catching offenders who violate the terms of their sentence. So as Feeley and Simon (1990) allude to in discussing the "new penology," instead of a recidivist being a failure, a recidivist, in effect, becomes a success.

## How the Texas ISP Model Operates

The Texas ISP resembles the Georgia model. Under this model, an offender may enter the program in one of several ways. First, an offender may be sentenced to a prison term, then be removed from incarceration and placed in an ISP through an amended sentence order. Secondly, an offender may be placed in an ISP after serving the prison portion of a split sentence. Thirdly, an offender may be placed in an ISP by way of a revocation order, usually resulting from technical or misdemeanor violations of a regular probation sentence. Fourthly, an offender may be placed in an ISP through direct sentence. It is this fourth method which has opened the Georgia model to charges of net-widening.

Aware of the prospect that ISPs might be used for "lightweight" offenders, Texas policy makers have instituted guidelines for admission to their ISP. Eligibility for placement in the program is restricted to offenders diverted from incarceration in the Texas Department of Criminal Justice (TDCJ) by:

1. Being placed on probation and ordered into the ISP by the court; or
2. Being placed on probation after incarceration (shock probation) and ordered into the ISP by the court; or
3. Being continued on probation by the court after a revocation hearing as the result of a subsequent arrest, behavior seriously in conflict with the conditions of probation, or failure to report to the probation officer, in lieu of revocation and incarceration in TDCJ; and
4. Demonstrating one or more of the indicators of need (Adult Probation Department, 1988).

Some of the "indicators of need" leave a loophole for the judge to place an offender in the ISP who might not indeed be prison-bound. For example, indicators of need include a "documentable alcohol or drug dependency problem," and "seriousness of the current offense." Plus, judges are not prohibited from sentencing an offender to the intensive supervision program simply because the offender does not meet the suggested criteria. This leaves the sentencing of ISP offenders totally within the discretion of the local judge, who may or may not observe the guidelines.

Since the initiation of the ISP in 1981, there has been a gradual increase in the number of persons diverted to the program. The total number of persons in the ISP for the FYs 1982–1990 is depicted in Table 1. The numbers illustrate the growing use of the program as an alternative to incarceration.

Table 1: Participants in Texas Intensive Supervision Program (by Fiscal Year)

| Fiscal Year | Total participants |
|-------------|--------------------|
| 1982 | 2,197 |
| 1983 | 4,657 |
| 1984 | 6,937 |
| 1985 | 8,069 |
| 1986 | 8,310 |
| 1987 | 9,872 |
| 1988 | 11,653 |
| 1989 | 13,572 |
| 1990 | 14,498 |

Source: Community Justice Assistance Division of Texas

The overall characteristics of those who have participated in the ISP, in Texas, for the years 1988 through 1990, is presented in Table 2. Most of the participants are male and over the age of twenty-five. More than 60 percent have an education level below a high school degree for all three years. The main offense category is dangerous drugs (more than 30 percent) followed by burglary. Last, the majority have a risk level of maximum and a need level of medium.

Table 2: Demographic Profile of Participants in Texas ISP
(1988–1991)

|  | 1990–91 | 1989–90 | 1988–89 |
|---|---|---|---|
| **Sex:** |  |  |  |
| Male | 14,206 (82%) | 12,652 (82%) | 11,556 (83%) |
| Female | 3,060 (18%) | 2,740 (18%) | 2,444 (17%) |
| **Race:** |  |  |  |
| White | 7,214 (42%) | 6,882 (45%) | 6,622 (47%) |
| Black | 5,930 (34%) | 5,014 (33%) | 4,167 (30%) |
| Hispanic | 4,024 (23%) | 3,434 (22%) | 3,148 (22%) |
| Other | 126 (.7%) | 74 (.5%) | 65 (.5%) |
| **Age:** |  |  |  |
| 17–19 | 1,261 (07%) | 1,167 (08%) | 291 (02%) |
| 20–24 | 4,727 (27%) | 4,031 (26%) | 3,577 (26%) |
| 25–29 | 3,823 (22%) | 3,517 (23%) | 3,483 (25%) |
| 30–34 | 3,094 (18%) | 2,909 (19%) | 2,936 (21%) |
| 35 + | 4,385 (25%) | 3,778 (25%) | 3,716 (27%) |
| **Education Level:** |  |  |  |
| < 8th Grade | 2,252 (13%) | 2,001 (13%) | 1,912 (14%) |
| 9th–11th | 8,060 (47%) | 7,226 (47%) | 6,663 (48%) |
| High School | 4,416 (26%) | 3,940 (26%) | 3,385 (24%) |
| Some College + | 2,548 (15%) | 2,227 (14%) | 2,032 (15%) |
| **Risk Level at Assessment:** |  |  |  |
| Maximum | 8,802 (57%) | 8,270 (59%) | 7,765 (60%) |
| Medium | 5,199 (34%) | 4,534 (33%) | 4,164 (32%) |
| Minimum | 1,427 (09%) | 1,107 (08%) | 932 (07%) |
| **Needs Level at Assessment:** |  |  |  |
| Maximum | 3,080 (20%) | 3,175 (23%) | 3,060 (24%) |
| Medium | 9,279 (60%) | 8,413 (61%) | 7,670 (60%) |
| Minimum | 3,004 (20%) | 2,280 (16%) | 2,085 (16%) |
| **Primary Offenses:** |  |  |  |
| Dangerous Drugs | 5,789 (34%) | 5,346 (35%) | 4,594 (33%) |
| Burglary | 2,808 (16%) | 2,671 (18%) | 2,577 (19%) |
| Traffic | 1,353 (08%) | 1,051 (07%) | 1,010 (07%) |
| Assault | 1,194 (07%) | 979 (06%) | 888 (06%) |
| Stolen Vehicle | 1,051 (06%) | 863 (06%) | 814 (06%) |

Source: Community Justice Assistance Division of Texas

As of June 30, 1991, Texas adult probation officials were supervising 8,662 ISP offenders. Of that number, 5,112 (59 percent) were placed in intensive supervision through direct sentence. The rest entered the ISP as a result of revocation proceedings, or by being discharged from shock probation. The large percentage of offenders in the ISP through direct sentence is an indicator that judges may be placing offenders in the program who are not really prison-bound. This position is supported by Petersilia and Turner (1990A) in one of the seminal works of ISP evaluation:

> In Georgia . . . judges were permitted to directly sentence offenders to the ISP program, being instructed to do so only for offenders who would have been imprisoned had they not been sentenced to intensive supervision. . . . Half of the ISP participants in Georgia got there by direct sentence and half by amended sentence. Thus, it appears that judges were using (more severe) ISP sanctions to enhance the supervision of offenders who might otherwise have been granted (less severe) routine probation (i.e., net-widening). (Petersilia and Turner, 1990A: 2)

It appears that although Texas probation officials have tried to build anti-net-widening measures in the ISP criteria, it may be politically impractical to totally eliminate the threat. Whether or not net-widening of the sort mentioned here is actually occurring is an empirical question which has not been fully addressed. However, it does appear that the current admission criteria of the Texas ISP create conditions favorable to net-widening.

Though it may be contrary to the original intent of the legislation which created the ISP, Texas officials are using it as a reintegrative program for those who are sentenced to shock probation. Offenders sentenced to shock probation serve a brief period of incarceration. Upon court order, they are released from custody very early in their sentence and placed under supervision. Harris County probation officials began noticing that offenders released from jail or the county boot camp program encountered difficulty in readjusting to life in the community. Now, all graduates of the Harris County boot camp program must serve a portion of their sentence under the guidelines of a program called Super-Intensive Probation, or SIP. The conditions of SIP are even more stringent than those of the standard ISP, as offenders are often required to report every day and maintain a daily itinerary. So it appears that intensive probation is not only being used as (theoretically) a prison diversion tool, or a probation enhancement tool, but now is being used to provide a smooth transition into community life for those just released from incarceration.

Once an offender is placed on ISP, the conditions he/she is subjected to are not radically different from those in other states. Though Texas adopted the Georgia model of intensive supervision, reporting requirements are less stringent for Texas ISP clients than Georgia's. For the first thirty to forty-five day period, Texas ISP clients are required to report bi-weekly. Georgia requires three to five weekly contacts during the first few months of supervision. Texas is also less stringent than New Jersey, which requires twelve face-to-face contacts per month. Texas ISP probationers may have their reporting requirements lessened after the first forty-five day period; where Georgia and New Jersey usually require the initial phase to last up to six months (Jones, 1991).

Like ISP offenders in other jurisdictions, Texas sometimes requires its offenders to either perform community service work, submit to random drug tests, abide by a curfew, submit to electronic monitoring or house arrest, or a combination of these conditions.

In order to examine a program's effectiveness, one must look at the numbers: How many offenders are being served, what kind of offenders are being served, and how many offenders are successfully or unsuccessfully completing the program?[6]

## The Future of ISP in Texas

The ISP is in little danger of extinction in Texas, nor in any other jurisdiction. The fiscal necessities which drove its creation will drive its survival. As long as crowding in prisons and jails remains a problem, the ISP will survive. Even if the retributive attitudes of its citizenry do not survive, the ISP will continue to function. Though the ISP is primarily a punitive mechanism, it could just as easily become a rehabilitative one.

Researchers and policy makers are discovering that ISPs may not be achieving all of their original goals, but they are nonetheless achieving some goals. Tonry (1990) suggests that ISPs serve latent functions. He states that ISPs serve "bureaucratic and organizational goals by enabling probation administrators to be 'tough on crime' and thereby increase the institutional and political credibility of probation" (p. 174). Indeed, with the decline of the rehabilitative ideal in the 1970s, probation had fallen on hard times before the prison crowding crisis necessitated the creation of "alternatives to incarceration." In accordance with Feeley and Simon's (1990) idea of the "new penology," and as we suggested earlier, a failure, i.e., a recidivist, in probation, can now be considered a success. A recidivist demonstrates to the public and policy makers that probation can be used as a crime-fighting mechanism.

Becoming more credible with the public increases the clout probation administrators have at budget appropriation time. Plus, as ISP probation officials get more entrenched in the bureaucracy, it will get more and more difficult to get them out (assuming anyone wanted them out). Bureaucratic programs and agencies tend to get stronger as they get larger.

If one steps outside discussions about ISPs from an organizational viewpoint and examines the survival of ISPs from an administration of justice view, he/she should still conclude that ISPs will survive. ISPs have become a part of the sentencing schemes of judges, and they have become a component in what Morris and Tonry (1990) refer to as part of a rational sentencing system. Morris and Tonry view the recent influx of intermediate sanctioning mechanisms as ways to fill the long-present void between regular probation and prison. With ISPs and other intermediate sanctions, judges can avoid the problem of being too rough, and at the same time, too soft on criminals (Morris and Tonry, 1990).

What implications does the survival of ISPs have for society as a whole? Authors who raise this question often answer it in a very negative way. The implications of net-widening—unnecessarily bringing more offenders under the net of social control—were discussed earlier. What we did not discuss was the implications that community-based sanctions such as ISPs have on third parties, people who are not officially under some sort of correctional supervision. Third parties most often affected by such sanctions are those individuals who live with the offender, such as parents, spouses, and children. An ISP impacts their lives also. Thomas Blomberg of Florida State University states that community-based sanctions are gradually graying the lines between prison and the community. His claim is that we are extending the net of control and becoming a "minimum security society" (Blomberg, 1987; Blomberg et al., 1991). Blomberg illustrates this point with a story he related at the 1991 American Society of Criminology conference. Here is a paraphrase of his story:

> During the course of our research (on Florida's Community Control, or house arrest, Program), a probation officer told us this story. The officer had been supervising a certain offender, a young adult man who lived with his parents. The officer had explained to the probationer, with his family members present, when he could go somewhere, where he could go, and so forth. This probationer's father phoned the officer one Friday night. The father asked the officer something like, "What about going to a movie? Is that okay?" The officer replied that the terms of the Community Control Program were quite explicit; going to a movie was not allowed. The father said okay, and hung up. Right away, the officer asked himself the question: who was the father talking about? He immediately phoned the father back. Sure enough, the father, who was not on probation, was asking his son's probation officer if he, the father, could go to a movie.

The intrusion into this family's life was so complete that it seems they had forgotten who was on probation.

Some writers, including Gordon (1990), blame a combination of factors, including the retributive mood of the public and advances in electronic monitoring, for this increased intrusion. But von Hirsch (1990) warns against what he calls the "intrusiveness is a matter of technology" fallacy. According to von Hirsch, intrusion is not dependent upon the sophistication of technology employed but, instead, "the extent to which the practice affects the dignity and privacy of those intruded upon" (p. 165). He claims that frequent, unannounced home visits are just as intrusive and undignifying as electronic monitoring devices.

So what is the key to having an effective, humane ISP in Texas or any other state? As mentioned earlier, Pearson and Harper (1990) and Petersilia and Turner (1990b) warn against totally forsaking the treatment approach. Von Hirsch (1990) states that an ISP must let the offender maintain some sense of dignity if the government expects him/her to conform to societal norms.

As states, especially punitive-oriented ones like Texas, are simultaneously trying to figure ways of dealing with prison crowding and keeping a retributive public satisfied, the suggestions made by other researchers should be kept in mind. It appears that using ISPs strictly as a prison alternative, even in theory, may soon become an idea of the past. Von Hirsch (1990: 165) warns against the "anything-but-prison" fallacy. Those who subscribe to the anything-but-prison fallacy maintain that an offender should not complain about the treatment he/she is receiving while under community supervision, since prison is always the unpleasant alternative. If the ISP is destined to become a permanent intermediate sanction rather than a prison alternative, it should receive the same scrutiny from researchers, policy makers, administrators, and civil liberties groups as traditional sanctions such as the death penalty, prison, and regular probation.

NOTES

1. In addition to *Ruiz v. Estelle*, 503 F. Supp. 1265 (S.D. Texas, 1980), which practically revolutionized the administration of Texas prisons, the list includes *Cruz v. Beto*, 603 F. 2d 1178 (5th Cir., 1979), which concerned freedom to engage in religious practices. *Guajardo v. Estelle*, 580 F. 2d 748 (5th Cir., 1978), involved mail privileges; and *Estelle v. Gamble*, 429 U.S. 97 (1976), concerned proper medical treatment. Litigated reform in Texas prisons is discussed at length by Crouch and Marquart (1989) and Martin and Ekland-Olson (1987).

2. For comparisons, the District of Columbia was excluded. The total control rate for DC in 1989 was 5.62 and inmates per 100,000 of the district population in 1990 was 1,225.2.

3. A great deal of the information in this section is taken from Crouch and Marquart (1989).

4. Texas, like many states, employs a risk/needs classification instrument to determine the amount of supervision a probationer should have. Those with the highest risk or need scores are placed under maximum supervision. So Fields was trying to see how ISP offenders compared with the toughest clientele that regular probation had to offer.

5. The term "net-widening" is a frequent topic of discussions, both theoretical and empirical, of diversion and prison alternative programs (Blomberg, 1980; Austin and Krisberg, 1981; Decker, 1985; Gordon, 1990; Morris and Tonry, 1990). Walker (1989) uses the phrase "expanding net syndrome" to explain the same phenomenon. Basically, net-widening refers to the notion that judges utilize prison alternative programs on low-risk offenders who, prior to the institution of the program, would have exited the system under less punitive means. Meanwhile, judges continue to sentence prison-bound offenders to terms of incarceration. Hence, more people are brought under the net of formal control.

6. Our definition of success merely means that an offender successfully completed the ISP. In order to effectively gauge the amount of positive impact a program has had on individual offenders, one should track those who complete the program for a one- to two-year period, as some researchers are doing with boot camp offenders. Tracking offenders goes beyond our purposes here, but hopefully more ISP research will be devoted to this area.

# REFERENCES

Adult Probation Department (1988). "Intensive Supervision Probation Policies and Procedures," 12 and 278th District, Texas. Unpublished training material.

Austin, James, and Barry Krisberg (1981). "Wider, Stronger, and Different Nets: The Dialectics of Criminal Justice Reform." *Journal of Research in Crime and Delinquency* 18 (1): 165–196.

Blomberg, Thomas G. (1980). "Widening the Net: An Anomaly in the Evaluation of Diversion Programs." In M. W. Klein and K. S. Teilman (eds.), *Handbook of Criminal Justice Evaluation* (pp. 572–592). Beverly Hills, CA: Sage.

——— (1987). "Criminal Justice Reform and Social Control: Are We Becoming a Minimum Security Society?" In J. Lowman, R. J. Menzies and T. S. Palys (eds.), *Transcarceration: Essays in the Sociology of Social Control* (pp. 218–226). England: Gower Press.

Blomberg, Thomas G., William Bales, and Karen Reed (1991). "Intermediate Punishment: Redistributing or Extending Social Control?" Paper presented at American Society of Criminology annual meeting, San Francisco, CA (November).

Bureau of Justice Statistics (1991). *Correctional Populations in the United States, 1989*. Washington, DC: U. S. Department of Justice.

——— (1992). *Census of State and Federal Correctional Facilities, 1990*. Washington, DC: U. S. Department of Justice.

Coyle, Edward (1990). *Alternatives to Incarceration Programs in New Jersey*. Newark: Criminal Disposition Commission.

Crouch, Ben M., and James W. Marquart (1989). *An Appeal to Justice: Litigated Reform of Texas Prisons*. Austin, TX: University of Texas Press.

Crouch, Ben M., Mark Jones, and James Marquart (1991). "The Devaluation of Prison as a Sanction: Inmates' Perceptions of Punishment in Texas." Paper presented at the American Society of Criminology annual meeting, San Francisco, CA (November).

*Cruz v. Beto*, 603 F. 2d 1178 (5th Cir., 1979).

Decker, Scott A. (1985). "A Systematic Analysis of Diversion: Net-Widening and Beyond." *Journal of Criminal Justice* 13: 207–216.

Erwin, Billie S. (1990). "Old and New Tools for the Modern Probation Officer." *Crime and Delinquency* 36 (1): 61–74.

*Estelle v. Gamble*, 429 U. S. 97 (1976).

Farnworth, Margaret, and Vincent West (1991). *Texas Crime Poll.* Huntsville, TX: Sam Houston State University Press.

Feeley, Malcolm M., and Jonathan Simon (1990). "The New Penology: Reformulating Penal Objectives and Implications for Penal Growth." Unpublished paper.

Fields, Charles B. (1984). "The Intensive Supervision Probation Program in Texas: A Two-Year Assessment." Unpublished doctoral dissertation, Sam Houston State University, Huntsville, TX.

Gordon, Diana R. (1990). *The Justice Juggernaut: Fighting Street Crime, Controlling Citizens.* New Brunswick, NJ: Rutgers University Press.

*Guajardo v. Estelle*, 580 F.2d 748 (5th Cir. 1978).

Hume, Wendelin, Vincent West, and Margaret Farnworth (eds.) (1990). *Texas Crime Poll.* Huntsville, TX: Sam Houston State University.

Jones, G. Mark (1991). "Intensive Probation Supervision in Georgia, Massachusetts, and New Jersey." *Criminal Justice Research Bulletin* 6 (1): 1–9.

Martin, Steve, and Sheldon Ekland-Olson (1987). *Texas Prisons: The Walls Came Tumbling Down.* Austin, TX: Texas Monthly Press.

Morris, Norval, and Michael Tonry (1990). *Between Prison and Probation: Intermediate Punishments in a Rational Sentencing System.* New York: Oxford University Press.

Nidorf, Barry J. (1991). "'Nothing Works' Revisited." *Perspectives* 15 (3): 12–13.

Pearson, Frank S., and Alice Glasel Harper (1990). "Contingent Intermediate Sentences: New Jersey's Intensive Supervision Program." *Crime and Delinquency* 36 (1): 75–86.

Petersilia, Joan, and Susan Turner (1990A). *Diverting Prisoners to Intensive Probation: Results of an Experiment in Oregon.* Santa Monica, CA: Rand Corporation.

———— (1990B). *Intensive Supervision for High-Risk Probationers: Findings from Three California Experiments.* Santa Monica, CA: Rand Corporation.

Reynolds, Carl (1989). "H.B. 2335: The 1989 Criminal Justice Reform Legislation." Unpublished manuscript.

*Ruiz v. Estelle*, 503 F. Supp. 1265 (S.D. Texas, 1980).

Texas Department of Criminal Justice (1990). *1990 Annual Report.*

Tonry, Michael (1990). "Stated and Latent Functions of ISP." *Crime and Delinquency* 36 (1): 174–191.

von Hirsch, Andrew (1990). "The Ethics of Community-Based Sanctions." *Crime and Delinquency* 36 (1): 162–173.

Walker, Samuel (1989). *Sense and Nonsense about Crime: A Policy Guide*, 2nd ed. Pacific Grove, CA: Brooks Cole.

Williams, Frank P., III, Charles M. Friel, Charles B. Fields, and William V. Wilkinson (1982). *Assessing Diversionary Impact: An Evaluation of the Intensive Supervision Program of the Bexar County Adult Probation Department*. Huntsville, TX: Sam Houston State University.

# CHAPTER FOUR

# Examining the Factors Related to Success or Failure with Felony Probationers: A Study of Intensive Supervision

*Edward J. Latessa*
*Jill A. Gordon*

Ohio, like many other states, is currently experiencing an ever-increasing prison population. Despite spending more than $500 million on new penal institutions, Ohio still has a shortage of prison space. In an attempt to reduce some of the burden brought on by this crisis, Ohio has developed a probation subsidy program designed to offer local counties funding to reduce state commitments through pilot probation programs. In 1985, Cuyahoga County developed an intensive supervision program (ISP). The focus of this program is to reduce the county commitment rate without seriously increasing the risk to the community.

Intensive supervision programs are a prevalent alternative used by virtually every state. It is essential to evaluate these types of programs, not only in terms of outcome, but also to identify the type of offender who is successful and unsuccessful. This chapter will examine these issues in one ISP located in Cuyahoga County (Cleveland), Ohio.

## Issues in Intensive Supervision

Intensive probation is defined by Clear and Cole as "Probation granted as an alternative to incarceration under conditions of strict reporting to a probation officer with limited caseload" (1986: 518). Bennett describes intensive supervision as an "attempt to place some offenders who had been sentenced to prison in an alternative without danger to the community" (1984: 9). These definitions illustrate the changing nature of intensive supervision. It originally was used to increase surveillance of offenders already on regular probation. Today, ISPs are being used to reduce prison populations by diverting offenders into the community who would otherwise be in prison (Clear and Hardyman, 1990; Latessa, 1986). Indeed, intensive probation is not a new concept. There are those who would argue that what is considered intensive supervision today is really what supervision was meant to be when it was originally conceived (Rothman, 1980).

The new version of probation has helped reestablish probation within the system of justice. Furthermore, intensive supervision provides politicians with a "get tough" policy while diverting offenders from institutions. For example, the Georgia program clearly states that its purpose is to "increase the heat on probationers" (Erwin, 1986: 17). These two combined components have proven to be acceptable by both liberals and conservatives, and this may help explain its widespread implementation (Byrne, 1990). ISPs also appear to be a more cost effective alternative to incarceration (Erwin and Bennett, 1986; Latessa, 1987; Noonan and Latessa, 1987; U.S. Department of Justice 1988; Byrne, 1990).

With this more intense form of probation supervision, both the offender and the probation officer become more accountable for their activities. This is a major factor in making intensive supervision acceptable to judges as an alternative to incarceration (Bennett, 1984: 9). The intensive supervision probation officer, because of reduced caseloads, has more weekly contacts with the offender than a regular probation officer. These contacts include visits, telephone calls, and assistance in providing services such as unemployment, welfare, job training, educational assistance, and alcohol and drug programs. The combination of closer surveillance and better services places the intensive probationer under tighter control than he/she would be if on regular probation (Hardyman, 1984: 2).

Throughout the years various forms of intensive supervision have been tested. Although there has been a great deal of interest and research on the effects of intensive supervision (Robinson et al., 1969; Gottfredson and Neithercutt, 1974; Sasfy, 1975; Banks, et al., 1977; Fallen et al., 1981; Gettinger, 1983), many of the early efforts were of questionable value (Adams and Vetter, 1974; Latessa, 1979; Fields, 1984).

The four major issues surrounding the use of intensive supervision have been the effectiveness question, the caseload size and classification issue, the debate over the number and quality of contacts, and more recently, the treatment versus control issue.

The question of effectiveness has gone largely unanswered. Much of the prior research has used recidivism as the primary if not sole measure of effectiveness. There is no conclusive evidence that intensive supervision will result in lower recidivism rates (Byrne, 1990). However, there appears to be some success with "specially" selected offenders (Banks et al., 1977; Latessa and Vito, 1984), but overall anticipated reductions in recidivism have not materialized. Studies that have included cost, social adjustment, and commitment rates as indicators of effectiveness have demonstrated more success and impact (Latessa, 1987; Erwin and Bennett, 1986; Pearson, 1987).

As far as caseload size is concerned, experiments with intensive supervision have resulted in lower numbers of offenders per officer. Caseload size ranges from ten per officer to fifty, with the average around twenty-five. While large caseloads are often cited as a reason for high failure rates, researchers have not found a strong relationship between caseload size and recidivism. The crucial operational issue has been the dilemma of accurately selecting cases appropriate for higher levels of supervision. The most widely used screening techniques involve either (or both) risk or need assessment instruments (Baird, 1982). This issue has become even more complex as states have attempted to "divert" offenders from prison. If that is a program goal then it is important that offenders be diverted from prison, and that intensive supervision not simply be provided to offenders that would normally receive regular supervision. Indeed, there are many who feel that we should focus our efforts on the most recalcitrant offenders (Gendreau and Ross, 1987). Thus, it is important to identify the factors and characteristics that distinguish successful from unsuccessful offenders.

As expected, the number of contacts with clients has increased under intensive supervision, but the question of whether "intensity" should simply involve increasing the number of contacts received still remains. Recently, Georgia and New Jersey have instituted intensive supervision programs that assign two officers caseloads of between ten and twenty-five, with contacts required on at least a daily basis (Bennett, 1984). It appears, however, that the primary purpose of these contacts is for surveillance, not treatment. It should also be noted that both of these states have centralized state probation services. It is unlikely that local probation departments could provide the same level of service in a cost-effective manner without state subsidies. There is also some evidence that increasing supervision levels lead to more technical violations. However, it should be noted that researchers have not established a clear relationship between the number of contacts and probation outcome.[1]

Recently there has been renewed attention to the debate over the purpose of providing increased supervision. Supporters of a control/surveillance approach point to the Georgia model as an example of a program that emphasizes community safety. Others believe that a treatment/assistance model is ultimately the way to ensure public safety through rehabilitation (Clear and Latessa, 1989). The philosophy of the program can have strong implications for evaluations. Programs that are designed to "control" offender behavior might reasonably measure effectiveness by the number of offenders caught violating their probation. It is also reasonable to expect treatment-oriented programs to measure success through reduced recidivism rates.

These issues raise a number of important concerns about intensive supervision. Perhaps the most enigmatic is the interpretation of effectiveness. Clearly, we may need to consider the possibility that program effectiveness may not necessarily translate into reduced levels of recidivism. Higher failure rates may result because of the type of offenders being selected and the tighter controls that are being exercised in intensive supervision programs. In other words, if ISPs are giving offenders a "last chance," and using strict control requirements to meet the objective of public protection, higher revocation rates should not be unexpected. Indeed, this may mean that the program is "effective."

This study will explore the issue of program effectiveness by examining the provisions of intensive supervision in Cuyahoga County, Ohio. Crucial to this debate is an identification of the type of offenders being diverted, their likelihood of failure, and the identification of factors related to program outcome.

## Cuyahoga County's Probation and Intensive Supervision Program

Cuyahoga County includes the city of Cleveland and serves a population of nearly 1.5 million residents. In 1984, the Cuyahoga County Adult Probation Department put into effect the ISP. This program was part of a probation subsidy agreement entered into with the Ohio Department of Rehabilitation and Correction. The program has three basic goals: (1) to protect society and preserve public safety, (2) to develop each offender's ability to become a self-reliant and contributing member of society, and (3) to provide a sentencing alternative to incarceration.

There are three ways in which an individual can enter the program:

1. Direct sentence by the judge.
2. Cases diverted from the state prison system as a result of an amended sentence (shock probation).[2]
3. Cases from general probation that become probation violators.

Presently there are ten officers with an average caseload of approximately thirty-five offenders. At a minimum, the officer's are to contact each offender once each week. Other requirements include weekly payments of restitution and court costs, urinalysis (announced and unannounced), employment/vocational or educational training, and any other stipulations imposed by the court.

Individuals assigned to the ISP must complete between six months and one year in the program. Upon completion the offender is transferred to regular probation for an extended period of time.

In comparison, the group on regular probation must report to their assigned probation officer twice during the first thirty days and thereafter as instructed. All fines, court costs, and restitution are to be paid in monthly installments as directed.

## Methodology

A quasi-experimental design was used for this study. A random sample of offenders sentenced to the ISP between April 1990 and June 1991 were included. Comparison cases were randomly selected from the balance of the department's caseloads. Similar data were gathered on both groups from an equivalent time frame. There are a total of 401 ISP and 404 comparison cases included in this study. Data related to demographic characteristics, criminal history, problem areas, and classification were used to describe the various groups.[3]

The outcome measures used in this study were designed to gauge the performance of the offenders while under supervision. The outcome indicators included arrests, convictions, technical violations, and offender status. In addition, an analysis was conducted to identify the factors significantly related to success or failure. Success is defined as "released from probation" or "still under supervision" at the time of the follow-up. Failure included those offenders who were "revoked" or incarcerated on a new offense." In addition, those "absconding" from probation were included in the failure group and as a separate definition of failure.

Comparisons between the two groups were conducted through analysis of variance and chi-square. Discriminant function analysis was used to identify the factors predicting success and failure on the recidivism measure.

# Results

The results from this study are of four major types: (1) a description of the samples and identification of significant relationships between background characteristics outcome (success or failure),[4] (2) differences between the ISP and comparison groups with regard to these background variables, (3) follow-up data concerning criminal behavior and probation status, and (4) identification of factors related to success and failure of the two groups in terms of probation status.

## Background Characteristics

Table 1 presents the background characteristics of the various groups. These data were gathered at the time of admission to probation. The demographic data indicates that approximately 80 percent of each group was male, and that 70 percent or more of each group was black. The average age for all groups was thirty, approximately 65 percent of each group was single, and the average educational level for both groups was eleven years.

Table 1: Background Characteristics—ISP and Comparison Groups

| Factor | ISP Group | Comparison |
|---|---|---|
| | N (%) | N (%) |
| Sex: | | |
|     Male | 326 (81%) | 323 (80%) |
|     Female | 75 (29%) | 81 (20%) |
| Race: | | |
|     Black | 298 (74%) | 283 (70%) |
|     White | 103 (26%) | 119 (30%) |
| Age: | | |
|     18–21 | 51 (13%) | 72 (18%) |
|     22–28 | 150 (37%) | 130 (32%) |
|     29–35 | 107 (27%) | 100 (25%) |
|     36 + | 93 (23%) | 100 (25%) |
| Education: | | |
|     < High School | 215 (54%) | 200 (50%) |
|     High School Grad | 147 (37%) | 145 (37%) |
|     Post High School | 38 ( 9%) | 52 (13%) |
| Marital Status: | | |
|     Single | 261 (66%) | 255 (64%) |
|     Married | 135 (34%) | 142 (36%) |
| Length of Residence:* | | |
|     < 1 year | 210 (53%) | 97 (29%) |
|     1–2 years | 67 (17%) | 71 (22%) |
|     2–3 years | 55 (14%) | 50 (15%) |
|     Over 3 years | 65 (16%) | 111 (34%) |
| Employed at Entry:* | | |
|     Yes | 116 (31%) | 191 (50%) |
|     No | 254 (69%) | 188 (50%) |
| PSI Recommendation:* | | |
|     Probation | 182 (48%) | 293 (77%) |
|     Incarceration | 175 (46%) | 59 (16%) |
|     Other | 20 ( 6%) | 28 ( 7%) |

* Factors were statistically significant at .05 or greater

(N may not equal 401 ISP and 404 Comparison Group due to missing data.)

Two factors resulted in significant differences: length of residence and employment at entry to supervision. Forty-seven percent of the ISP group had resided at the same residence for more than one year versus 70 percent of the comparison group. Similarly, the employment category resulted in a significant difference, with only 31 percent of the ISP group employed at entry compared to 50 percent of the comparison group. With regard to the pre-sentence investigation (PSI) recommendation, the ISP group was less likely to be recommended for probation and more likely to be recommended for incarceration than the comparison group. This is not surprising, given the goal of the program to divert offenders from incarceration.

Table 2: Factors Associated with Failure on Probation—
Combined ISP and Comparison Groups

| Factor | Statistical Test Result | Significance |
|---|---|---|
| Number of Prior Felony Convictions | $F = 20.5$ | .000 |
| Number of Institutional Commitments | $F = 4.5$ | .035 |
| Number of Prior Felonies While Under Supervision | $F = 12.4$ | .000 |
| Number of Times on Probation | $F = 17.7$ | .000 |
| Previous Conviction for Same Offense | $X^2 = 11.9$ | .000 |
| Prior Juvenile Record | $X^2 = 11.2$ | .000 |
| Risk Score | $F = 57.8$ | .000 |
| Needs Score | $F = 74.7$ | .000 |
| Age | $F = 5.0$ | .000 |
| Race | $X^2 = 14.3$ | .000 |
| Marital Status | $X^2 = 6.2$ | .013 |
| PSI Recommendation | $X^2 = 32.5$ | .000 |
| Prior Drug History | $X^2 = 33.3$ | .000 |
| Prior Alcohol History | $X^2 = 14.4$ | .000 |
| Needs Assistance in Employment | $X^2 = 45.8$ | .000 |
| Needs Assistance in Academics | $X^2 = 19.8$ | .000 |
| Needs Assistance in Substance Abuse | $X^2 = 57.8$ | .000 |
| Needs Assistance in Domestic Relations | $X^2 = 11.0$ | .000 |

In order to determine the importance of differences between the two groups, an initial analysis was conducted on the total sample to identify significant relationships between demographic, criminal history, and special problems/needs characteristics, and probation outcome during the follow-up period. As illustrated in Table 2, eighteen background factors proved to be significantly related to probation outcome. Individuals in the sample were more likely to fail while under supervision if they had more involvement with the criminal justice system, a history of substance abuse, higher needs, and a recommendation for incarceration. In addition, younger, black, and single offenders were more likely to fail on probation.

Table 3: Factors Associated with Failure on Probation—
ISP and Comparison Groups

| Factor | ISP | Comparison |
|---|---|---|
| Number of Prior Felony Convictions** | 1.91 | .93 |
| Number of Institutional Commitments** | .61 | .25 |
| Number of Prior Felonies While Under Supervision* | .57 | .37 |
| Number of Times on Probation** | 1.52 | 1.24 |
| Risk Score** | 16.56 | 10.13 |
| Needs Score** | 18.36 | 11.50 |
| Previous Conviction for Same Offense** | 29.6% | 19.0% |
| Prior Juvenile Record* | 35.6% | 24.0% |
| Prior Drug History* | 73.8% | 65.1% |
| Needs Assistance in Employment** | 59.7% | 45.2% |
| Needs Assistance for Substance Abuse** | 60.8% | 49.0% |

* $p < .01$
** $p < .001$

Note: PSI recommendation was also significant (See Table 1)

In order to facilitate the comparison of the ISP and comparison groups in terms of the outcome measure, the groups were assessed for differences in background characteristics significantly related to failure while under supervision. The results of this analysis are presented in Table 3, and reveal significant differences between the ISP and comparison samples on eleven of the eighteen factors associated with outcome.

In all of the criminal justice history areas the ISP group reported significantly more prior involvement with the criminal justice system. Further, the ISP group was more likely to have a history of substance abuse, more employment needs, and more needs overall than the comparison group. These data suggest that the ISP group had a higher a priori chance of experiencing failure while under supervision than the comparison group.

## Performance on Probation

In order to gauge the performance of the two groups while under supervision, several outcome measures were examined. The average length of supervision was approximately nine months for each group. Data were gathered with regard to arrests, convictions, technical violations, and probation status.

Table 4: Percentage Arrested, Convicted, or Technical Violation Filed While Under Supervision—ISP and Comparison Groups

| Factor | ISP | Comparison |
|---|---|---|
| Misdemeanor Arrest | 4.7% | 1.5% |
| Misdemeanor Conviction | 2.0% | 1.5% |
| Felony Arrest | 10.7% | 9.9% |
| Felony Convictions | 6.0% | 6.7% |
| Total Arrests | 13.7% | 11.4% |
| Total Convictions | 6.7% | 8.2% |
| Technical Violations[*] | 47.9% | 33.2% |

[*] $p < .05$

Table 4 presents the arrests, conviction, and technical violation data for the two groups. Arrests and convictions were divided into misdemeanors and felonies as well as totals. Overall, nearly 14 percent of the ISP group were arrested and 6.7 percent were convicted, versus 11.4 percent arrested and 8.2 percent convicted for the comparison group. None of the differences were statistically significant. Nearly 48 percent of the ISP group had a technical violation filed. This is in contrast to the comparison group, with a 33 percent rate. This difference was significant, and is consistent with results from other studies of intensive supervision which have found that higher levels of supervision lead to high technical violation rates.

Finally, the probation outcome of the two groups was examined. Three distinct groups were examined; "successful," defined as those offenders released from supervision or still under supervision at the time of the follow-up; "revoked," which included offenders incarcerated as a result of a technical violation or a new offense; and "absconders," which included all offenders that had a capias issued. There were two reasons to examine absconders separately. First, absconders are often returned to supervision (especially if they do not commit a new offense). Second, there may be factors associated with this unique category of failures that set them apart from those incarcerated.

The data in Table 5 indicates that the ISP group reported significantly more "failures" than the comparison group. Approximately 45 percent of the ISP were classified as successes, versus 77 percent of the comparison group. The ISP group were revoked at twice the rate as the comparison group and more than 31 percent absconded. When the categories revoked and absconded are combined, more than 55 percent of the ISP group versus 23 percent of the comparison group failed while under supervision.

Table 5: Probation Outcome

| Outcome | ISP | Comparison |
|---|---|---|
| Successful[*] | 44.7% | 77.0% |
| Revoked | 23.7% | 10.4% |
| Absconded | 31.8% | 12.7% |

[*] Successful includes released from supervision and still under supervision

## Factors Related to Outcome

A final set of analyses was conducted to identify the factors related to probation outcome. Three separate analyses were conducted. First, the total sample was dichotomized into those who were successful or those who failed (including absconders) while under supervision. Second, the total sample was divided into three groups: success, revoked, and absconded. Third, success and revoked were examined separately. Discriminant function analysis was used to identify those characteristics which predicted group membership.

The following variables were included as independents in the discriminant analysis: group, sex, race, age, marital status, education level, number of prior felony convictions, previous commitment to a penal institution, degree of felony, number of prior felonies while under supervision, times on probation, juvenile record, previous conviction for the same offense, multiple charges, employment status at the time of arrest, length of residence, assessed as needing assistance in employment, academics, domestic relations, substance abuse, drug history, PSI recommendation, risk and needs scores, and whether they receive employment, educational, drug or alcohol service.

Results from the discriminant analysis are presented in Tables 6, 7, and 8. As indicated in Table 6, the absconded group is included in the category of "failure." Five factors were found to predict outcome. Those with a higher needs assessment score, those in the ISP group, those that did not require employment assistance, those whose PSI recommendation was for incarceration, and those who did not require assistance for substance abuse were more likely to "fail" while under supervision. Overall, these five factors correctly classified 70.45 percent of grouped cases in terms of these two outcomes.

When the absconder group was broken out separately and examined in Table 7, four of the five factors were similar. The only new predictor was "previously convicted of the same offense." Successful cases were less likely to have been previously convicted of the same offense than those revoked or absconded. It is interesting to note that the absconder group had the highest needs score. Overall, these five factors correctly classified 57 percent of the grouped cases.

Table 6: Discriminant Function Analysis for Success/Failure[**]

| Factor[*] | Mean | Standard Deviation | Lambda |
|---|---|---|---|
| Needs Score: | | | |
| Success | 12.85 | 8.59 | .87 |
| Failure | 19.49 | 8.44 | |
| Group:[1] | | | |
| Success | 1.54 | .49 | .82 |
| Failure | 1.20 | .40 | |
| Needs Assistance for Employment:[2] | | | |
| Success | 1.57 | .49 | .80 |
| Failure | 1.29 | .45 | |
| PSI Recommendation:[3] | | | |
| Success | 1.21 | .41 | .79 |
| Failure | 1.46 | .50 | |
| Needs Assistance for Substance Abuse:[2] | | | |
| Success | 1.55 | .49 | .78 |
| Failure | 1.29 | .45 | |

[*] All factors statistically significant

[**] Failure is defined as revoked, incarcerated, or absconded

[1] ISP = 1 Comparison = 2

[2] Yes = 1 No = 2

[3] Probation = 1 Incarceration = 2

Classification Results:

| | *Success* | *Failure* |
|---|---|---|
| *Success* | 318 (72.1%) | 123 (27.9%) |
| *Failure* | 88 (32.2%) | 185 (67.8%) |

70.45% Correctly Classified

Table 7: Discriminant Function Analysis for
Success/Revoked/Absconded

| Factor[*] | Mean | Standard Deviation | Lambda |
|---|---|---|---|
| Needs Score: | | | |
| Success | 12.85 | 8.59 | .86 |
| Revoked | 18.16 | 8.99 | |
| Absconded | 20.45 | 7.88 | |
| Group:[1] | | | |
| Success | 1.54 | .49 | .82 |
| Revoked | 1.20 | .40 | |
| Absconded | 1.44 | .49 | |
| Needs Assistance for Employment:[2] | | | |
| Success | 1.57 | .49 | .78 |
| Revoked | 1.32 | .47 | |
| Absconded | 1.26 | .44 | |
| PSI Recommendation:[3] | | | |
| Success | 1.21 | .41 | .80 |
| Revoked | 1.50 | .50 | |
| Absconded | 1.44 | .49 | |
| Previous Conviction for Same Offense:[2] | | | |
| Success | 1.84 | .36 | .77 |
| Revoked | 1.62 | .48 | |
| Absconded | 1.72 | .45 | |

[*] All factors statistically significant

[1] ISP = 1 Comparison = 2

[2] Yes = 1 No = 2

[3] Probation = 1 Incarceration = 2

| Classification Results: | | *Success* | *Revoked* | *Absconded* |
|---|---|---|---|---|
| | *Success* | 292 (65.9%) | 74 (16.7%) | 77 (17.4%) |
| | *Revoked* | 34 (28.8%) | 45 (38.1%) | 39 (33.1%) |
| | *Absconded* | 44 (28.2%) | 40 (25.6%) | 72 (46.2%) |

57.04% Correctly Classified

Finally, only those cases that were classified as successes
or were revoked from probation are examined in Table 8. Once

again five predictors were found. Group, PSI recommendation, and employment assistance were again present. Two new factors emerged: risk score and education level. Those with a higher risk score were more likely to be revoked. Risk replaced needs as the strongest predictor. Education was also significant; those with less education were more likely to succeed. Nearly 70 percent of the groups were correctly classified with this model.

Table 8: Discriminant Function Analysis for Success/Revoked

| Factor* | Mean | Standard Deviation | Lambda |
|---|---|---|---|
| Risk Score: | | | |
| Success | 11.72 | 7.71 | .91 |
| Revoked | 17.65 | 9.01 | |
| Group:[1] | | | |
| Success | 1.54 | .49 | .87 |
| Revoked | 1.20 | .50 | |
| PSI Recommendation:[2] | | | |
| Success | 1.21 | .41 | .85 |
| Revoked | 1.50 | .50 | |
| Needs Assistance for Employment:[3] | | | |
| Success | 1.57 | .49 | .83 |
| Revoked | 1.32 | .47 | |
| Education Level: | | | |
| Success | 11.29 | 2.09 | .82 |
| Revoked | 11.37 | 1.76 | |

* All factors statistically significant

[1] ISP = 1 Comparison = 2

[2] Probation = 1 Incarceration = 2

[3] Yes = 1 No = 2

Classification Results:

| | Success | Revoked |
|---|---|---|
| Success | 320 (71.6%) | 127 (28.4%) |
| Revoked | 44 (37.0%) | 75 (63.0%) |

69.79% Correctly Classified

## Summary and Conclusions

There are a number of limitations to this study that hinder its generalization to a wider population. First, the samples were taken from one jurisdiction. Probation services are often markedly different from one locale to another, both in terms of the type of supervision offered and the types of cases under supervision. We also know that probation agencies have different policies that affect outcome, for example, the time it takes to be declared an absconder. Second, the assessment of program outcome is restricted by virtue of the ex post facto nature of the measures. It is possible that changes in staff or programs at the probation department may render the results of this test ungeneralizable to current populations. Finally, the relatively short follow-up period is too brief to obtain a complete picture of probation outcome. With these limitations in mind the following conclusions can be reached.

While there were a number of similarities between the ISP and comparison groups with regard to background variables, several differences existed. Offenders in the ISP sample had less stable residence, were less likely to be employed at entry, and were more likely to be recommended for incarceration.

Based on group characteristics at intake, an a priori assumption that the ISP group would demonstrate a higher rate of recidivism seems reasonable. There were a total of eighteen factors associated with failure for both groups. Eight of these factors could be classified as "criminal history," seven as "needs areas," and three as demographic. There were significant differences between the two groups in eleven of these factors. The ISP group had considerably more prior involvement with the criminal justice system, exhibited more prior involvement in drugs, was in need of more services, and was assessed as higher risk/needs than the regular probationers. These data support the contention that the ISP group was in need of more intensive supervision and treatment than the regular probation sample and was more likely to fail under supervision. These data also support the contention that ISP offenders in Cuyahoga County were being diverted from a state commitment. This is an important point since it helps confirm the assumption that these offenders were given a "last chance" and were more likely to be revoked from probation.

The factors examined for the follow-up found no significant differences between the two groups in terms of new arrests or convictions. However the ISP group did report significantly more technical violations. This is consistent with other intensive supervision programs, which usually report higher technical violation rates than regular probation. Overall, a fairly low number of offenders was arrested or convicted. These data also support the contention that there was less tolerance of nonconformity to stricter probation supervision. Simply stated, ISP offenders were not arrested or convicted at higher levels, but were significantly more likely to be revoked for technical violations.

The discriminant analyses of factors associated with outcome revealed a few surprises. When the failure group included revoked and absconded, three "need" factors predicted outcome. Similarly, when the absconder group was broken out separately, two "need" factors remained in the model. In both instances the "needs scores" were the strongest predictors. When the absconders were eliminated, the risk score replaced the needs score as the strongest factor.

The findings from the discriminant analyses indicate that a general assessment of risk alone may not adequately identify those most likely to fail on ISP. That is, rather than viewing ISP placement as a punitive (more intrusive) or incapacitative (more controlling) sanction for convicted offenders, placement in a program should also be guided by an assessment of client needs. It is possible that ISP intervention can reduce the likelihood of negative outcome through meeting the treatment needs of residents.

The results from this study illustrate the difficulties in evaluating the effectiveness of intensive supervision. On the one hand, the new generation ISP programs are expected to divert higher risk offenders than would normally be found on probation caseloads. In order to satisfy the demand for public safety, stricter controls and conditions are placed on these offenders. It should come as no surprise, then, when these offenders fail at a higher rate than regular probationers. On the other hand, programs that do not demonstrate "success" are often the targets of criticism and elimination.

NOTES

1. There is some evidence that suggests that increased services and contacts do in fact enhance the social adjustment of the offender. There is little evidence, however, that they have a positive impact on recidivism. See Bennett (1987).

2. In Ohio, shock probation is an early release program that grants the sentencing judge the discretionary authority to release an offender on probation. For a thorough discussion of shock probation in Ohio, see Vito and Allen (1981).

3. Risk/needs classification assessment was based on the Wisconsin model.

4. For this analysis, success was defined as still under supervision or successfully released from supervision. Failure included those offenders whose probation was revoked, those incarcerated for a new offense, and those that absconded.

REFERENCES

Adams, R., and H.J. Vetter (1974). "Effectiveness of Probation Caseload Sizes: A Review of the Empirical Literature." *Criminology* 9: 333–343.

Baird, C. (1982). "Probation and Parole Classification: The Wisconsin Model." In American Correctional Association (ed.), *Classification as a Management Tool: Theories and Models for Decisionmakers.* College Park, MD: Author.

Banks, J., A.L. Porter, R. Rardin, T. Silen, and V.E. Unger (1977). *Summary: Phase I Evaluation of Intensive Probation projects.* Washington, DC: U.S. Government Printing Office.

Bennett, L.A. (1984). "Practice in Search of Theory: The Case of Intensive Supervision." Paper presented at the annual meeting of the Academy of Criminal Justice Sciences, Chicago, IL (March).

——— (1987). "A Reassessment of Intensive Service Probation." In B.R. McCarthy (ed.), *Intermediate Punishments: Intensive Supervision, Home Confinement and Electronic Surveillance.* Monsey, NY: Criminal Justice Press.

Byrne, James M. (1990). "The Future of Intensive Supervision and the New Intermediate Sanctions." *Crime and Delinquency* 36(1): 6–41.

Clear, T.R., and G.F. Cole (1986). *American Corrections.* Belmont, CA: Brooks/Cole.

Clear, T.R., and P.L. Hardyman (1990). "The New Intensive Supervision Movement." *Crime and Delinquency* 36: 42–60.

Clear, T.R., and E.J. Latessa (1989). "Probation Officer Roles in Intensive Supervision: Surveillance versus Treatment." Paper presented at the annual meeting of the Academy of Criminal Justice Sciences, Washington, DC (March).

Erwin, B.S. (1986). "Turning up the Heat on Probationers in Georgia." *Federal Probation* 50 (2): 16–24.

Erwin, B.S., and L.A. Bennett (1986). "New Dimensions in Probation: Georgia's Experience with Intensive Probation Supervision (IPS)." *Research in Brief.* Washington, DC: National Institute of Justice.

Fallen, D.C., J. Apperson, J. Holt-Milligan, and J. Roe (1981). *Intensive Parole Supervision.* Olympia, WA: Department of Social and Health Services.

Fields, C.B. (1984). "The Intensive Supervision Probation Program (ISP) in Texas: A Two-Year Assessment." Unpublished doctoral dissertation, Sam Houston State University, Huntsville, TX.

Gendreau, P., and R.R. Ross (1987). "Revivification of Rehabilitation: Evidence from the 1980s." *Justice Quarterly* 3: 349–408.

Gettinger, S. (1983). "Intensive Supervision: Can It Rehabilitate Probation." *Corrections Magazine* (April): 7–17.

Gottdfredson, D., and M. Neithercutt (1974). *Caseload Size Variation and Difference in Probation/Parole Performance.* Pittsburgh, PA: National Center for Juvenile Justice.

Hardyman, P.L. (1984). "Intensive Supervision: What It Is and How It Can Be Evaluated." Paper presented at the annual meeting of the Academy of Criminal Justice Sciences, Chicago, IL (March).

Latessa, E.J. (1979). "Intensive Supervision: An Evaluation of the Effectiveness of an Intensive Diversion Unit." Unpublished doctoral dissertation, Ohio State University, Columbus, OH.

———— (1986). "The Cost Effectiveness of Intensive Supervision." *Federal Probation* 50: 70–74.

———— (1987). "The Effectiveness of Intensive Supervision with High-Risk Probationers." In B.R. McCarthy (ed.), *Intermediate Punishments: Intensive Supervision, Home Confinement and Electronic Surveillance.* Monsey, NY: Criminal Justice Press.

Latessa, E.J., and G.F. Vito (1984). "The Effects of Intensive Supervision on Shock Probationers." Paper presented at the annual meeting of the Academy of Criminal Justice Sciences, Chicago, IL (March).

Noonan, S., and E.J. Latessa (1987). "Intensive Probation: An Examination of Recidivism and Social Adjustment." *American Journal of Criminal Justice* 12 (1): 45–61.

Pearson, F.S. (1987). "Taking Quality into Account: Assessing the Benefits and Costs of New Jersey's Intensive Supervision Program." In B.R. McCarthy (ed.), *Intermediate Punishments: Intensive Supervision, Home Confinement and Electronic Surveillance.* Monsey, NY: Criminal Justice Press.

Robinson, J., L.T. Wilkins, R. Carter, and A. Wahl (1969). *The San Francisco Project: A Study of Federal Probation and Parole.* Berkeley, CA: University of California at Berkeley, School of Criminology.

Rothman, D. (1980). *Conscience and Convenience: The Discovery of the Asylum and Its Effects on Progressive America.* Boston, MA: Little, Brown.

Sasfy, J. (1975). *An Experimentation of Intensive Supervision as a Treatment Strategy for Probationers.* Washington, DC: Mitre Corporation.

U.S. Department of Justice (1988). *Intensive Probation and Parole (ISP).* Washington, DC: Bureau of Justice Statistics.

Vito, G.F., and H.E. Allen (1981). "Shock Probation in Ohio: A Comparison of Outcomes." *International Journal of Offender Therapy* 25: 70–76.

# PART TWO

# Targeting Special Offender Populations

# CHAPTER FIVE

# Intensive Supervision for Drug-Involved Probationers

*Christine Curtis*
*Darlanne Hoctor*
*Susan Pennell*

Probation has become the sentence of choice due to severe prison and jail crowding. Nationwide, prison population levels doubled in the past decade without a commensurate rise in capacity. Many U.S. jails are overcrowded and are under federal court orders to limit capacity. The probation population has doubled in the past ten years, with no significant increase in staffing. Almost two-thirds of all convicted offenders are placed on probation, yet probation receives less than one-third of the correctional resources. According to the Bureau of Justice Statistics, at the end of 1980, 1.1 million adults were on probation in the U.S. By the end of 1990, probation populations increased 139 percent to more than 2.7 million adults (Jankowski, 1991). In California, probation services were responsible for 305,700 offenders in 1990, an increase of 102 percent since 1980 (Renshaw, 1982; Jankowski, 1991). A Rand study found that the majority of felons placed on probation in California constitute a serious threat to the public, as 65 percent of those studied were rearrested and 34 percent were sentenced to jail or prison for new crimes (Petersilia et al., 1985).

Within this context, intensive, surveillance-oriented, community corrections programs have emerged as an intermediate sanction between regular probation and incarceration. The primary goals of intensive probation cited by proponents are to reduce prison crowding by diverting offenders from incarceration, avoid the exorbitant costs of building and sustaining prisons, prevent the stigmatizing effects of imprisonment, rehabilitate the offender, demonstrate the potential of probation, and promote public safety by ensuring surveillance of offenders supervised in community settings who are at high risk of continued criminal activity (Byrne et al., 1989; Clear and Hardyman, 1990). However, there are differences across intensive supervision programs (ISPs). Some probation programs incorporate drug treatment and employment assistance, while others focus solely on combatting future criminal activity.

The need to intervene in the lives of drug-involved offenders has been well-documented in the literature. Extensive research indicates that drug abusers constitute a significant proportion of the offender population, that they are responsible for a considerable amount of crime, and that their involvement in criminal activities is highly correlated with their drug use. In addition, treatment of the substance abuser can, according to research findings, reduce and sometimes eliminate drug usage, thus reducing the cost of drug-related criminal activity. Since decreases in drug use have been shown to lead to a reduction in criminality, public safety objectives of the criminal justice system may be best served by incorporating mandatory drug treatment into intensive supervision for high-risk probationers (National Task Force on Correctional Substance Abuse Strategies, 1991; Gerstein and Harwood, 1990; Leukefeld and Tims, 1988; Lipton and Wexler, 1987; Wexler and Williams, 1986; Wexler, Lipton, and Foster, 1985).

## Current Research

Probationers in Recovery (PIR) is an intensive probation program in San Diego County which requires offenders to participate in intensive drug treatment and drug testing. PIR probation caseloads are limited, enabling probation officers to provide increased contacts with clients. Probation and drug treatment staff work cooperatively to enforce probation conditions and participation in the treatment program. Graduated sanctions, including increased drug-use monitoring, curfew, and return to custody, are additional tools used to increase accountability.

The San Diego Association of Governments' Criminal Justice Research Division is conducting research for the National Institute of Justice (NIJ) to evaluate the effectiveness of the PIR program. The research incorporates a quasi-experimental design to compare program activities and outcomes among matched groups of high-risk probationers receiving different services and levels of supervision. Characteristics of offenders and features of program activities that contribute to successful outcomes are examined.

Study results will provide information needed by policy makers to make decisions regarding cost-effective use of intensive supervision programs and alternative sanctions. The effectiveness of the PIR program will be assessed in terms of community control of offender behavior and protection of the safety of the community through the utilization of graduated sanctions, expanded use of drug testing, reduced caseloads, and intensive supervision. In addition, detailed information regarding program participants and the impact of intensive supervision on their behavior and life patterns will be provided.

## Literature Review

Faced with increasing probation populations, correctional officials have been searching for innovative and effective approaches to assessing, treating, managing, and controlling the diverse offender group. Charles B. DeWitt, NIJ's director, states that "intermediate punishments can provide the means to hold offenders accountable for their illegal action and achieve the goal of increasing public safety" (U.S. Department of Justice, 1990).

Community supervision programs emphasizing reduced caseloads and increased levels of client supervision have operated since the early 1980s. Early intensive supervision programs were based on the assumption that increased offender supervision would lead to rehabilitation of parolees and probationers. Research showed that this objective was not realized (Smith, 1988). Early research on intensive supervision programs attempted to discover the "correct" number of clients to place on a caseload. Researchers found that

- Intensive supervision is difficult to achieve.
- Intensity of supervision is not merely a result of smaller caseloads.
- Close contact does not guarantee greater success.
- Intensive supervision produces an "interaction effect," by which treatment helps some types of offenders but hurts the chances of success for others.

Despite early research findings, intensive supervision became popular as an alternative to prison in the latter half of the 1980s.

Several points supporting intensive supervision programs have been presented in the literature. Many of the new intensive probation programs claim to deliver "tough" conditions with increased supervision and enforcement that will ensure community safety (Clear and Hardyman, 1990). Intensive supervision is considered to be one method toward reinstalling judicial and public confidence in the ability of probation to serve the needs of the community. In addition, some evaluations report that intensive supervision can successfully keep "specially" chosen offenders in the community with a minimal risk of their being arrested for further crimes (Byrne et al., 1989; Latessa, 1987).

In order to provide a cost-effective sentencing option satisfying punishment, public safety, and treatment objectives, the following objectives for intensive supervision need to be met, according to Smith (1988):

- Provide a cost-effective community option for offenders who may otherwise be incarcerated.
- Administer sanctions appropriate to the seriousness of the offense.
- Promote public safety by providing surveillance and risk control strategies indicated by the risk and needs of the offender.

- Increase the availability of treatment resources to meet offenders' needs.
- Promote a crime-free lifestyle by requiring offenders to be employed, perform community service, make restitution, and remain substance free.

The last four elements are consistent with the goals of the PIR program being evaluated.

## Intensive Supervision Probation Programs

There are variations across and within jurisdictions as to what is included in intensive supervision programs. Generally, the specified offender populations are targeted for intensive levels of supervision and surveillance. Most intensive supervision programs establish certain criteria for exclusion. Reasons for exclusion often include a violent current offense, a long criminal record, or an otherwise unusual risk to the community (Clear and Hardyman, 1990). Increased supervision is usually combined with other conditions of probation or parole, such as curfew, restitution, community service work, drug and alcohol testing, substance abuse treatment, and an employment or educational requirement. Intensive supervision programs also limit caseloads to a maximum level considerably below that of traditional supervision, permitting an increased number of contacts with the offender and employers, more frequent alcohol and drug testing, and closer observance of participation in treatment. Typically, offenders are required to complete a minimum amount of time in the program before being either released from supervision or released to a period of regular probation or parole supervision (GAO-PEMD, 1990).

A number of intensive probation programs have been evaluated, but only recently has the research begun to emphasize drug treatment as a key program element. Evaluations of two of the first ISPs provide an assessment of the effectiveness and costs of intensive supervision as diversion from state prison in Georgia and as an early release mechanism after a relatively short prison term in New Jersey (Pearson and Harper, 1990, Erwin, 1990). Both the Georgia and New Jersey research studies report positive results in terms of recidivism and cost savings (Erwin, 1990; Pearson, 1987). The New Jersey intensive supervision program includes relatively low-risk offenders, with less than half convicted of a drug offense (Pearson, 1987). A comparison of risk levels shows that, proportionately, the Georgia program serves a somewhat higher risk population; however, approximately one-third are classified as minimum risk (Byrne et al., 1989).

With regard to drug offenders in the Georgia intensive supervision program, Erwin states that the level of need for drug treatment was not met in many cases due to the lack of resources. Despite this, the research concludes that the highest success rate was for those convicted of drug-related offenses (Erwin, 1990). This conclusion suggests that an ISP may be an effective option for offenders with drug problems, and that the potential for success of programs with an intensive drug treatment program may be even greater.

The Massachusetts ISP was designed to provide community supervision for high-risk offenders typically placed on probation rather than as a diversion or early release from custody, although 44 percent of the sample received split sentences including some jail time. This population is similar to the probationers selected for the PIR program being evaluated. However, PIR only includes high-risk drug offenders. The Massachusetts study found that the level of supervision provided had an indirect effect on subsequent recidivism. Key factors related to reduced recidivism were improvements in employment status and reductions in substance abuse, suggesting a need for sufficient resources to provide employment opportunities and substance abuse treatment programs (Byrne et al., 1989). The research on the PIR program will further assess this hypothesis.

An Ohio program serving high-risk probationers was evaluated by Latessa (1987). Results suggest that there was no significant difference between the ISP and control groups on recidivism and social adjustment. However, Latessa notes that the level of supervision for the ISP groups was below program objectives, which could have affected the success rates for this group. He concludes that the effectiveness of an ISP is dependent on the caseload size, classification of offenders, and the number and quality of contacts.

The Rand Corporation has completed evaluations of a number of intensive probation programs funded by the Bureau of Justice Assistance. In general, their findings show that ISPs did not reduce recidivism, as measured by technical violations and new arrests. The Rand researchers offer the following factors that may impact the success of ISPs: conditions imposed by programs and the extent of compliance; personal offender traits that are correlated with success; and the issue of adequate drug treatment (Petersilia and Turner, 1990).

Despite recent findings that show limited success of selected intensive probation programs in reducing recidivism, it is important to continue to look for alternatives that are effective with specific types of offenders. The literature supports the incorporation of drug treatment components and employment assistance within intensive probation, as is the case in the PIR program.

## Drug Treatment

The impact of substance abuse on crime is significant. Individuals with established patterns of both drug abuse and criminality have been shown to have increases or reductions in criminality with corresponding increases or reductions in drug abuse (Field, 1989). Some experts suggest that substance abuse accelerates the level of criminal activity among individuals already involved in crime. Drug addicts participate in criminal activity three to five times as often as arrestees who do not use drugs, and they are arrested more frequently than arrestees not involved with drugs. Most drug-involved offenders pursue a continuing cycle of crime, arrest, conviction, incarceration or community service, release, and return to crime (National Task Force on Correctional Substance Abuse Strategies, 1991).

A study on incorporating drug treatment in criminal sanctions, conducted by Visher (1990) for the National Institute of Justice, found that drug treatment, coupled with other sanctions, appears to be the most promising alternative for handling drug-involved offenders. According to the study, drug-involved offenders in drug treatment commit fewer crimes and use drugs less often than those not in treatment. Because drug use and criminal behavior are common after release, post-release supervision or aftercare is an essential component of treatment to support changes in behavior. The relapse prevention component of the PIR program addresses this issue.

Visher (1990) also notes that drug treatment programs as part of the sanctions imposed on drug-involved offenders are critical in achieving the public safety objective. The study emphasizes the importance of compulsory or enforced drug treatment and drug testing for drug-involved offenders who are under legal supervision by the criminal justice system. Visher's evidence suggests that early intervention and treatment can benefit young drug-involved offenders with no heroin use and no prior treatment history.

Additional literature indicates that compulsory treatment has several advantages. It directs drug abusers into treatment, keeps drug abusers in treatment longer, makes treatment available before a crime has been committed, and contains the addict through the drug treatment program rather than only providing punishment (Leukefeld and Tims, 1988).

The major issues outlined in this review of recent research will be addressed through an assessment of PIR.

- To assess the level of actual program delivery, the analysis will include measurement of actual surveillance and treatment provided by the program.
- Through a comparison with probationers on regular high-risk probation, the effectiveness of PIR program components will be determined, including caseload size, classification of offenders, and number and quality of contacts.
- The impact of employment assistance, program fees, graduated sanctions within a drug treatment program, and the compulsory nature of PIR will be evaluated.
- A profile of the "successful" probationer will be described for identification of offenders most appropriate for the program.

The final evaluation of PIR will provide an extensive assessment of the issues related to intensive probation, drug treatment, and relapse prevention as components of a comprehensive program to meet the increasing demand for probation services with limited resources.

# Program Description

As mentioned previously, PIR is an intensive supervision program including drug treatment for high-risk offenders which serves San Diego County. Offices are located in the northern and southern areas of the county. The program was originally implemented in the city of Vista in November 1989 and was expanded to National City in April 1991. The San Diego County Probation Department enforces the conditions of the probation sentence and the requirements of drug treatment, while Mental Health Systems, Inc., a community-based organization, provides the drug treatment component.

## *Goals and Objectives*

The goal of PIR is to address the multifaceted problems of the chemically dependent criminal population, to remove from the community clients who continue to use illegal drugs and/or participate in criminal activity, and to concentrate on supervising and treating those who remain in the community. The focus is primarily on rehabilitation rather than deterrence. The primary objectives of the program are to:

- provide concentrated probation supervision for drug-involved offenders to decrease further substance abuse and related criminality;
- provide in-depth assessment to assure that appropriate sanctions and treatment are provided;
- promote public safety by providing surveillance and risk control strategies as indicated by the risk and needs assessment of the participating probationer;

- identify and remove from the community those offenders who continue their substance abuse and criminality;
- satisfy participant needs through increased availability of service and treatment resources;
- promote a crime- and drug-free, productive lifestyle;
- develop procedures and supervision strategies which can be used to enhance the effectiveness of conventional probation operation;
- provide a variety of sanctions to effect control including, but not limited to, residential treatment, electronic surveillance, house arrest, work projects, curfews, and urinalysis testing; and
- provide graduated levels of supervision appropriate to the needs and risks of offenders.

## Target Population

The purpose of PIR is to identify adult probationers who are drug-involved and provide appropriate, intensive case action planning, supervision, and treatment. Offenders are selected for entrance to the PIR program according to the following screening criteria:

- high-risk offenders, based on risk/needs scores, with a primary presenting problem of drug abuse;
- drug testing/alcohol conditions assigned by the court;
- not participating in a state-mandated intensive program for alcohol offenders;
- not an illegal alien;
- not on state parole or federal probation;
- not a transient;
- not a known psychotic/chronic schizophrenic; and
- no excessive criminal/violent history.

Offenders in the PIR program are drawn from existing probation caseloads; placement is not a sentencing option or alternative to incarceration. Probation supervision is expanded to include more frequent drug testing than regular probation supervision for high-risk offenders, additional contacts with probation officers, and graduated punishments (for example, residential treatment, work projects, curfews, phone check-in, additional Narcotics or Alcoholics Anonymous (NA/AA) meetings, extended time in the PIR program, and local custody with substance abuse programs). Due to this increased supervision, caseloads have been limited to fifty clients per probation officer.

The program staff assess offenders' needs and motivation to determine the appropriate supervision level and drug treatment. Drug treatment personnel and probation staff work cooperatively in a shared office space to assess the needs of PIR participants and to intervene in their lives while maintaining the safety of the community. A primary objective of PIR is to hold each probationer accountable for inappropriate behavior while enabling staff to continue to work with the offender toward a crime-free and drug-free lifestyle. Through a balanced use of intensive probation supervision and drug treatment, it is expected that the offender will address substance abuse and the associated problems of social dysfunction and criminal activities.

## Program Components

The drug treatment component requires participants to attend two NA or AA classes per week, three PIR drug treatment meetings per week, and two individual meetings with a PIR drug counselor per month. Attendance at the "job club" is also required for probationers without employment. These sessions provide information on job search skills and allow time for job search activities. In addition, referrals by treatment staff to outside agencies are made as needed. The three PIR meetings each week focus on a variety of areas: drug education, the twelve-step recovery process, aggression replacement, improvement of social skills, self-esteem, alternatives to risk-taking behaviors, and "clean and sober" activities. Each client is required to pay $360 prior to completion of the program to offset the costs of providing the drug treatment service. This initial phase of the program lasts at least six months. The time spent in the program depends on the responsiveness of the client. In order to successfully complete the PIR program, a client must:

- be drug and alcohol free;
- attend at least two NA/AA meetings per week;
- have a NA/AA sponsor;
- be employed;
- be crime free;
- have a home group;
- attend a step study group weekly;
- complete PIR homework;
- complete step one through step three of the twelve steps;
- begin relapse prevention classes;
- pay the $360 fee for participation in the PIR program; and
- develop a reentry plan with the counselor.

On completion of the initial phase of the program, the probationer continues treatment through two relapse prevention classes per week for up to six months and remains involved in an NA or AA recovery program.

The probation component focuses on providing public protection and the prevention of probation violations related to substance abuse. Probation officers utilize a case action plan for supervision and treatment. The case action plan may include, but is not limited to, activities undertaken by the probation officer to ensure that the probationer remains free of substance abuse, remains crime free, is employed, performs community service, and provides restitution to victims where applicable. The plan also provides for such activities as drug testing, drug treatment (e.g., residential treatment, detoxification), law enforcement and electronic surveillance, home confinement, pre-employment training, referral to social service agencies and outpatient clinics, family counseling, transportation, recreation, education, curfews, telephone contact, written reports, participation in self-help organizations, prevention of delinquent association, liaison with family and employer, referral to Department of Rehabilitation and Employment Development Department, and AIDS training.

PIR attempts to increase user accountability through limited caseloads, intensive supervision, mandatory drug treatment, and graduated punishments. As mentioned, the goal of PIR is to balance the enforcement and treatment needs for chemically dependent offenders. Initially, there is a greater need for an emphasis on law enforcement and surveillance. As the client becomes involved in the treatment process, the balance shifts more toward treatment. By utilizing an integrated approach in which treatment of drug-involved offenders is shared by the criminal justice system and the treatment community, PIR seeks to address the dual needs of protecting the public while providing treatment to the chemically dependent, criminally active population.

## Program Evaluation

As discussed in the previous section, the PIR program differs from current probation for high-risk offenders with respect to the systematic partnership between surveillance and treatment, and the degree of intensity of both accountability and treatment for the offender. While regular high-risk caseloads are subject to surveillance and control procedures that exceed those in regular probation, they do not integrate the treatment and other support services provided through PIR. Due to limited resources, regular high-risk probation supervision is not consistently able to balance risk control and risk reduction, and frequently must opt for the control function. Research has demonstrated that without adequate resources such as drug treatment, intensive probation becomes less effective with drug-involved offenders. The purpose of the evaluation is to test this assertion by evaluating the effectiveness of PIR.

The evaluation is a quasi-experimental design comparing program activities and outcomes for two matched groups of high-risk probationers receiving different levels of service and supervision. The purpose of this research is to describe two types of probation services, to determine if expected service levels are implemented as designed, and to assess the effectiveness of drug treatment within an intensive probation program. The experimental group includes 222 probationers assigned to the PIR program. The control group consists of 164 probationers assigned to regular high-risk probation caseloads.

It is hypothesized that:

- The provision of drug treatment within the PIR program will reduce subsequent drug use and criminal behavior of high-risk probationers.
- Successful outcomes of reduced drug use and criminality are associated with characteristics of offenders and program services.

The following research objectives address expected results and outcomes of the PIR program:

- Determine if the PIR program was implemented as designed, including screening criteria, caseloads, level of drug testing, graduated sanctions for violations, and treatment program delivery.
- Assess the violation and return-to-custody rates of intensive probation for high-risk offenders in two groups.
- Determine the relative effectiveness of two types of probation for high-risk offenders in reducing drug use and criminal behavior, improving life skills, changing lifestyles, and increasing employment or educational opportunities.
- Assess the characteristics of high-risk probationers who successfully complete probation without becoming involved in the criminal justice system during or after release from probation. The comparison will include sociodemographic characteristics, drug and criminal behavior patterns, and daily life patterns.
- Compare the relative costs of both types of intensive probation for high-risk offenders, in terms of program costs and the costs associated with subsequent criminal behavior.

In addition to addressing these objectives, the research will answer the following questions regarding intensive supervision for high-risk, drug-involved offenders:

- What types of interventions, including drug testing and treatment, lead to successful results for high-risk probationers?
- What are the characteristics of probationers who remain drug-free after intervention?
- Is there an association between reduced drug use and criminal behavior after intervention?
- How does intervention affect daily life patterns of offenders? How is this related to successful outcomes?
- What specific intervention strategies are effective with particular types or classifications of offenders?
- Which graduated sanctions are effective alternatives to revocation for probation violators?
- What are the appropriate measures of success during and after intervention?
- What are the financial costs and public safety benefits of providing drug treatment to high-risk probationers?
- What is the most cost-effective approach to drug treatment for specific types of high-risk probationers?

The research methodology will focus primarily on rehabilitation and specific deterrence of the probation intervention programs for specific types of offenders, with a subjective assessment of the extent to which probation for high-risk offenders meets the perceived public demand for punishment and retribution.

## Methodology

To fit the research to the program and develop methods for addressing the similarities and differences between alternative probation programs, a quasi-experimental design is being used. Random assignment of subjects is not possible because all eligible probationers in the areas served by PIR are being placed in the program. To randomly assign some PIR eligible probationers to an alternative program would reduce the viability of the PIR program and increase the cost per probationer.

Although the value of a true experimental design is not to be underestimated, a carefully controlled quasi-experimental design can effectively address the research question of "what works with high-risk, drug-involved offenders." According to Visher, "not all research problems are suitable for randomized field experiments" (1990). This quasi-experimental design will contribute to the body of knowledge concerning intervention with drug-involved offenders through intensive probation. Information on programs like PIR is vital to justice administrators faced with crowded jails and limited resources. In addition, this study will augment the body of research concerned with evaluation methodologies for determining program effectiveness.

The primary research design to assess program impact is a non-equivalent control group design. The experimental and control groups were matched using the PIR screening criteria. The two groups differ in terms of the level of probation supervision and the services delivered. Clients in the PIR program receive one face-to-face contact with a probation officer every week, six drug tests per month, and collateral contacts as needed. Probationers in the control group have been chosen from the Central San Diego County Probation Office. The control group was selected from the two supervision levels for high-risk probationers which are the source for PIR cases (Level I and Level II). Level I caseloads include up to fifty probationers and require two face-to-face contacts with the probation officer, one drug test, and two collateral contacts per month. Level II caseloads have up to 100 probationers who are subjected to one face-to-face contact with their probation officer per month, one drug test every two months, and one collateral contact per month. The probation department has two additional supervision levels for lower risk probationers which involve minimal levels of supervision (Table 1).

The primary differences between the experimental and control groups are that the experimental group receives higher levels of contacts with probation officers, drug testing, intensive drug treatment, and sanctions for violations. Both groups attend NA/AA meetings and are referred to appropriate community service agencies. The level of supervision for the control and

Table 1: Supervision Levels for Felony Probationers, San Diego County, 1991

| | PIR | | Level I | Level II | Level III | Level IV |
|---|---|---|---|---|---|---|
| | Phase I[1] | Phase II | | | | |
| Face-to-Face Contacts | 1 per week | 2 per month | 2 per month | 1 per month | As needed | As needed |
| Drug Testing | 2 per week[2] | 2 per month | 1 per month | 1 at 2 mos. | As needed | As needed |
| Collateral Contacts | As needed | As needed | 2 per month | 1 per month | 1 at 6 mos. | As needed |
| Case Reviews | 90 days | 90 days | 6 months | 6 months | 12 months | Mid-term |
| Caseload per Officer | 50 | 50 | 50 | 100 | 500 | 500 |

[1] At least first four months of program.

[2] During first thirty days. Due to financial constraints, this was changed in May 1991 to six per month.

experimental groups can change during the probation period as a result of reclassification to higher or lower levels.

Determination of selection criteria for study groups is critical in setting up evaluations of intensive supervision programs. Byrne, Lurigio, and Baird (1989) note that using risk score as the sole selection criteria identifies a control group that is comparable on one dimension only. Further, evaluation and program limitations may result from the lack of perfectly matched comparison groups (Latessa and Travis, 1988). This evaluation uses the multidimensional set of PIR screening criteria as the basis for selecting the experimental and control groups.

To test the comparability of the groups, the final analysis will include a comparison of the equivalency of the experimental and control groups on a number of measures, including the PIR screening criteria, age, sex, offense, and drug use patterns. Inclusion of both Level I and Level II probationers in the control group will result in some variation in the level of service for these cases. This will allow a comparison of outcome measures for inmates classified at two different risk levels. This will be useful in identifying service level needs for different populations. The analysis will also address within-group variations in supervision levels as well as sanctions related to changes in level of supervision during the program due to reclassification.

The evaluation includes collection of data from drug treatment and probation case files and state criminal history files of probationers in the experimental and control groups, observation of PIR program activities, interviews with criminal justice personnel, and interviews with a subsample of probationers in the experimental and control groups (about 100 in each group). Interviews with the experimental and control groups occur upon assignment to community supervision and eight months later when they have completed or are nearing completion of the PIR program.

Prior to assessing the results and outcomes of the PIR program, the final evaluation will document the implementation of the program delivered to both the control and experimental groups in terms of procedures, policies, and activities during the study period. Both types of probation services will be described. In addition, researchers will determine if expected service levels were met. Changes in the implementation process for either the experimental or control group could affect study results and are currently being documented. Program implementation and operation will be evaluated within the context of organizational theory as discussed by other authors in the field of community corrections (Petersilia, 1990; Corbett et al., 1987).

## In-Program Performance

Most high-risk probationers have probation grants of three or five years. For the experimental group, the first eight months (approximately) includes participation in the PIR program, while the control group receives the regular probation service for high-risk Level I and II probationers during the comparable eight-month period. This eight-month time frame is the study period for the analysis of program implementation and in-program performance of probationers. The analysis of in-program performance will be based on post-test non-equivalent control group design with measures taken at the end of the eight-month period.

A central issue in assessing differences related to in-program performance is the level of supervision and control. It is likely that a higher proportion of probationers in the experimental group will have technical violations because of the greater frequency of testing and contacts with probation and treatment staff. This result could be interpreted as "successful" implementation of the program because a greater percentage of the violations were detected, assuming that *actual* violation rates are the same for both groups. For this reason, the interpretation of results will take into account subjective assessments of program staff and interviews with probationers regarding technical violations and new offenses. This component of the analysis is included as documentation of program delivery, reasons for dropout rates, and factors which could affect program outcomes after release, in addition to an assessment of program success. Data on characteristics of probationers collected from case records and offender interviews will be used to assess differences in program completion rates for specific categories of offenders (for example, type of offense, type of drug used).

The following issues addressed in offender interviews relate to the analysis of in-program performance:

- offender characteristics which may affect success rates
- detected and undetected technical violations, including new offenses and drug use
- level of program participation and commitment to the program
- criminal and drug use history
- daily life-patterns associated with successful completion of probation, such as interaction with family members and friends
- opinions regarding the need for treatment and type of treatment provided

## Post-Release Behavior

After probationers complete or graduate from PIR, they are placed on regular probation. For this research project, a follow-up period of six months will be used to evaluate the effectiveness of PIR in reducing future drug use and criminality for the experimental and control groups. The follow-up period represents the six months following the first eight months of probation. The research design includes pre-post-test and post-test only measures for the experimental and control groups.

The typical measure of rehabilitation has been recidivism, or commission of new offenses. In this study, additional measures will be included to assess drug use patterns as well as positive lifestyle changes, such as employment and school attendance. Results on outcome measures will be compared for subjects in the experimental and control groups. Analysis of program outcomes will assess the effects of graduated sanctions, as well as other features of the probation programs. The final analysis will also include a subjective assessment of relationship stability and involvement in positive activities (e.g., recreation, hobbies) based on probation officer reports and offender interviews.

For purposes of the research, successful completion of the PIR program is determined by the fact that the probationer remains drug free, completes the program, and is classified to regular high-risk probation. An unsuccessful client is one who commits a new offense, returns to custody while in the program, and/or continues drug use. A regression analysis will be performed to determine the characteristics of probationers who successfully complete probation during the study periods.

The costs associated with the PIR program and the probation program for the control group will be computed, including salaries and benefits, operating costs, and costs associated with treatment provided by outside agencies. The costs will include the amounts associated with sanctions imposed, such as court processing, drug treatment, and jail. Total program costs will be divided by the number of probationers successfully completing each program. The cost per successful probationer will be compared for the experimental and control groups. Even if the total costs of PIR are greater than the regular high-risk probation program for Level I and II offenders in the study groups, a higher success rate could result in average costs equal to or less than traditional program services.

The costs will also be assessed for subcategories of offenders to determine if the probation programs are more cost-effective for specific probationers based on type of drug used, offenses committed, and other factors which may affect program outcomes. As suggested by Todd Clear, saving money may be a goal that is contradictory to the goal of rehabilitation. A more important issue may be determining the appropriate level of intervention needed to attain positive results for specific types of drug users or offenders (Clear and Hardyman, 1990).

## Evaluation Results

Sample selection for the experimental and control groups occurred from February through December 1991. Based on monthly reports prepared by probation department staff, 292 probationers entered the North County PIR program during this time frame, and 288 entered the South Bay program. To increase the comparability of the experimental and control groups, only probationers with new grants from the court and those just released from local custody were included in the study groups. The PIR program also accepts probationers who have failed in other programs by testing positive for drugs and who have previously been in PIR and failed to comply with program conditions. Sample selection yielded 222 experimental cases and 164 control cases. Intake interviews were conducted with approximately the first 100 probationers assigned to the experimental and control groups. This section presents results of 100 interviews with probationers in PIR. Data for cases in the control group have not yet been analyzed.

Since complete data for all sample cases were not available, information on characteristics of probationers in PIR were compiled from probation department monthly reports. Data on gender and ethnicity in Table 2 represent the caseload at the end of the sample selection period (December 31, 1991). Because monthly figures are based on a summary of the active caseload for each month, a combined total of all participants during the sample selection period could not be compiled. The gender of participants in North County and South Bay is similar; about eight out of ten participants were male. The expansion of PIR to the South Bay has extended the delivery of service to differing ethnic populations. Participants in the North County program were predominantly white (68 percent), while a greater percentage of South Bay were minorities (65 percent). The differences reflect the composition of the population in the areas served.

Table 2: Characteristics of PIR Program Participants,
December 1991

| Characteristics | North County | South Bay |
|---|---|---|
| Gender | | |
| Women | 15% | 20% |
| Men | 85% | 80% |
| Ethnicity | | |
| White | 68% | 35% |
| Black | 8% | 21% |
| Hispanic | 23% | 42% |
| Other | 1% | 2% |
| Total Participants | 136 | 151 |

# Results of the Intake Interviews with Probationers

On September 30, 1991, the intake interviews with probationers were completed. A primary purpose of this interview is to obtain the perceptions of offenders with respect to probation supervision and drug treatment, as well as information on sociodemographic characteristics, knowledge of probation conditions, prior criminal history, lifestyle, drug use patterns, services needed, and level of support from family and friends. The follow-up interview consists of questions to assess changes in opinions, level of program participation and commitment to the program, probation violations, new offenses, sanctions imposed, drug use, and changes in lifestyle, support groups, and service needs.

The intake interview results presented are from the responses of 100 probationers in the experimental group and focus on characteristics of PIR participants, criminal history, drug use patterns, drug treatment, and opinions regarding drug use.

## *Characteristics of PIR Probationers*

Table 3 presents characteristics of respondents from both PIR program sites, North County and South Bay. Almost all of those interviewed were 36 years of age, or under. This includes the age range usually considered to be high risk for crime and drug use. More than half the probationers at both sites were 30 years of age or younger.

Table 3: Characteristics of PIR Participants Interviewed,
San Diego County, February–September 1991

|  | North County | South Bay |
|---|---|---|
| Age | | |
| 19–24 | 27% | 37% |
| 25–30 | 39% | 24% |
| 31–36 | 27% | 31% |
| Over 36 | 6% | 8% |
| Marital Status | | |
| Single | 67% | 65% |
| Married | 2% | 8% |
| Separated | 14% | 16% |
| Divorced | 18% | 4% |
| Other | 0% | 6% |
| Highest Grade Completed | | |
| Less than 12 | 51% | 55% |
| 12 or more | 49% | 45% |
| Current Employment Status | | |
| Employed | 31% | 24% |
| Not employed | 69% | 76% |
| Current Charge* | | |
| Drug Possession | 55% | 31% |
| Drug Sales | 22% | 29% |
| DUI | 4% | 0% |
| Person/Property | 27% | 35% |
| Other | 25% | 27% |
| Total Interviewed | 51 | 49 |

* The respondent could indicate multiple charges for the current offense.

About two-thirds of the respondents were single, never having been married. Most of the remainder were divorced or separated. Only a small percentage were married at the time of the interview (2 percent at North County and 8 percent at South Bay). About one in three probationers at both sites lived with their parents at the time of intake, and one in five lived with a spouse or significant other (not shown in table).

In addition, the majority of the respondents had less than 12 years of school and more than two-thirds were unemployed. The education level of these probationers could affect their chances of obtaining employment, which research indicates is a critical factor in rehabilitation. Also, these findings suggest that the PIR program must provide adequate employment services, if the objectives related to employment are to be met.

## Current Offense

More than half the probationers at the PIR sites reported that they were on probation for drug- or alcohol-related offenses (77 percent at North County and 60 percent in South Bay). The differences between the program sites may be somewhat misleading as a measure of drug use patterns. Table 4 presents self-reported offenses committed within six months prior to the current probation term, including offenses which did not result in arrests. The data show that prior drug offenses for both groups were very similar with regard to drug sales, drug use, other drug violations, driving under the influence (DUI), and alcohol offenses. Eighty-six percent of the respondents at both sites admitted to offenses related to drug use during the six-month period.

Table 4: Criminal History Six Months Prior to Current Offense,
PIR Participants Interviewed,
San Diego County, February–September 1991

| Offense Committed | North County | South Bay |
|---|---|---|
| Vandalism | 8% | 16% |
| Probation Violation | 37% | 29% |
| Motor Vehicle Theft | 10% | 8% |
| Shoplift | 8% | 12% |
| Other Theft | 8% | 16% |
| Drug Sales | 53% | 55% |
| Drug Use | 86% | 86% |
| Other Drug Violation | 8% | 12% |
| DUI | 53% | 45% |
| Alcohol Offense | 6% | 6% |
| Burglary | 4% | 6% |
| Robbery | 0% | 6% |
| Assault | 12% | 14% |
| Other Offenses | 16% | 7% |
| Total Interviewed | 51 | 49 |

Note: The respondent could indicate multiple offenses committed during the six
months prior to the current offense.

The data on current and prior charges also indicate that
many of these probationers were also involved in property
offenses. Very few reported current or prior violent offenses,
since the program screens for this type of offense history. For the
most part, the data on charges indicate the PIR screening criteria
related to offense have been implemented appropriately. This
will be confirmed when data are collected from probation files
and state criminal history records.

## Drug Use

Table 5 summarizes data on self-reported drug use
histories, which also indicates that these probationers have
extensive drug history. Most have tried cocaine, amphetamines,
marijuana, hallucinogens, and alcohol. In South Bay, a majority

had also tried PCP and heroin. The drug used by most probationers during the six months prior to the current probation term at both sites was amphetamines (77 percent in North County and 55 percent in South Bay). Differences in drug use among different ethnic groups has been confirmed in the Drug Use Forecasting (DUF) program in San Diego (Pennell et al., 1991). The PIR data show that the type of drug reflects the ethnic composition of the communities served. A higher proportion of the PIR participants in South Bay were Hispanic, and this group had a greater tendency to use heroin. The probationers in North County were predominantly white, a group that uses amphetamines and marijuana more frequently than other ethnic groups.

Almost all the PIR probationers interviewed stated that they had served time in custody on their current offense, which could include pretrial custody time. The majority received some type of drug treatment while in custody (61 percent in North County and 72 percent in South Bay). Of those receiving treatment, almost all participated in Narcotics or Alcoholics Anonymous. The North County PIR participants were more likely to receive education and counseling programs while in custody, which may reflect the facility in which they were incarcerated. Two honor camps in San Diego have extensive drug treatment programs.

Almost half the PIR probationers stated that they still needed treatment at the time of intake (45 percent in North County and 53 percent in South Bay). It is interesting that, when asked what the best type of drug program is for someone in their circumstances, the highest response was for Narcotics or Alcoholics Anonymous (96 percent in North County and 97 percent in South Bay). This may be associated with the fact that most respondents had personal experience with these programs. Other respondents recognized the need for different kinds of treatment, including education and counseling.

Table 5: Drug Use History
PIR Participants Interviewed, San Diego County,
February–September 1991

| Ever Tried | North County | South Bay |
|---|---|---|
| Heroin | 20% | 53% |
| Cocaine | 88% | 84% |
| Amphetamines | 92% | 84% |
| Marijuana | 96% | 96% |
| Hallucinogens | 75% | 51% |
| PCP | 35% | 63% |
| Alcohol | 98% | 100% |
| Total Interviewed | 51 | 49 |
| Drug Used Past Six Months | | |
| Heroin | 11% | 33% |
| Cocaine | 20% | 17% |
| Amphetamines | 77% | 55% |
| Marijuana | 48% | 33% |
| Hallucinogens | 5% | 7% |
| Other | 9% | 5% |
| Total Respondents | 44 | 42 |
| Drug Treatment in Custody | | |
| Served time in custody | 100% | 94% |
| Drug program in custody | 61% | 72% |
| Type of program in custody | | |
| NA/AA | 96% | 97% |
| Education | 50% | 42% |
| Counseling | 25% | 6% |
| Other | 4% | 3% |
| Total Respondents | 28 | 33 |

Note: Percentages based on multiple responses.

## Opinions Regarding Drug Use

Table 6 presents PIR probationers opinions regarding drug use. Respondents provided a number of reasons for using drugs. The most frequently mentioned reasons at both sites were the feeling they got from drugs, the ability to escape by using drugs, and the role of drugs in terms of gaining social acceptance.

Respondents were also asked about the best and worst things about using drugs. More than one-third of the respondents at both sites indicated that there are no good things about using drugs. Other categories mentioned most often included the feeling received from drugs and the energy level, which may be associated with use of stimulants. Escape, attainment of social acceptance, and financial gain were also mentioned more often than other categories. The worst things about using drugs included the effects on health and emotional stability, legal problems, poor relationships with family and friends, and financial strains. The responses to these two questions may point to the need for self-esteem and support systems in the provision of drug treatment, as well as opportunities for employment.

Respondents cited a number of factors that would help them stop using drugs, with 30 percent or more at both sites indicating self-motivation, family issues including support and regaining custody of children, and incarceration. Approximately one in five also noted the potential benefits of drug treatment.

Table 6: Opinions Regarding Drug Use,
PIR Participants Interviewed,
February–September 1991

| Reasons for Drug Use | North County | South Bay |
|---|---|---|
| Social Acceptance | 24% | 24% |
| Familial Pressures | 6% | 2% |
| Escape | 29% | 39% |
| Feeling | 43% | 41% |
| Financial Pressures | 16% | 2% |
| Fun | 10% | 10% |
| Energy | 12% | 14% |
| Habit | 8% | 14% |
| Power | 6% | 6% |
| Personal Decision | 12% | 6% |
| Other | 12% | 22% |
| Total Respondents | 49 | 46 |
| Best Things About Drug Use | | |
| Nothing | 34% | 41% |
| Social Acceptance | 12% | 6% |
| Escape | 14% | 12% |
| Feeling | 30% | 41% |
| Financial Gains | 14% | 10% |
| Fun | 6% | 0% |
| Energy | 18% | 22% |
| Habit | 2% | 2% |
| Power | 4% | 8% |
| Other | 6% | 4% |
| Total Respondents | 50 | 46 |
| Worst Things About Drug Use | | |
| Employment Difficulties | 2% | 4% |
| Poor Friendships | 20% | 16% |
| Poor Family Relations | 16% | 29% |
| Legal Problems | 42% | 35% |
| Financial Strain | 12% | 20% |
| Health Consequences | 48% | 61% |
| Everything | 8% | 10% |
| Emotional Strain | 24% | 37% |

| Reasons for Drug Use | North County | South Bay |
|---|---|---|
| Crime Forced | 18% | 2% |
| Nothing | 0% | 2% |
| Other | 16% | 14% |
| Total Respondents | 50 | 46 |
| How to Stop Drug Use | | |
| Drug Treatment | 18% | 21% |
| Education | 0% | 2% |
| Employment | 10% | 6% |
| Family | 36% | 30% |
| Financial Change | 6% | 4% |
| Friends | 6% | 6% |
| Self | 38% | 43% |
| Incarceration | 30% | 36% |
| Change in Environment | 2% | 2% |
| Health Risk | 4% | 6% |
| Religion | 0% | 9% |
| Nothing | 6% | 0% |
| Other | 6% | 11% |
| Total Respondents | 50 | 47 |

Note: Percentages based on multiple responses.

## Conclusion

The preliminary analysis of interview results suggests a number of factors that should be considered in developing programs for drug offenders and issues that require more extensive evaluation. The respondents indicated that incarceration may be a factor in eliminating drug use (about one-third of the respondents stated that incarceration would stop them from using drugs). This result may be related to the probationer's unwillingness to take responsibility for personal drug use. While incarcerated, there is no personal control over drug use, and thus no responsibility. On the other hand, they may not have experienced alternative solutions to their drug problem. On orientation to the PIR program, participants seem to be hopeful that their probation term will help them (approximately 80 percent of the respondents at both sites). Further, the lack of self-esteem and support systems revealed during these interviews suggests possible components necessary for effective treatment, such as focusing on self-help and friendship groups. Also, education and employment opportunities may be a key factor associated with recovery and positive lifestyle changes.

The final evaluation of PIR will determine if the program achieves the goal of reducing drug use and recidivism among drug-involved offenders. Since the program design differs from other projects evaluated in the literature, this assessment will add to the body of knowledge regarding the types of interventions that may be effective in intensive probation programs for a specific population of offenders. The preliminary data presented show that PIR probationers have extensive drug histories and have been involved in various other types of offenses, including property crimes. Other research has shown that drug offenders may reduce criminal activity when drug use decreases or stops. The association between drug use and crime is a key issue of the research being conducted. The study will also provide an in-depth examination of the characteristics of probationers who succeed on regular probation and PIR. The results will provide guidelines for assigning offenders to intensive probation based on the effectiveness of the PIR screening criteria in identifying appropriate candidates for ISP. Through the examination of the use of graduated sanctions in combination with drug treatment, knowledge about the optimum mix of punishments for the drug-involved offenders will be expanded. Finally, the cost analysis will provide valuable information for corrections administrators in maximizing their resources within fiscal restraints.

## REFERENCES

Byrne, J. M., A. J. Lurigio, and C. Baird (1989). "The Effectiveness of the New Intensive Supervision Programs." *Research in Corrections* 2 (2): 1–48.

Clear, T.R., and P. L. Hardyman (1990). "The New Intensive Supervision Movement." *Crime and Delinquency* 36 (1): 42.

Corbett, R.P., D. Cochran, and J.M. Byrne (1987). "Managing Change in Probation: Principles and Practice in the Implementation of an Intensive Probation Supervision Program." In Belinda R. McCarthy (ed.), *Intermediate Punishment: Intensive Supervision, Home Confinement and Electronic Surveillance* (pp. 51–66). Monsey, NY: Willow Tree Press.

Erwin, B.S. (1990). "Old and New Tasks for the Modern Probation Officer." *Crime and Delinquency* 36 (1): 61–74.

Field, G. (1989). "The Effects of Intensive Treatment on Reducing the Criminal Recidivism of Addicted Offenders." *Federal Probation* 53: 51–56.

Gerstein, D.R., and H.J. Harwood (eds.) (1990). *Treating Drug Problems.* Washington, DC: National Academy Press.

Jankowski, L. (1991). "Probation and Parole 1990." *BJS Bulletin.* Washington, DC: Bureau of Justice Statistics. (NCJ-133285) (November).

Latessa, E.J. (1987). "The Effectiveness of Intensive Supervision with High-Risk Probationers." In Belinda R. McCarthy (ed.), *Intermediate Punishments: Intensive Supervision, Home Confinement, and Electronic Surveillance* (pp. 99–112). New York: Criminal Justice Press.

Latessa, E.J., and L.F. Travis (1988). "The Effects of Intensive Supervision with Alcoholic Probationers." *Journal of Offender Counseling, Services and Rehabilitation* 12 (2): 175–190.

Leukefeld, C.G., and F.M. Tims (eds.) (1988). "Compulsory Treatment: A Review of Findings." In *Compulsory Treatment of Drug Abuse: Research and Clinical Practice* (pp. 236–251). Rockville, MD: National Institute on Drug Abuse.

Lipton, D.S., and H.K. Wexler (1987). "Recidivism Reduction for Incarcerated Drug Offenders." Submitted to the National Institute of Justice to be published as a chapter in their monograph series.

National Task Force on Correctional Substance Abuse Strategies (1991). *Intervening with Substance-Abusing Offenders: A Framework for Action.* Washington, DC: National Institute of Corrections.

Pearson, F.S. (1987). *Research on New Jersey's Intensive Supervision Program* (Grant No. 83–IJ-CX-K027). National Institute of Justice. Washington, DC: U.S. Government Printing Office.

Pearson, F.S., and A.G. Harper (1990). "Contingent Intermediate Sentences: New Jersey's Intensive Supervision Program." *Crime and Delinquency* 36 (1): 75–86.

Pennell, S. B., C.E. Curtis, and D. Hoctor (1991). *Crime in the San Diego Region: Mid-year 1991.* San Diego: San Diego Association of Governments.

Petersilia, J. (1990). "Conditions that Permit Intensive Supervision Programs to Survive." *Crime and Delinquency* 36 (1): 126–145.

Petersilia, J., and S. Turner (1990). *Intensive Supervision for High-Risk Probationers: Findings from Three California Experiments* (Contract # 86–SD-CX-0015). Washington, DC: U.S. Government Printing Office.

Petersilia, J., S. Turner, J. Kahan, and J. Peterson (1985). *Granting Felons Probation: Public Risks and Alternatives.* Santa Monica, CA: Rand Corporation.

Renshaw, B. (1982). "Probation and Parole 1981." *BJS Bulletin.* Washington, DC: Bureau of Justice Statistics. (NCJ-83647).

Smith, C.P. (1988). *Intensive Supervision Probation and Parole (ISP).* Washington, DC: National Institute of Justice.

U.S. Department of Justice (1990). "Conference Focuses on Filling the Void Between Prison and Probation." In *Research in Action.* Washington, DC: National Institute of Justice. (NCJ-126159) (November/December).

U.S. General Accounting Office (GAO-PEMD). (1990). *Intermediate Sanctions and Their Impacts* (DHHS Publication No. B-239626). Washington, DC: U.S. Government Printing Office.

Visher, C.A. (1990). "Incorporating Drug Treatment in Criminal Sanctions." In *Research in Action.* Washington, DC: National Institute of Justice (Summer).

Wexler, H.K. and R. Williams (1986). "The Stay'n Out Therapeutic Community: Prison Treatment for Substance Abusers." *Journal of Psychoactive Drugs* 18 (3): 221–229.

Wexler, H.K., D. S. Lipton, and K. Foster (1985). *Outcome Evaluation of a Prison Therapeutic Community for Substance Abuse Treatment:*

*Preliminary Results* (Grant No. GR 1 R 18 DA 03310–01). Washington, DC: U.S. Government Printing Office.

# CHAPTER SIX

# Drug Abuse Treatment and Community Corrections: Findings from the Kentucky Substance Abuse Program

## *Gennaro F. Vito*

In the past two decades, the ethos of corrections shifted from rehabilitation to emphasize elements of retribution. Deterrence, "just deserts," and incapacitation became dominant themes. The history of corrections has incessantly shifted between the two extremes of this philosophical continuum. Lately, the assumed causal factor in crime was substance abuse. For this reason, correctional treatment is enjoying a renaissance. This chapter focuses upon one such effort—the Kentucky Substance Abuse Program (KSAP).

## Substance Abuse, Crime, and Community Corrections

There is a remarkable link between substance abuse and crime. Offenders who abuse drugs or alcohol are likely to continue their criminal behavior. Drug abuse is highly correlated with frequent criminal activity, including violent crime, habitual offending, and delinquency (Gropper, 1985; Blumstein et al., 1986; Inciardi, 1986; Wish and Johnson, 1986; Graham, 1987; Chaiken and Johnson, 1988). In addition, alcoholic offenders are disproportionately involved in violent crime (Collins, 1986).

A survey of state prisoners in 1979 revealed that inmates had "an excessive pre-prison involvement with alcohol" and that "illegal drug use is about as pervasive among inmates as alcohol" (Bureau of Justice Statistics, 1983a: 2; 1983b: 5). By 1986, this pattern of inmate substance abuse had worsened (Innes, 1988). Thirty-five percent of the inmates admitted that they were under the influence of drugs at the time of their offense. Forty-three percent of the inmates stated that they were using illegal drugs on a daily or almost daily basis before their arrest.

Recent results from the national Drug Use Forecasting program (DUF) revealed that the level of substance abuse among booked arrestees ranged from 30 percent in Omaha to 78 percent in San Diego (National Institutes of Justice, 1991). There was some evidence that marijuana and cocaine use declined over a three-year period (1988 to 1990). Yet, self-reported alcohol use among male arrestees was higher than tested levels of cocaine, marijuana, and opiate use (Visher, 1991).

Offenders under community supervision also have high rates of substance abuse. A national study (Hubbard et al., 1989) reported that more than 30 percent of the clients in residential and outpatient substance abuse treatment were referred by the criminal justice system. In their study of offenders on intensive supervision in California, Petersilia and Turner (1990) reported that 50 percent of the clients needed drug treatment. Few of these offenders received treatment and eventually they committed new drug-related offenses.

Based on these studies, a clear need for treatment exists. One method in place is the Treatment Alternatives to Street Crime (TASC) program. The TASC model typically provides: monitoring of the client through drug testing, identification of the nature of the substance abuse problem, a thorough assessment and referral for treatment, a supervision strategy that makes use of the information provided by continued testing and performance in the treatment program, and close collaboration between officers, clients, and treatment providers (Weinman, Bowen, and Mueller, 1990: 51).

## Treatment Program Results

Treatment for drug abusing offenders can be effective. For example, a New York City study of a methadone maintenance program discovered that those clients who stayed with the treatment were less involved in criminal activity (Hunt, Lipton, and Spunt, 1984). A research compendium of forty-one treatment programs (Hubbard et al., 1989) reported significant decreases in heroin and cocaine use among clients in treatment for at least three months. In their review of the treatment literature, Gendreau and Ross (1987: 385) found that "addicts who stay the course of treatment or re-enroll after initial failure can decrease their drug intake and reduce criminal offenses." Similarly, a review of drug abuse treatment programs concluded that, despite modality, the longer a client remains in treatment, the greater the probability of success (Anglin and Hser, 1990: 439).

In a Houston, Texas, program, Wheeler and Rudolph (1990) found that probationers who tested positive for drugs were more likely to fail on probation. Drug offenders also committed a substantially higher percentage of technical violations. However, they also discovered that drug offenders who did not participate in a treatment program had a higher rate of success (57 percent) versus those who did take part in treatment (43 percent).

These research findings run counter to the "nothing works" conclusion regarding correctional treatment. This observation was credited to the late Robert Martinson (1974) who later recanted and noted that, among other things, parole supervision was effective. However, this message helped fuel the "get tough" movement toward fixed and determinate sentencing (Sanchez, 1990). It was difficult for rehabilitation rationale to survive under this punitive orientation. A problem like substance abuse demands a treatment approach. Substance abuse treatment can be structured within a supervisory plan to provide service and establish clear lines of responsibility for both the client and the officer.

## Program Description

The Kentucky Substance Abuse Program (KSAP) is specifically designed to handle several common problems that officers face in the attempt to provide treatment services to their clients (Vito, 1989a: 67):

1. Provide meaningful feedback to the officer concerning the performance of clients in the program. Such immediate feedback is not typically offered by private or public substance abuse programs and officers are often frustrated over the lack of information.
2. Provide substance abuse counseling services in the form of "self-help" sessions to help clients deal with the problems caused by substance abuse. Through group interaction and discussion with the group leader, the common problems of probationers and parolees are shared in the hope that possible solutions can be found.
3. Provide meaningful service to officers as well. KSAP gives officers the opportunity to make referrals to the program and, in effect, to maintain program "ownership." The officers are supplied with data concerning the performance of their clients and the opportunity to utilize the program as an alternative to revocation in handling substance abuse problems.

In sum, KSAP is designed to make another supervision tool (substance abuse treatment) available to probation and parole officers and their clientele.

The KSAP treatment plan has twenty-four, once per week counseling sessions. The sessions follow a roundtable format led by the group leader. While the sessions are highly confrontational, a compassionate concern for the client's well-being is also presented. Typically, the sessions last for a minimum of one hour.

KSAP also conducts an initial assessment of clients to determine the nature and extent of their substance abuse problem, plus any other emotional or psychological needs that could impact on their treatment. The screening tools used by the program include the Minnesota Multiphasic Personality

Inventory (MMPI) and the Substance Abuse Subtle Screening Inventory (SASSI). If necessary, psychological treatment is also provided.

The program consists of three basic phases that are designed to develop and enhance the client's ability to cope with life's problems and deal with an addictive personality structure. Specifically:

> PHASE I is an eight-week basic indoctrination section that highlights the establishment of a rapport between the offender and the group leader. The leader follows the offender's treatment plan with attention given to such areas as pride, ego, self-respect, dignity, and self-esteem. Discussions follow offenders' perceptions of why they are where they are and their feelings toward the program and their probation/parole officer. More in-depth assistance is offered in Phase II.
>
> PHASE II is an eight-week intensive block that focuses on individual problems within the group. Remedial actions are monitored by the group itself under the direction of the group leader. Job and emotional problems, the need to modify behavior, develop living skills, deal with personal tragedy, and change one's environment are targeted for resolution.
>
> PHASE III is an extended, action-oriented eight-week period. Here, the group collectively monitors an individual's ability to cope with problems. The group offers support to deal with such difficulties as divorce, death, suicide, broken homes, and other emotional problems. Group leaders are available after each session for individual counseling. Each session centers on individual problems rather than a planned discussion on a particular topic.

All clients are required to go through the three-phase program. The final phase also emphasizes getting the client involved in outside programs at Alcohol or Narcotics Anonymous.

In the third year of program operations, drug testing became a key feature of program operations. The initial test is used as a part of the referral process. Subsequent testing indicates continued use or abstinence by the client. The KSAP lab and its operator are certified by the American Correctional

Association to deal with testing in the correctional system. In addition, KSAP is certified to operate both the Syva Emit Plus and Abbott ADX systems. Test results are reported to the probation/parole officer.

## Research Findings

These findings are drawn from published research based upon evaluations of the Kentucky Substance Abuse Program. As we shall see, such applied research efforts do not always meet the methodological requirements of true experiments. Therefore, the findings do not always meet the traditional standards of methodological proof. Threats to validity are demonstrably present and may be just as responsible as the program for the research results. But KSAP has always demonstrated the ability to treat those offenders with the most deleterious substance abuse history who also demonstrated the greatest risk of returning to crime—in other words, clients with substance abuse and personal problems that guarantee continued problems with the law. Table 1 is a summary of reincarceration rates under the first four years of KSAP operations.

### First Year Results

The research design for the first year of KSAP followed a quasi-experimental format (Vito, 1989a). Probation/parole officers in Louisville, Lexington, and Covington, Kentucky, were asked to screen their caseloads for substance abuse problems and then make referrals to KSAP. The lists compiled by the officers became the source for a matched comparison group. Subjects were randomly selected in proportion to the number of clients that each officer had referred to KSAP.

Table 1: Summary of Published Reincarceration Rates Under the
Kentucky Substance Abuse Program[1]

| Year of Operation and Reincarceration Result | *KSAP Graduates* N | % | *KSAP Exits* N | % | *Comparison Group* N | % |
|---|---|---|---|---|---|---|
| 1st Year: | | | | | | |
| Treatment Only | | | | | | |
| Yes | 5 | 3.6 | 38 | 35.2 | 19 | 8.3 |
| No | 134 | 96.4 | 70 | 64.8 | 230 | 91.7 |
| 2nd Year: | | | | | | |
| Treatment Only | | | | | | |
| Yes | 47 | 9.7 | 172 | 36.6 | N/A | |
| No | 437 | 90.3 | 298 | 63.4 | | |
| 3rd Year: | | | | | | |
| Testing + Treatment | | | | | | |
| Yes | 3 | 3.0 | 40 | 17.5 | 30 | 5.9 |
| No | 98 | 97.0 | 189 | 82.5 | 476 | 94.1 |
| 4th Year: | | | | | | |
| Testing + Treatment | | | | | | |
| Yes | 2 | 1.7 | 67 | 24.8 | 9 | 0.8 |
| No | 114 | 98.3 | 203 | 75.2 | 1,161 | 99.2 |
| Grand Mean Incarceration Rate: | 6.8% (57/840) | | 27.0% (291/1,077) | | 2.0%(39/1,906) | |

[1] Reincarceration = return to prison for a violation of the conditions of
supervision or a new felony. The follow-up period for each study was a
maximum of one year.

Recidivism was defined as reincarceration for a new crime
or a technical violation through July 1, 1987. This time frame
provided at least six months of follow-up after program
completion. The measure of service delivery is program
completion ("KSAP Graduates"). The assumption is that clients
who complete the program will perform better than those who
do not (see Vito, 1982).

The research compares the performance of three groups:

1. Clients who completed KSAP ("Graduates").
2. Clients who did not complete the program ("Exits").
3. Members of the matched comparison group.

With some modifications, this design was followed for each of the four years reported here.

As Table 1 demonstrates, the KSAP graduates had the lowest rate of reincarceration (3.6 percent) during the first year of program operations. This recidivism rate was markedly lower than that registered by either the KSAP exit group (35.2 percent) or the comparison group (8.3 percent).

## Second Year Results

The second publication (Vito, 1989b) is actually a long-term follow-up of persons referred to KSAP from the beginning of the program July 1, 1986, through March 1, 1988. The original matched comparison group was not a part of this extension of the research. Recidivism was still defined as reincarceration for a new crime or technical violation. The length of the follow-up period varied from six to twenty months after the original KSAP referral.

In Table 1, we see that the reincarceration rates of the KSAP graduates (9.7 percent) was more than three times lower than that of the KSAP exits (36.6 percent). Clients who completed KSAP were much less likely to recidivate.

## Third Year Results

Beginning with the third year of program operations, drug testing became a key component of KSAP. In fact, drug testing was the crucial feature of this new project. Housed entirely in Louisville, this extended program sought to determine the level of substance abuse in the entire caseload. Once detected, a positive test resulted in a referral to KSAP for treatment. Therefore, the research design for the third and fourth years follows the original in terms of tracking the KSAP graduates and exits. At this point, the comparison group consists of those clients who tested negative for substance abuse. The follow-up period for both the third and fourth years was one year.

Again, the data in Table 1 reveal that KSAP graduates had the lowest reincarceration rate. The exits had the highest rate of reincarceration (17.5 percent), followed by the comparison group (5.9 percent), and the graduates (3.0 percent).

Although the clients who completed KSAP (graduates) had the lowest rate, it was also determined that the three groups were not comparable. For these reasons, it was necessary to use a multivariate statistical technique to control for the differences between groups. This analysis revealed that the exit group (who left KSAP before completion) was most likely to be reincarcerated. Again, the reincarceration results support the conclusion that clients with substance abuse problems who complete KSAP are more likely to avoid reincarceration.

## Fourth Year Results

Here, the research design from the third year was repeated (Vito et al., forthcoming). The KSAP group is subdivided into two parts: (1) those clients who completed the program ("graduates"), and (2) those who did not complete the program ("exits"). The comparison group consists of clients who were tested (mostly negative) but not referred to treatment. As Table 1 reveals, the comparison group had the lowest rate of reincarceration (0.8 percent) followed closely by the KSAP graduates (1.7 percent). KSAP exits had the highest rate of recidivism (24.8 percent).

Because the three groups were different in nature and construction, a multivariate analysis (discriminant function analysis) was conducted to more accurately compare recidivism rates. The following attributes were observed of the clients that returned to prison:

- The greater the number of positive tests for cocaine, the greater the likelihood of reincarceration.
- The greater the number of positive tests for marijuana, the greater the likelihood of reincarceration.
- Parolees, rather than probationers, were more likely to be reincarcerated.
- Exits, rather than graduates or comparison group members, were more likely to be reincarcerated.

.– ...ultivariate results confirmed that the exit group, despite the differences between the three groups, had the highest rate of recidivism. If clients with a substance abuse problem completed KSAP, they were less likely to be reincarcerated.

## Conclusion

The overall conclusion is that community corrections clients who completed the Kentucky Substance Abuse Program were much less likely to be reincarcerated. Over the entire four-year period, the KSAP graduates had a lower average reincarceration rate (6.8 percent) than the exit group (27 percent). The comparison group had the lowest average rate (2 percent) but they were much less likely to have a severe substance abuse problem.

But, there are several methodological limitations upon this finding (Cook and Campbell, 1979; Vito, Latessa, and Wilson, 1988). First, the evaluations failed to follow an experimental design (see Petersilia, 1989). Program administrators were reluctant to assign clients randomly to treatment. Therefore, it was necessary to conduct the analysis on non-equivalent groups. The comparison groups always had a less severe substance abuse problem than the clients referred to KSAP. The exit group had been exposed to the treatment, confounding our ability to determine its effect.[1] Also, the addition of drug testing to the program operations makes it difficult to determine whether the recidivism outcomes are due to the effect of treatment or testing. The use of multivariate statistical analysis provides some measure of control over these limitations.

Other problems relate to the unique nature of the clients referred to KSAP. "Regression to the mean" is a potential validity issue. These clients had such severe substance abuse problems and prior records that they almost had to improve. For this reason, they may have been amenable to treatment, had "hit bottom" and were ready to change (see Orsagh and Marsden, 1985).

In the future, an extended follow-up of these groups is planned to determine if there is a long-term treatment effect. The testing and treatment program is now in its fourth year and it was extended to other Kentucky locations in 1992. This database will answer more questions about the effectiveness of drug testing. Nevertheless, the findings concerning KSAP are remarkably consistent with those of other drug treatment programs. If such programs are made available to offenders, they can make a difference. The effectiveness of treatment for offenders with substance abuse problems cannot be overlooked.

## NOTES

1.   However, "skimming" was not an issue here. KSAP officials do not have the authority to remove a client from the program. This authority rests entirely with the probation/parole officer.

## REFERENCES

Anglin, M.D., and Y. Hser (1990). "Treatment of Drug Abuse." In M. Tonry and N. Morris (eds.), *Drugs and Crime* (pp. 393–460). Chicago: The University of Chicago Press.

Blumstein, A., J. Cohen, J.A. Roth, and C.A. Visher (eds.) (1986). *Criminal Careers and "Career Criminals," Volumes I and II.* Washington, DC: National Academy Press.

Bureau of Justice Statistics (1983a). *Prisoners and Alcohol.* Washington, DC: Author.

——— (1983b). *Prisoners and Drugs.* Washington, DC: Author.

Chaiken, M.R., and B.D. Johnson (1988). *Characteristics of Different Types of Drug-Involved Offenders.* Washington, DC: National Institute of Justice.

Collins, J.J. (1986). "Relationship of Problem Drinking to Individual Offending Sequences." In A. Blumstein et al. (eds.), *Criminal*

Careers and "Career Criminals," Volume II (pp. 89–120). Washington, DC: National Academy Press.

Cook, T.D., and D.T. Campbell (1979). *Quasi-Experimentation: Design and Analysis Issues for Field Settings*. Boston: Houghton Mifflin.

Gendreau, P., and R.R. Ross (1987). "Revivification of Rehabilitation: Evidence from the 1980s." *Justice Quarterly* 4: 349–408.

Graham, M.G. (1987). "Controlling Drug Abuse and Crime: A Research Update." *NIJ Reports*. Washington, DC: U.S. Department of Justice.

Gropper, B.A. (1985). *Probing the Link Between Drugs and Crime*. Washington, DC: National Institute of Justice.

Hubbard, R.L., M.E. Marsden, J.V. Rachal, H.J. Harwood, E.R. Cavanaugh, and H.M. Ginzburg (1989). *Drug Abuse Treatment: A National Study of Effectiveness*. Chapel Hill: University of North Carolina Press.

Hunt, D.E., D.S. Lipton, and B. Spunt (1984). "Patterns of Criminal Activity Among Methadone Clients and Current Narcotics Users Not in Treatment." *Journal of Drug Issues* 14: 687–702.

Inciardi, J.A. (1986). *The War on Drugs*. Palo Alto, CA: Mayfield.

Innes, C.A. (1988). *Drug Use and Crime*. Washington, DC: Bureau of Justice Statistics.

Martinson, R. (1974). "What Works?—Questions and Answers About Prison Reform." *The Public Interest* (Spring): 22–54.

National Institute of Justice (1991). *Drugs and Crime, 1990 Annual Report*. Washington, DC: U.S. Department of Justice.

Orsagh, T., and M.E. Marsden (1985). "What Works When: Rational Choice Theory and Offender Rehabilitation." *Journal of Criminal Justice* 13: 269–278.

Petersilia, J. (1989). "Implementing Randomized Experiments: Lessons From BJA's Intensive Supervision Project." *Evaluation Review* 13: 435–458.

Petersilia, J., and S. Turner (1990). "Comparing Intensive and Regular Supervision for High-Risk Probationers: Early Results from an Experiment in California." *Crime and Delinquency* 36: 33–51.

Sanchez, J.E. (1990). "The Uses of Robert Martinson's Writings on Correctional Treatment: An Essay on the Justification of Correctional Policy." *Journal of Contemporary Criminal Justice* 6 (3): 127–138.

Visher, C. (1991). "Self-Reported Use of Alcohol by DUF Arrestees." In National Institute of Justice, *Drugs and Crime, 1990 Annual Report* (pp. 22–23). Washington, DC: U. S. Department of Justice.

Vito, G.F. (1982). "Does it Work? Problems in the Evaluation of Correctional Treatment Programs." *Journal of Offender Counseling, Services, and Rehabilitation* 7 (1): 5–22.

——— (1989a). "The Kentucky Substance Abuse Program: A Private Program to Treat Probationers and Parolees." *Federal Probation* 53 (1): 65–72.

——— (1989b). "The War on Drugs—The Kentucky Substance Abuse Program." *Corrections Today* 51 (3): 34–37.

Vito, G.F., E.J. Latessa, and D.G. Wilson (1988). *Introduction to Criminal Justice Research Methods*. Springfield, IL: Charles C. Thomas.

Vito, G.F., D.G. Wilson, and T.J. Keil (1990). "Drug Testing, Treatment, and Revocation: A Review of Program Findings." *Federal Probation* 54 (3): 37–43.

Vito, G.F., S.T. Holmes, T.J. Keil, and D.G. Wilson (1992). "Drug Testing in Community Corrections: A Comparative Program Analysis." *Journal of Crime and Justice* XV(1): 63–90.

Weinman, B., V. Bowen, and J.A. Mueller (1990). "Coordinated Interagency Drug Training and Technical Assistance Project." *APPA Perspectives, Special Issue, Substance Abuse: Strategies for Community Corrections Agencies* 14 (4): 51–53.

Wheeler, G.R., and A.S. Rudolph (1990). "Drug Testing and Recidivism of Houston Felony Probationers." *APPA Perspectives, Special Issue, Substance Abuse: Strategies for Community Corrections Agencies* 14 (4): 36–43.

Wish, E.D., and B.D. Johnson (1986). "Impact of Substance Abuse on Criminal Careers." In A. Blumstein et al. (eds.), *Criminal Careers and "Career Criminals," Volume II* (pp. 52–88). Washington, DC: National Academy Press.

# CHAPTER SEVEN

# Community Corrections for Spouse Abusers

*Sue Mahan*
*Lori Leigh Osta*

The focus of this chapter is on people convicted of battery of a spouse. It reports on an experimental program being developed in response to changes in the Florida state criminal law with regard to handling domestic violence. There are three questions which are given attention in this chapter: (1) What characteristics and situations are shared by offenders in domestic violence cases? (2) What is known about programs offered as dispositions in cases involving domestic batterers? (3) What policy and procedural innovations are necessary to develop intermediate sanctions for correction of batterers?

Gender differences are important in this investigation about battering. Both males and females are being arrested for battery of their spouses, although many more males than females are the offenders, and many more females than males are victims of domestic abuse.

The focus of the experimental program being described in this chapter is on offenders, but the genesis of the program comes from a concern for victims and for ending the trauma and abuse they receive. With that goal in mind, it is important to examine the importance of gender in the situations of offenders of both sexes. This indicates that the needs and experiences of women convicted for battering are significantly different from those of male batterers. The needs of women who are reported to be the offenders in domestic violence cases emerge as important concerns calling for a great deal more study and evaluation.

The present analysis resulted from an increased interest in questions of policy about domestic abuse following the amendment of domestic violence statutes in Florida which became effective in January 1992. The amended Florida Statute 741.30 directs police officers to make an arrest charging battery of a spouse or misdemeanant battery. The arrest does not require the consent of the victim nor does it consider the relationship of the parties. Not only husbands and wives are subject to the statute, but also others living together in the same house. A pro-arrest stance resulted in a large increase in cases of domestic violence being processed by the criminal justice system.

This chapter examines the first six months after the implementation of Florida Statute 741.30 in the seventh judicial circuit in Florida. In addition to the pro-arrest and pro-prosecution stance taken by law enforcement, the chief judge issued an administrative order mandating that those arrested for domestic battery, a misdemeanor, would be held without bond until the first court appearance. In this central Florida jurisdiction, the first six months following the change in this state statute showed a drastic change in the processing of domestic abuse cases.

The present study is a preliminary one. The investigation of family battering in this Florida judicial circuit is ongoing and the life situation it provides presents a perfect field laboratory in which to study administrative, political, and personal implications of domestic abuse policy.

## (1) What Characteristics and Situations Are Shared by Offenders in Domestic Violence Cases?

Terminology used to describe violence in intimate relationships varies and represents differing perspectives toward the phenomenon. For instance, *romantic violence* is used by the organization of Batterers Anonymous (Hamm, 1991), and *conjugal violence* has been used by humanist psychologists (Okun,

1986). Terms used to describe the crime do not simply raise semantic issues; they can also impact treatment. Battered women active in the social movement against domestic violence use the term *wife abuse* to define a criminal activity and feel it should be treated as a crime. On the other hand, there are those who oppose treating battering as a criminal activity who prefer the use of the term *domestic disturbance* (Loseke, 1991).

According to the National Commission on the Causes and Prevention of Violence, nearly one-fifth of all Americans approve of slapping one's spouse on appropriate occasions. Appropriate occasions include holidays when episodes of violence seem to cluster (Gelles, 1987).

Cross-cultural research has shown that contextual factors which are especially important for domestic violence are: violence in the family of orientation in which the abuser grew up, stress, and an aggressive personality style in interaction with marital strife and alcohol use. These are factors which make violence between spouses likely (Levinson, 1989). Those most likely to continue to abuse their spouses are those who have problems with alcohol and witnessed violence between their own parents (DeMaris and Jackson, 1987).

Husbands are only rarely assaulted by their wives (Dobash and Dobash, 1977). Studies show that when incidents of violence by wives toward husbands do occur, the vast majority of these women are attempting to protect themselves from abuse initiated by their spouses (Gelles and Straus, 1988).

The majority of abusers have a prior criminal history, although most charges against them are misdemeanors (Roberts, 1987). Often, the abuser maintains a public image as a friendly, caring person (Adams, 1989), and there is some dispute about whether or not batterers act violently toward individuals outside their home (Walker, 1989, 1984; Ptacek, 1988). But sources agree that male batterers are likely to abuse more than one woman and that their abusive behavior is likely to reoccur. It is commonly believed that, once begun, a pattern of escalating violence over the course of abuse is common (Okun, 1986). Yet, Feld and Straus (1991) found a transient pattern of escalating and desisting of battering. Nevertheless, researchers point out that serious, repetitive episodes of abusive behavior stem from the batterer, not from the relationship (Walker, 1989).

No characteristic of victims appears to precipitate any measurable degree of woman battering. No factors have been consistently found to increase a woman's risk of abuse (Stark and Flitcraft, 1988). Research has shown that abusive men with alcohol or drug problems are apt to abuse their partners both when drunk and when sober; they are violent more frequently and inflict more serious injuries on their partners than abusive men who do not have a history of alcohol or drug problems (Browne, 1987; DeMaris and Jackson, 1987).

Results support the belief that batterers as a group are a violent population (Walker, 1989), and the particularly vicious batterer usually has a long violent history (Browne, 1987). Experts working with abusive men agree that they greatly underreport their violent actions (Frieze and Browne, 1987). The abuser's tendency to minimize problems is comparable to the denial problems of alcohol or drug abusers (Adams, 1989). In one study, batterers consistently rated themselves as less dangerous and more motivated for treatment than did their therapists (Tsoi-Hoshmand, 1987). Victims report much higher levels of violence than assailants.

Those looking for the psychopathological roots of battering have traced male violence to a vulnerable self-concept; a complex of helplessness, powerlessness, or inadequacy; conflicts over being dependent; traditional attitudes, particularly about sex; pathological jealousy; fear of abandonment alternating with a desire for control over women and children; an inability to communicate feelings or to identify feelings in others; and a lack of assertiveness (Stark and Flitcraft, 1988). Common characteristics of batterers include: minimalization and denial of the violent behavior, dependency and jealousy, low self-esteem, and physical or sexual abuse during childhood (Sonkin et al, 1985). Researchers have found that the result of violent men in unstable relationships is likely to be homicide (Silverman and Mukherjee, 1987). Most domestic homicides by both males and females are committed with firearms (Howard, 1986).

It is safe to say that batterers, in general, have a strong need to control others (Allen et al, 1989). Caesar (1986) refers to a group of serious batterers as "tyrants" and describes them as passive, dependent, depressed, and repressed. Men in this group had alcohol problems, a history of marital violence in their family of origin, were confused about their masculine identity, and were married to women who were passive and dependent and had a prior history of being abused.

In order to assess the dangerousness of batterers, an investigation must determine the following: the frequency and severity of violent incidents, if the offender threatens to kill, if the victim threatens suicide, the offender's drug or alcohol use, and forced or threatened sexual acts, if any (Sonkin, 1986).

## (2) What Is Known about Programs Offered as Dispositions in Cases Involving Domestic Batterers?

The criminal justice system is interactive. Not only do officials react to legal changes, their acts also cause changes in family situations and actions. When the law is changed, countless people are affected far beyond the few who commit the crimes of domestic abuse and witness them. Criminal justice, human services, and emergency intervention personnel are directly affected on all levels. Those indirectly affected by family violence are innumerable.

Researchers have examined the interactive nature of the system and the situation. For example, a study showed that officers trained in the dynamics of family violence were less likely to arrest batterers when responding to a report of domestic violence. These law enforcement officers were trained to use a service response to family violence and mediate or separate the disputants (Breci, 1989).

The results of mediation training for police officers were not viewed positively by all those affected by the policy. The National Women Abuse Prevention Project declared that mediation is totally inappropriate and potentially dangerous in cases where battering has occurred. They see it as a poor substitute for adjudication (Exchange, 1988–89). Typically, police are called only after the damage has been done (Gelles, 1987).

Training for police officers answering a domestic disturbance call is explicit. Police officers must first put an end to the violence or potential violence, then gather information regarding the nature of the conflict. Both sides are to be heard separately. Nevertheless, discretion is necessary since the officer must then decide whether to leave the scene, mediate the quarrel, persuade one party to leave, or arrest one or more parties (Schonborn, 1975). Arrest is more likely when the officer has met a direct threat to his/her safety, when a felony has been committed, when a weapon is present, or when there is a perceived likelihood of further violence (Johnson, 1990).

Some police officers, prosecutors, and judges believe that, from a legal standpoint, spouse abuse should not include criminal punishment but rather be viewed as a potential cause for divorce. The extent to which professionals consider domestic violence to be a crime varies dramatically (Crowley, 1990).

Some research has shown that enforcement of arrest policies, coordinated with aggressive prosecution, is related to significantly less recidivism among batterers (Steinman, 1991). Statutes which mandate police officers to arrest and which require prosecutorial review of suspected abuse cases have been recommended, along with other statutory changes, to facilitate the enforcement of assault laws against offending partners (Schonborn, 1975; Crowley, 1990). A four-year study of a pro-arrest policy in one urban area found that the number of victims who reported battering increased when the law went into effect. Some residents of the area predicted a lowering of calls when victims realized that reports would result in arrest, but the rate of reporting did not decrease over the length of the study. The researchers also found that, despite police officers' negative attitudes about using criminal charges, victims made positive reports of the pro-arrest stance and there was a reduction in police calls and violence associated with police intervention (Jaffe et al., 1986).

The results of pro-arrest policies and mandatory arrest laws have been questioned despite these positive reports. Miller (1992) points out that a policy of pro-arrest in domestic abuse cases is likely to have a significantly different impact depending on the socioeconomic status of the batterer and the victim. Other researchers have noted that the policy of pro-arrest can have different results depending on the length of time the offender is kept in custody. Sherman et al. (1991) found that the deterrent effect of short-term arrest ended after thirty days, and after that time there may even be an increase in the amount of violence. They conclude: ". . . a little jail time can be worse than none."

Some authors conclude that an important deterrent to domestic violence is the personal humiliation of the arrest (Williams, 1989). A valid measure of deterrence must address the perceptions held by assaulters concerning the consequences of battering within their life circumstances. Consequences of arrest are not only the direct costs of processing, but also the indirect costs of stigmatization, damage to relationships, and jeopardization of opportunities (Williams and Hawkins, 1989). It is not surprising that researchers have found that arrest can contribute to attitudinal change (Barnett et al., 1988). But it is not clear what impact attitudinal change may have on a violent family life immediately or in the long run.

Regardless of the psychological dynamics involved with a policy of pro-arrest, the U. S. Department of Justice (1979) has made it clear that it is the responsibility of local justice agencies to ensure that laws governing spouse abuse are enforced, to develop victim advocacy programs, and to provide training for criminal justice officials. The criterion for success in treatment programs for domestic abusers is the complete cessation of violence and threats of violence while the offender is participating in the program and during follow-up contacts (Brygger and Edleson, 1987).

Numerous programs were developed during the 1980s to provide therapy for batterers (U. S. Department of Health and Human Services, 1989; Roberts, 1982). Cognitive, affective, and behavioral therapies have been applied (Steinfeld, 1989). Treatment for batterers developed from clinical intuition, clinical style, and personal understanding rather than from research data (Sonkin, 1988).

Most treatment programs for abusers are designed for the use of male offenders rather than female offenders (Steinman,

1991). Therapy for women involved in domestic violence aims to provide support systems and a group forum for discussing problems and examining alternatives. Men's groups focus on dynamics of intimate relationships, techniques for control of violent behavior, and the treatment of alcoholism or drug abuse (Dreas et al., 1982).

A study of the psychohistories of male batterers suggests that male battering may be understood best from the point of view of cultural definitions of manhood and structural constraints that operate when striving for manhood (Harris and Bologh, 1985). According to Gondolf and Hanneken (1987), treatment for batterers needs to address a sense of inadequacy associated with a failed macho self-image and the need to redefine manhood. The patriarchal structure of society which has condoned violence against women since ancient times is the root cause of male battering (Martin, 1976).

Sexist attitudes contribute to the likelihood of battering. Studies of cultural differences in males' sexist attitudes have shown that Hispanic batterers are more likely to have sexist attitudes than blacks, and black batterers' attitudes are more sexist than whites (Douglas et al., 1986).

In some programs, anger control groups with couples rather than individuals have claimed to reduce or eliminate family violence (Deschner et al., 1986). Therapy for couples presumes that the abuse represents a fixed pattern of behavior based on an interaction between the partners rather than the characteristics of the batterer (Geller, 1982).

Despite numerous reports about programs for batterers using anger management training, emotional awareness training, exploration of personal and family histories, emotional expressiveness training, building social support systems, exploration of sex roles, problem-solving skill training and communication skill training, the relative effectiveness of the various treatment methods has not been determined (Eddy and Myers, 1984; Geffner and Rosenbaum, 1990). Gondolf reports that the results of at least one research project have led to cautions against treatment programs such as anger control. Warnings have been raised that treatment must not diffuse the responsibility nor prolong the batterer's denial (Gondolf and

Russel, 1986). Clinicians note that at least half of the small percentage of abusive men who receive treatment continue their violent behavior with new partners (Walker and Browne, 1985).

Using the self-help model of treatment, Batterers Anonymous members attend meetings once a week with other batterers who have the common goal of eliminating their abusive behaviors (Goffman, 1984). The effectiveness of self-help treatment programs is based on the willingness of offenders to admit their problems and to learn alternative means of dealing with their domestic conflicts.

Presumably volunteers are the most amenable candidates for treatment (Bersani et al., 1988). Gondolf cautions that court mandated counseling of batterers is diverse in practice, beset with substantial dropouts, and offers an uncertain outcome (1991). But some programs have shown favorable results with court-ordered participants, which suggest that batterers need not be volunteers to benefit from training in nonviolence (DeMaris and Jackson, 1987).

Surveys indicate that common methods among counseling programs for men who batter include: cognitive restructuring, communications skill-streaming, stress reduction, relaxation, and sex-role resocialization (Gondolf, 1987). An effective treatment technique is "time out." Evidence shows that psychoeducational groups which teach techniques such as "time out" can effectively help abusive men eliminate violence in their relationships (Rosenbaum, 1986).

# (3) What Policy and Procedural Innovations Are Necessary to Develop Intermediate Sanctions for Correction of Batterers?

Following the implementation of a strong pro-arrest and pro-prosecution policy toward spouse battery in Florida's Seventh Judicial Circuit, it became evident that there was a need for a treatment program which offered an intermediate sanction for the increasing numbers of individuals convicted of battery in this jurisdiction. At the beginning of 1991, when the new law went into effect, there were essentially three choices of court-ordered treatment for batterers; treatment ranged from release with a warning, to long-term counseling, to spending time in jail in extreme cases.

While these three alternatives proved satisfactory in some cases, a need for intermediate sanctions became evident. Simply releasing convicted batterers without continued observation and attention to the problem of violence is not an appropriate sanction for most batterers. Long-term counseling may not provide the immediate crisis intervention which is called for in the short term. Jail terms for batterers may simply exacerbate economic and personal problems which may have caused the violence in the first place.

As a result of the need for intermediate sanctions, the PAVE Program was developed. PAVE has as its goal "Providing Alternatives to Violence Through Education" for first-time offenders convicted of simple battery arising from spouse abuse.

The original impetus for creating PAVE came from the director of a private community corrections organization operated by the Salvation Army. PAVE is one of several misdemeanor corrections programs offered as part of a larger Life Management Program which also handles prostitutes and shoplifters, among others. From the outset there was no funding for PAVE; it was clear that the program would have to be self-sustaining. Offenders were to be charged a fee of $50 to complete PAVE, but batterers could not be excluded from the program if they were unable to pay. From the outset it was also clear that the program would be dependent on volunteers both for clerical work and for professional presentations.

The ideas and concepts which were used in developing the PAVE program were taken from the educational curriculum called *Power and Control: Tactics of Men Who Batter*, prepared by the Domestic Abuse Intervention Project in Duluth, Minnesota. The philosophy of the Duluth project calls for a clear community commitment to hold batterers accountable for their further use of violence. They recommend a much larger system of controls placed on batterers to confront their use of violence. The PAVE program is based on the same philosophical perspective that intermediate sanctions are appropriate only in a larger system which includes short-term and long-range sentences as well.

The goal of the PAVE program is to teach—it is an educational approach. Lessons present spouse abuse as a crime and teach techniques for alternative behaviors. There are eight, two-hour lessons in PAVE related to the eight themes addressed by the Duluth curriculum.

1. Legal Ramifications: This course is taught by volunteers from the state attorney's office and the clerk of the court's office. A panel explains the Florida statute and the criminal treatment for convicted batterers. The goal is to give batterers an idea of what they can expect from the criminal justice system.
2. Resolving Conflicts: This course is taught by volunteers from the field of human relations. Two facilitators demonstrate techniques for mutually satisfying conflict resolution. The goal is to give batterers practice in dealing with conflict without coercion and threats.
3. Communications: This course is taught by volunteers who work as counselors. An instructor provides examples of open, non-intimidating communication. The goal is to teach batterers more effective communications skills.
4. Substance Abuse and Violence: This course is taught by volunteers from drug and alcohol rehabilitation programs. An instructor explains the links between substance abuse and violence and provides alternatives to addictive behavior. The goal is to encourage batterers to take responsibility for alcohol and drug problems.
5. Economic Partnership: This course is taught by volunteers who are money managers. An instructor describes the negative effects of using the family income as an excuse to abuse a spouse and explains money plans to address economic problems which may contribute to domestic violence. The goal is to teach offenders how to make a democratic family money plan.
6. Responsible Parenting: This course is taught by volunteers from parenting programs. An instructor covers family stress and nonviolent techniques for disciplining

children. The goal is to teach batterers the importance of responsible parenting.

7. Defusing Anger: This course is taught by volunteers who are instructors in yoga, Tai Chi, or physical education along with training in social psychology. Instructors address denial and blaming others for anger and demonstrate exercises which help to keep anger under control. The goal is to teach batterers the relationship between physical and emotional reactions to anger.

8. Family Dynamics: This course is taught by family counselors. The instructor covers family systems and family roles. The goal is to teach batterers how to make family decisions together.

The eight lessons are presented in separate formats. Convicted batterers assigned to the program may begin with whichever lesson is being taught during the week they are assigned. They must attend all eight sessions in order to complete the program, and if they fail to attend after being assigned to PAVE, the sentencing judge is notified. Dropouts face being resentenced to spend time in jail for being in violation of their court-ordered probation stipulations.

The instructors for PAVE are professionals whose voluntary participation was solicited because of their expertise in the eight areas covered by the lessons. Volunteers were encouraged to develop their own lesson plans. Instructors are asked to provide a written outline of their presentation, but they are free to develop the class however they wish. Maintaining high standards of quality for class presentations was considered very important to success for PAVE, but only a few instructors were dropped from the PAVE program because their lessons were not appropriate or their class presentations did not address PAVE goals.

A second important aspect of the PAVE program is the entrance interview. During this initial screening by interviewers at the Salvation Army Life Management Program, the convicted batterer completes a social history and a behavior checklist which assesses the extent of the battery. During this initial interview the intake worker takes note of personal factors and the offender's perception of the situation. The first interview provides the batterer with a brief orientation to PAVE and directions for completing the program. The first individual meeting is also important for eliciting cooperation from court-ordered offenders.

An exit interview is another significant part of the PAVE program. The batterer is asked to complete the behavior checklist again and to evaluate the PAVE program. Comments and suggestions are also solicited during the exit interview.

The first PAVE class covering legal ramifications was held on April 23, 1991. Consecutive classes in circles of eight have been held on a weekly basis since. A preliminary assessment of the program is possible after six months of operation, but there are too few completed cases for statistical analysis this early in the history of PAVE. The present analysis does not pretend to be a full-scale evaluation of PAVE after only a few months of operation, but some interesting findings have been collected from ongoing evaluation of the PAVE program which will provide the basis for continuing long-term study.

As mentioned earlier, checklists of abusive behaviors are administered at the entrance and exit interviews (see Appendix). Lower scores after completing the program may demonstrate improvement and less extensive problems with battering. Of thirty-four cases, twenty-four batterers scored lower on the exit interview, eight scored higher, and two remained the same.

Convicted batterers are asked to complete brief evaluations at the end of every class session they attend. High scores on class evaluations may show a positive response to PAVE lessons. When a significant number of batterers make negative evaluations of particular class sessions, changes can be made before the class is offered again.

During exit interviews, batterers who have completed the program evaluate PAVE and are asked for comments on any aspect of the program. Positive evaluations of the program may indicate that PAVE is useful and meeting abusers' needs. Of twenty-two completed termination questionnaires, twenty-one were positive in all three categories; one questionnaire was negative in two out of three categories. The negative evaluation was offered by a woman convicted for battering. She said that "the speakers seemed to think we were all uneducated, drug abusing, out of control 'deralics'." Her comments and others given by the three females (compared to approximately fifty men) who have finished the eight PAVE classes indicate the need for consideration of gender differences among convicted batterers in the development of treatment programs.

Observations of PAVE classes allow close examination of the characteristics and responses of convicted batterers ordered to attend PAVE, thus providing information for ongoing evaluation. Observations also help determine if the goals of PAVE are being addressed in the various class sessions. When batterers assigned to the program give negative evaluations of classes, observations by the director provide an explanation and direction for improvement.

Monthly reports show the number of batterers assigned to PAVE, as well as how many complete or drop out of the program. In addition, official arrest statistics can provide information about the cases of battery of a spouse reported in the jurisdiction. Statistical comparisons with other jurisdictions and other policies are planned.

## Policy Implications

Three of the five judges who are responsible for the court orders which are the basis for PAVE as an alternative sanction in the Seventh Judicial Circuit were interviewed after PAVE had been in operation for six months. The judges generally supported the program, but all three voiced legal concerns with the criminal treatment of spouse batterers. Their concerns are directed at the pro-arrest/pro-prosecution policy. For one, there is concern that victims do not really want batterers to be arrested, and fewer will report abuse if they know their spouses will be treated like criminals. Another concern has to do with holding accused batterers without bail and mandating arrest in every case. There is concern that the present policy is illegal and deprives the accused of certain constitutional rights. A third concern is that the increase in arrests for spouse abuse means that numerous petty cases can be brought to court, and the prosecution is faced with numerous reports impossible to substantiate.

The policy of pro-arrest/pro-prosecution in domestic violence is meant to deter offenders from further violence. Deterrence is a perceptual process, and costs to the convicted batterer can only be estimated. Economic costs are not the only ones faced by convicted batterers, but they are important to questions of policy. For example, when asked to approximate the cost of an arrest for battery to the offender, judges agreed that an appearance in the Seventh Judicial Circuit would be likely to cost the defendant at least $500 or $600. Of that amount, approximately $50 goes for bail; court costs are likely to be more than $115; prosecution and police investigation costs add at least another $100; convicted offenders sentenced to probation must pay $40 per month, and most are sentenced to six months probation. Those sentenced to the PAVE program are also expected to pay a $50 administrative charge. For offenders with private attorneys, fees can run as high as $3,000 in battery cases, but private attorneys are not common. In other cases, convicted batterers may be assessed a fine of up to $1,000, and they may be ordered to pay for property damage or medical costs of the victim, as well as other restitution. Outside the criminal justice system, the costs of lost wages to the offender are also likely to be significant, and there are, no doubt, many other personal costs which can be considered important for deterrence.

The judges agree that the implications of monetary loss for deterrence of spouse abuse are complex. They pointed out that many domestic disputes arise from economic problems. They note a general relationship between the rate of spouse battery and cases of abuse they hear with the rate of unemployment and other economic indicators. They agree that the cost of an arrest for batterers and their families is very high. In this jurisdiction, the cost of a policy of pro-arrest and pro-prosecution is passed on to offenders by the court, arresting agencies, the prosecution, and community corrections programs. Although the county system of criminal justice has absorbed the increase in offenders with very little strain, those arrested have definitely felt the economic impact.

It is possible that the economic cost may not only deter batterers, but also victims. Knowing that the abuser will be arrested and held in jail, and having an idea of the cost of the arrest to the family may lower the likelihood of the victim making a report. Arrests may not serve to protect victims, but rather add to the climate of fear.

The judges who were interviewed agreed they had observed important differences between males and females charged with battery of a spouse. The judges characterized gender differences in various ways. One judge thought female batterers suffer from alcohol and chemical dependency problems. Another pointed out that females who were arrested might have been acting in fear after a history of battering. And, a judge explained, women were being arrested along with their spouses in response to the mandatory arrest law. Whatever the reasons behind the number of women arrested for battery, the judges estimate that a woman is accused in about 10 percent of the cases of battery of a spouse heard in their courts. For this small proportion of female batterers corrections programs which emphasize gender are important.

All the judges who hear battery cases use the PAVE program as a sentencing alternative. The numbers of convicted batterers ordered to attend PAVE has continued to increase since April when the first class was held. The PAVE program developed several innovations aimed at meeting the needs of the courts and convicted batterers. Ongoing evaluation is crucial for maintaining the quality of the program. The initial screening of offenders and careful observation of classes which characterize the program during the first six months of operation are the basis for the success of PAVE. Indications of success include both positive responses from batterers who participate, and increasing numbers of court orders which include PAVE in the disposition of battery cases.

Innovations which contribute to success involve the use of volunteers and the rotating schedule of open classes. The philosophical underpinnings of PAVE are educational, although the program is part of the system of corrections in criminal justice. From a learning perspective, PAVE demonstrates that it is possible to provide short-term crisis intervention and skills training as an immediate alternative to violence.

## REFERENCES

Adams, D. (1989). "Identifying the Assaultive Husband in Court." *Boston Bar Journal* 2.

Allen, K., et al. (1989). "Interpersonal Behaviors of Male Batterers." *Journal of Interpersonal Violence* 4 (1): 79–89.

Barnett, O.W., et al. (1988). *Court Mandated Batterers' Attitudes Toward Violence.* Malibu, CA: Pepperdine University.

Bersani, C., H. Chen, and R. Denton (1988). "Spouse Abusers and Court Mandated Treatment." *Journal of Crime and Justice* 11 (1): 43–60.

Breci, M.G. (1989). "The Effect of Training and Police Attitudes Toward Family Violence." *Journal of Crime and Justice* 12 (1): 35–49.

Browne, A. (1987). *When Battered Women Kill.* New York: The Free Press.

Brygger, M.P., and J.L. Edleson (1987). "Domestic Abuse Project: A Multisystems Intervention in Women Battering." *Journal of Interpersonal Violence* 2 (3): 324–336.

Cesar, L.P. (1986). "Men Who Batter—A Heterogeneous Group." Paper presented at the annual meeting of the American Psychological Association, Washington, DC (August).

Crowley, J.E., et al. (1990). "Variations Across Agency Types in Perceptions of Seriousness of Family Abuse." *Journal of Criminal Justice* 18: 519–531.

De Maris, A., and J.K. Jackson (1987). "Batterers' Reports of Recidivism after Counseling." *Social Casework* 68 (8): 458–465.

Deschner, J.P., et al. (1986). "Treatment Model for Batterers." *Social Casework* 67 (1): 55–60.

Dobash, R.E., and R. Dobash (1979). *Violence Against Wives.* New York: The Free Press.

Douglas, M.A., et al. (1984). "Court Involved Batterers and Their Victims—Characteristics and Ethnic Differences." Paper presented at the annual meeting of the American Psychological Association, Toronto, Canada (August).

Dreas, G.A., et al. (1982). "Male Batterer—A Model Treatment Program or the Courts." *Federal Probation* 46 (4): 50–55.

Eddy, M.J., and T. Myers (1984). *Helping Men Who Batter—A Profile of Programs in the U.S.* Washington, DC: National Criminal Justice Reference Service.

Exchange (1988–89). "Working to Prevent Mediation of Domestic Violence Cases." *National Woman Abuse Prevention Project* 3 (1): 8–10.

Feld, S.L., and M.A. Straus (1991). "Escalation and Desistance of Wife Assault in Marriage." *Criminology* 27 (1): 141–159.

Frieze, I.H., and A. Browne (1989). "Violence in Marriage." In Lloyd Ohlin and Michael Tonry (eds.), *Family Violence*. Chicago: University of Chicago Press.

Geffner, R., and A. Rosenbaum (1990). "Characteristics and Treatment of Batterers." *Behavioral Science and the Law* 8 (2): 131–140.

Geller, J. (1982). "Conjoint Therapy—Staff Training and Treatment." In *Abusive Partner—An Analysis of Domestic Battering*. New York: Van Nostrand Reinhold.

Gelles, R.J. (1987). *The Violent Home*. Beverly Hills, CA: Sage.

Gelles, R.J., and M. Straus (1988). *Intimate Violence*. New York: Simon and Schuster.

Goffman, J.M. (1984). *Self-Help Counseling for Men Who Batter Women*. San Bernardino, CA: Batterers Anonymous Press.

Gondolf, E.W. (1987). "Evaluating Programs for Men Who Batter." *Journal of Family Violence* 2 (1): 95–108.

——— (1987). "A Victim-Based Assessment of Court-Mandated Counseling for Batterers." *Criminal Justice Review* 16 (2): 214–225.

Gondolf, E.W., and D. Russel (1986). "Case Against Anger Control Treatment Programs for Batterers." *Response to the Victimization of Women and Children* 9 (3): 2–5.

Gondolf, E.W., and J. Hanneken (1987). "The Gender Warrior: Reformed Batterers on Abuse, Treatment, and Change." *Journal of Family Violence* 2: 177–191.

Hamm, M.S. (1991). "Batterers Anonymous: Toward a Correctional Education to Control Romantic Violence." *Journal of Correctional Education* 2 (2): 64–73.

Hamm, M.S., and J.C. Kite (1991). "The Role of Offender Rehabilitation in Family Violence Policy." *Criminal Justice Review* 16 (2): 227–248.

Harris, R.N., and R.W. Bologh (1986). "Dark Side of Love—Blue and White Collar Wife Abuse." *Victimology* 10 (1–4): 242–252.

Howard, M. (1986). "Husband-Wife Homicide: An Essay from a Family Law Perspective." *Law and Contemporary Problems* 49 (1): 63–88.

Jaffe, P., et al. (1986). "The Impact of Police Charges in Incidents of Wife Abuse." *Journal of Family Violence* 1 (1): 37–49.

Johnson, I. (1990). "A Loglinear Analysis of Abused Wives' Decisions to Call the Police in Domestic Violence Disputes." *Journal of Criminal Justice* 18: 147–159.

Levinson, D. (1989). "Family Violence in Cross Culture Perspective." *Frontiers of Anthropology*, Volume 1. Newbury Park, CA: Sage.

Loseke, D.R. (1991). "Changing the Boundaries of Crime: The Battered Women's Social Movement and the Definition of Wife Abuse as Criminal Activity." *Criminal Justice Review* 16 (2): 249–262.

Martin, D. (1976). *Battered Wives*. San Francisco: New Glide.

Miller, S. (1992). "Arrest Policies for Domestic Violence and Their Implications for Battered Women." In Roslyn Muraskin and Ted Alleman (eds.), *It's A Crime: Women and Justice*. Englewood Cliffs, NJ: Regents-Prentice Hall.

Okun, L. (1986). *Woman Abuse—Facts Replacing Myths*. Albany, NY: SUNY.

Ptacek, J. (1988). "Why Do Men Batter Their Wives?" In Kersti Yillo and Michele Bograd (eds.), *Feminist Perspectives on Wife Abuse*. Newbury Park, CA: Sage.

Roberts, A.R. (1982). "National Survey of Services for Batterers." In *An Analysis of Domestic Battering*. New York: Van Nostrand Reinhold.

——— (1987). "Psychosocial Characteristics of Batterers." *Journal of Family Violence* 2 (1): 81–93.

Rosenbaum, A. (1986). "Group Treatment for Abusive Men." *Psychotherapy* 23 (4): 607–612.

Schonborn, K. (1975). *Dealing with Violence: The Challenge Faced by Police and Other Peacekeepers*. Springfield, IL: Bannerstone House.

Sherman, L., and R. Berk (1984). "The Specific Deterrent Effects of Arrest for Domestic Assault." *American Sociological Review* 49 (2): 261–272.

Sherman, L., et al. (1991). "From Initial Deterrence to Long Escalation: Short-Custody Arrest for Poverty Ghetto Domestic Violence." *Criminology* 29 (4): 821–849.

Silverman, R.A., and S.K. Mukherjee (1987). "Intimate Homicide: An Analysis of Violent Social Relationships." *Behavioral Sciences and the Law* 5 (1): 37–47.

Sonkin, D.J. (1988). "Male Batterer: Clinical and Research Issues." *Violence and Victims* 3 (1): 65–79.

Sonkin, D.J., D. Martin, and L.E. Walker (1985). *Male Batterer: A Treatment Approach.* New York: Springer.

Stark, E., and A. Flitcraft (1988). "Violence Among Intimates: An Epidemiological Review." In Vincent B. Van Hasselt et al. (eds.), *Handbook of Family Violence.* New York: Plenum Press.

Steinfeld, G.J. (1989). "Spouse Abuse: An Integrative-Interactional Model." *Journal of Family Violence* 4 (1): 1–23.

Steinman, M. (1991). "Arrest and Recidivism Among Woman Batterers." *Criminal Justice Review* 16 (2): 183–197.

Tsoi-Hoshmand, L.L.S. (1987). "Judgment of Anger Problems by Clients and Therapists." *Journal of Interpersonal Violence* 2 (3): 251–263.

U.S. Department of Health and Human Services (1989). *Therapy For Batterers.* Rockville, MD: National Criminal Justice Reference Service.

U.S. Department of Justice (1979). *Report from the LEAA Conference on Intervention Programs for Men Who Batter.* Rockville, MD: National Criminal Justice Reference Service.

Walker, L.E. (1984). "Eliminating Sexism to End Battering Relationships." Paper presented at the annual meeting of the American Psychological Association, Toronto, Canada (August).

———— (1989). *Terrifying Love.* New York: Harper and Row.

Walker, L.E., and A. Browne (1985). "Victimization by Intimates." *Journal of Personality* 53 (2):

Williams, K.R., and R. Hawkins (1989). "The Meaning of Arrest for Wife Assault." *Criminology* 27 (1): 163–181.

# Appendix
## CSR Abuse Index*

1. Do you continually monitor your wife's time and make her account for every minute (when she runs errands, visits friends, commutes to work, etc.)?
2. Do you ever accuse her of having affairs with other men or act suspicious of her?
3. Are you ever rude to your wife's friends?
4. Do you ever discourage her from starting friendships with other women?
5. Are you ever critical of things such as her cooking, her clothes, or her appearance?
6. Do you demand a strict account of how your wife spends money?
7. Do your moods change radically, from very calm to very angry (or vice versa)?
8. Are you disturbed by your wife's working or by the thought of her working?
9. Do you become angry more easily when you drink?
10. Do you pressure your wife for sex much more often than she likes?
11. Do you become angry if your wife does not want to go along with your request for sex?
12. Do you and your wife quarrel much over financial matters?
13. Do you quarrel much about having children or raising them?
14. Do you ever strike your wife with your hands or feet (slap, punch, kick, etc.)?
15. Do you ever strike her with an object?
16. Do you ever threaten her with an object or weapon?
17. Have you ever threatened to kill her or yourself?
18. Do you ever give your wife visible injuries (such as welts, bruises, cuts, etc.)?
19. Has your wife ever had to treat any injuries from your violence with first aid?

20. Has she ever had to seek professional aid for any injury at a medical clinic, doctor's office, or hospital?
21. Do you ever hurt your wife sexually or make her have intercourse against her will?
22. Are you violent toward your children?
23. Are you ever violent toward other people outside your home and family?
24. Do you ever throw objects or break things when you are angry?
25. Have you ever had any trouble with the police?
26. Has your wife ever called the police or tried to call them because she felt she or members of your family were in danger?

*Adapted from "CSR Abuse Index" in *The Family Secret: Domestic Violence in America,* by William A. Stacey and Anson Shupe. Boston: Beacon Press, 1983.

# CHAPTER EIGHT

# Electronic Monitoring of Juvenile Offenders: The Lake County, Indiana, Experience

*Sudipto Roy*

Court-ordered home detention and the use of electronic devices to monitor offender compliance with that court order has grown prodigiously over the last few years. Correctional systems around the country attempted to figure out a way to abate overcrowding in detention facilities and simultaneously maintain a reasonable degree of public safety. Technological advancement made practicable the use of electronic monitors for house arrest. Electronic monitoring was first used with adult offenders in the early 1980s, and a few years later, applications were instituted for juvenile offenders.

Although electronic monitoring programs for juveniles have propagated at a rapid pace, limited research has been conducted on the impact of these programs on the participants (Clarkson and Weakland, 1991; Vaughn, 1991). The growth of these programs calls for more studies concentrating on their impact. The purpose of this study is to focus on the impact of the electronic monitoring home detention program for juveniles in Lake County, Indiana. Established in February 1990, the impact of this program is measured in terms of offenders successfully completing their home detention and also offender recidivism both during the supervision and after their exit from the program.

## Electronic Monitoring for Juveniles

Empirical studies on the impact of these programs on the participants have been reported since the late 1980s. Most of the information available on these programs contains only reports on the number of juveniles successfully completing their programs; only a couple of studies focused on offender recidivism.

As for those studies reporting program completion figures, the percentages ranged from 53 percent to 95 percent. For instance, the aftercare electronic monitoring program operated in Kenosha County, Wisconsin, reported that successful completion figure decreased from 70 percent in 1987 to 53 percent in 1988 (for details on this study, see Editor, *Journal of Offender Monitoring*, 1990). On the other side of the spectrum, Vaughn (1991), in his survey of nine juvenile programs across the country, reported that successful completion percentages ranged from 70 percent to 95 percent; regarding offender recidivism, Vaughn concluded that "recidivism figures are not yet available" (p. 199). Also, Clarkson and Weakland (1991), focusing on the aftercare electronic monitoring program in Forsyth County, North Carolina, found that 68 percent of the youths were successful in completing the program. Furthermore, Charles (1989), in his study on the Allen County, Indiana, juvenile program reported a successful completion figure of 67 percent. Neither one of the last two studies mentioned included any follow-up of the participants for recidivism reports after their exit from the programs.

Regarding offender recidivism, two studies (one on electronic monitoring at the Orleans Parish Youth Study Center, New Orleans, and the other on the juvenile electronic monitoring in Kenosha County, Wisconsin) provided recidivism reports on the participants. The first study, conducted by the Office of Criminal Justice Coordination (1991), reported that 16 percent of the juveniles were rearrested during the program supervision; also, 38 percent of the youths were rearrested after their exit from the program. However, the researchers did not specify the length of follow-up in reporting rearrests. The second study

(Editor, *Journal of Offender Monitoring*, 1990) specified that 33 percent of the juveniles recidivated during the program.

Overall, it is apparent that very limited research has been conducted on the impact of these programs on juvenile offenders. Furthermore, it appears from the above discussion that "lowering offender recidivism" has not been an issue of concern for the evaluators. Information about program completion indicates an offender's behavior over a short period of time—only during the program supervision. Recidivism is a practical outcome measure for evaluating correctional programs, and as Rogers and Jolin (1989) point out, "recidivism is the standard by which correctional programs have traditionally been judged" (p. 143).

This study focuses on the impact of the Lake County program on the participating juveniles in terms of completing the program and also in terms of offender recidivism. The basic research questions in this study include the following: (1) from a pool of juveniles who participated in the program (from February 1990 to December 1991), how many were successfully discharged? (2) what variables are predictive of in-program success, as indicated by successful discharge status? and (3) what variables are predictive of post-program recidivism (during the follow-up period through the end of 1992), as measured by rearrests for committing new offenses?

## Overview of Lake County Program

The Superior Court of Lake County, Juvenile Division, established an Electronic Monitoring Home Detention Program (EMHDP) for juveniles in February 1990. The Home Detention Electronic Monitoring Unit of Lake County Community Corrections is responsible for administering the program and also for monitoring the participants. This program was instituted mainly to reduce overcrowding at the Lake County Juvenile Detention Center. Any juvenile, pursuant to Indiana Code 31–6–4–5 who is eligible for detention, is considered for EMHDP. However, no juvenile accused or adjudicated of a Class A felony is eligible for the program. Those juveniles accused or adjudicated of a Class B misdemeanor through a Class B felony, excluding any offense involving bodily injury or use of a deadly weapon, would be eligible. In making the decision, the juvenile court must consider the following: (a) whether the child, if not detained, would be a danger to the community, and (b) whether the child would be a danger to himself/herself. Status offenders as well as violators of court orders can be considered for the program. The primary group of status offenders that would be considered are runaways that can be detained pursuant to Indiana Code 31–6–4–5(c) for a period of 24 hours (Juvenile Center, 1991). Additionally, adjudicated runaways and truants can be held for a maximum of thirty days for violation of court order, pursuant to Indiana Code 31–6–7–16. Only juveniles who reside in Lake County and are between eleven and seventeen years of age are considered. Finally, all participants must pay a daily service charge of six dollars.

The program objectives emphasize financial responsibility of parents for supervising their child, parental responsibility and support for their child's compliance with program requirements, and close parent-child relationship to maintain normal home and school environment (Juvenile Center, 1991). They also stress close supervision of juveniles by officials making weekly visits (two/three times a week) to their homes, school, work places, etc., and making several personal phone contacts every week, in addition to those generated by the central computer. The Home Detention Electronic Monitoring Unit of the Lake County Community Corrections uses a passive system to monitor juveniles in the program. The central computer at the unit is programmed to make six daily (random) phone calls to the child's home and the child is required to appear before the camera device hooked up to the home phone. Voice and visual verification methods are used to insure offender compliance.

At a detention hearing, the judge or the magistrate decides whether a juvenile will be released to EMHDP. A juvenile can be removed from the program for violation of home detention rules (technical violation) and/or committing a new offense. Otherwise, the participants are discharged from the court by the judge or the magistrate, based on their compliance with program requirements.

# Methodology

The data were coded from the subjects' EMHDP files and also from their files maintained by the Superior Court Juvenile Division. The subjects were 144 juveniles court-ordered to EMHDP from February 1990 to December 1991. Afterwards, they were followed through the end of 1992 for recidivism reports.

One hundred and twenty-eight (88.8 percent) of the subjects were male. The majority of the subjects (76.4 percent) were nonwhites. At admission, subjects ranged in age from eleven to seventeen years, with an average age of almost sixteen years. Also, at admission, the majority of them (87.5 percent) had between nine and eleven years of education.

Ninety-four (65.3 percent) of the subjects were ordered to EMHDP for committing misdemeanor offenses. The length of program supervision on the subjects ranged from nine to sixty days, the mean being twenty-nine days. Only twenty-six (18.1 percent) juveniles had documented histories of substance abuse. Twenty-four (16.7 percent) of the youths had juvenile court records for prior offenses, and only twelve (8.3 percent) juveniles had records of prior detention.

The outcome measures included two components: completion of the program and offender recidivism after exit from the program. Although reducing recidivism among the participants was not a specified goal of EMHDP, arrests for committing recidivist offenses were included in the data to detect what effects the program might have had on offender recidivism. For the first component, completion of the program, the data were coded as "successful" and "unsuccessful." The second component, offender recidivism, refers to rearrest records of the participants during the follow-up period, after their exit from the program.

# Results

Regarding the first component of outcome measures, completion of the program, 125 (86.8 percent) juveniles received successful discharges from the program. Among the nineteen juveniles (13.2 percent) who were unsuccessful, twelve individuals were removed from the program for technical violations, and seven youths recidivated during the program.

As revealed by chi-square tests, the following independent variables were significant predictors of successful discharge status: prior offense, substance abuse, prior detention, and offense type (misdemeanor/felony) for court order to EMHDP. Juveniles with no prior offense records were more likely to receive successful discharge than those having such records ($X^2$=3.82, df=1, p=.05). Likewise, participants with no documented substance abuse history were more likely to be successfully discharged than ones with such history ($X^2$=8.006, df=1, p=.004). Furthermore, youths who had prior detention records were more likely to be successful in completing the program than others who did not have such records ($X^2$=4.13, df=1, p=.04). Finally, misdemeanants were more likely to get successful discharge than felony offenders ($X^2$=6.24, df=1, p=.04).

As mentioned earlier, 125 juveniles were successfully discharged from the program. Among these youths, 108 individuals (86.4 percent of those successfully discharged from the program) had no revocation or rearrest for violations of any kind transpiring during program supervision or follow-up. As revealed by rearrest data, these juveniles refrained from all violations for the entire time frame covered by the study. However, seventeen youths who were successfully discharged from the program, committed recidivist offenses during the follow-up period. The distribution of types of new offenses committed by them was: 29.4 percent felony, 47.1 percent misdemeanor, and 23.5 percent status offenses.

Only one background variable was significantly predictive of recidivism during the follow-up period. Juveniles who had documented records of substance abuse were more likely than others with no such records to be rearrested during the follow-up time frame ($X^2$=3.78, df=1, p=.05). In addition, individuals who received successful EMHDP discharges were less likely than those who received unsuccessful discharges to recidivate ($X^2$=8.59, df=1, p=.003).

To summarize the findings with respect to the basic research questions, the data indicated that 86.8 percent of the subjects court ordered to EMHDP were successfully discharged from the program. In addition, lack of prior offense records and substance abuse history, prior detention, and misdemeanor offenses committed for court order to EMHDP were predictive of in-program success. The only variables found to be predictive of reduced post-program recidivism were lack of substance abuse records and successful discharge from EMHDP.

## Conclusion

The Electronic Monitoring Home Detention Program for juvenile offenders in Lake County, Indiana, was initiated a little over three years ago. This study is a preliminary research focusing on the impact of the program on its participants since its inception. Among all the subjects who were court-ordered to the program during the first two years of its operation, 86.8 percent of them received successful discharges. At this early stage of the program, this successful completion figure seems commendable. One significant finding of this study was that juveniles who received successful discharges were less likely to recidivate than those unsuccessfully discharged. Only 13.6 percent of the subjects who successfully completed the program recidivated during the follow-up period. This finding supports Donnelly and Forschner's (1984) contention that in-program success should be associated with less post-program recidivism.

The findings from this study point to a number of interesting conclusions. First, one of the reasons for initiating the program in Lake County was to restrain overcrowding at the juvenile detention center. Since its inception, this program has helped the juvenile court to maintain the number of detainees at the center to its capacity (eighty bed spaces). On one side, the juvenile court has restrained overcrowding at the detention center by using this program. On the other side, due to the availability of this program, the court is utilizing this avenue to detain more juveniles at their homes, in addition to the detainees at the detention center. That is, even though the electronic monitoring program has curbed overcrowding at the detention center, its use has widened the net of juvenile detention in the county.

Second, the program objectives emphasize parental responsibility and support toward successful completion of their children's home detention requirements. Also, parents are responsible for payments of daily service charges. Given this context, "exit interviews" with parents as well as juveniles could be conducted to discover their perceptions about the program. Their notions about the program could provide some helpful suggestions to program administrators.

Third, we need to look at the issue of selecting juveniles for EMHDP. Substance abuse history, prior offense history, prior detention records, and the type of offense (misdemeanor) considered for the program reveal that the EMHDP involved mostly low-risk offenders. The data indicated that court officials in their final decision-making process selected mostly those juveniles who were anticipated to be successful in completing the program. This selective selection of juveniles resulted in almost 87 percent successful completion of the program requirements. There may be an explanation to account for this selective selection. It may reflect that at this early stage of the program, program administrators are emphasizing successful completion of the program by a high percentage of the participants. Selective inclusion of participants is one way to ensure a high success rate. As Rogers and Jolin (1989) maintain, "Administrators of electronic monitoring programs affect success rates by the selection methods they employ, and in the early days of any new program, administrators carefully select low-risk candidates to ensure initial success" (p. 150). This was found to be true by Friel, Vaughn, and del Carmen (1987) in their national survey on electronic monitoring programs. Also, selective selection may indicate skepticism on the part of the judge or the magistrate that the program can be effective in terms of participants completing the program and reducing recidivism among the participants.

It would be interesting to involve more high-risk juveniles in this program or make a balanced distribution of offenders (low-risk to high-risk) in the program first, and then evaluate the impact of the program on a more varied range of offenders. Involvement of various types of juvenile offenders (in terms of "risk") in this program would precipitate further evaluation.

# REFERENCES

Charles, M.T. (1989). "Electronic Monitoring for Juveniles." *Journal of Crime and Justice* 12 (2): 147–169.

Clarkson, J.S., and J.J. Weakland (1991). "A Transitional After-Care Model for Juveniles: Adapting Electronic Monitoring and Home Confinement." *Journal of Offender Monitoring* 4 (2): 2–15.

Donnelly, P.G., and B.E. Forschner (1984). "Client Success or Failure in a Halfway House." *Federal Probation* 48 (3): 38–44.

Editor (1990). "Monitoring Juvenile Offenders: The Kenosha County, Wisconsin, Experience." *Journal of Offender Monitoring* 3 (3): 2–7.

Friel, C.M., J.B. Vaughn, and R.V. del Carmen (1987). *Electronic Monitoring and Correctional Policy: The Technology and Its Application*. Washington, DC: National Institute of Justice.

Juvenile Center (1991). *Superior Court of Lake County Juvenile Division Annual Report*. Gary, IN: Juvenile Court Probation Department.

Office of Criminal Justice Coordination (1991). *Electronic Monitoring at the Youth Study Center: An Evaluation*. New Orleans, LA: Office of Criminal Justice Coordination.

Rogers, R., and A. Jolin (1989). "Electronic Monitoring: A Review of the Empirical Literature." *Journal of Contemporary Criminal Justice* 5 (3): 141–152.

Vaughn, J.B. (1991). "Use of Electronic Monitoring with Juvenile Intensive Supervision Programs." In T. Armstrong (ed.), *Intensive Supervision with High-Risk Youths*. Monsey, NY: Criminal Justice Press.

PART THREE

# New Models for Community Supervision

# CHAPTER NINE

# Punishment, Probation, and the Problem of Community Control: A Randomized Field Experiment on Absconder Location Strategies

*Faye S. Taxman*
*James M. Byrne*

More than 4 million adults were under some form of correctional control in the United States at the end of 1989. Nearly 3 million adults, or approximately 75 percent of the U.S. correctional population, were supervised in the community, either by probation (2,520,479) or by parole (456,797). The remaining offenders were admitted to prison (683,367) or jail (393,303). Despite the recent growth of the entire correctional population (e.g., a 34.6 percent increase between 1985 and 1989), the distribution of offenders under various forms of community supervision has remained remarkably stable over the past decade (Dillingham, 1990). What has changed is the movement of offenders from community to institutional control because of the increased use of probation and parole revocations.[1] Stated simply, offenders who fail while under community supervision constitute the fastest growing component of the prison and jail populations in this country.[2]

It has been argued that we currently have a prison crowding problem not because offenders are "getting worse" but because a "new punitiveness" now dominates the correctional landscape. This punitiveness can be found in both sentencing decisions and the dynamics of community control (Byrne, Lurigio, and Baird, 1989; Clear and Cole, 1990). Focusing on probation, it is apparent that judges are now using "split" sentences more often (Byrne and Pattavina, 1991) and setting more probation conditions (Clear, 1987; Taxman, 1990). These probation conditions are attempts to both punish (e.g., by using short periods of incarceration before probation, by requiring restitution to the victim, and by setting substantial fines) and control the lifestyles and behavior of probationers (e.g., by ordering drug testing, curfews, mandatory employment, and mandatory treatment). These changes in the imposition of probation sentences were highlighted in a recent report from the Bureau of Justice Statistics (BJS) on felony sentencing patterns in state courts (Dawson, 1990). The BJS report estimated that, in 1986, one in every five convicted felons received some form of split sentence, usually involving a period of jail time followed by probation supervision. Overall, "40 percent of all probationers were required to serve some amount of time in jail (28 percent) or prison (12 percent) in addition to their probation sentence" (Dawson, 1990: 1). Moreover, 48 percent of the convicted felons sentenced to probation had special conditions (described by Dawson as collateral penalties) established by judges at the time of sentencing. These conditions included restitution (36 percent of all probationers), fines (18 percent), and various forms of mandatory treatment (17 percent).[3]

How do probationers respond to this new mix of punishment and control? Not surprisingly, the answer seems to be that offenders are both absconding (i.e., failing to report) and/or being revoked (failing to comply with probation conditions and/or being arrested for new offenses) at disturbingly high rates.[4] For example, the results of a follow-up survey of 3,000 convicted felons placed on probation and "tracked" for at least two years revealed that about 9 percent of all probationers had absconded, while an additional 14 percent had their probation revoked (Dawson, 1990). If we assume for the moment that these survey results provide a reasonable estimate of probation failures nationwide, then it is possible to describe the size of the noncompliance problem faced by probation departments across this country. At present, we estimate that as many as one in every four felony probationers have failed to satisfy their probation conditions (e.g., drug testing, treatment, community service, fines)[5], while at least one in ten have simply absconded.

A similar pattern of failures exists for misdemeanor probationers (Byrne, 1986). Based on 1989 probation population estimates (including felons and misdemeanors), this would represent between 250,000 and 500,000 probation failures nationwide (Jankowski, 1990). As mentioned earlier, our current prison and jail crowding problem can be directly linked to changes in the form (e.g., the use of split sentences) and content (e.g., the number and type of special conditions) of probation sentences.[6] Ironically, resources for probation are being significantly reduced or are remaining stagnant during a "growth" period. Probation officers are handling larger caseloads, and these caseloads often include the need to monitor the offender's compliance with more (and varied) conditions than ever before.[7]

The increased use of multiple conditions of probation raises two obvious "enforcement" problems for both probation agencies and the judiciary. First, how should probation officers respond if an offender refuses to comply with the conditions of probation and absconds (i.e., he/she fails to report to probation and/or moves to a new residence without informing probation)? Secondly, how should a judge respond to noncompliance when (and if) the offender is subsequently apprehended? In this chapter, we will examine how one probation department (in Maricopa County, Arizona) decided to address both of these questions.

Focusing on the probation office response, this chapter presents the results of a randomized field experiment designed to test the effects of two different strategies for locating and apprehending absconders with a specialized probation-based warrants unit. One approach allows probation officers to use desk-style, or *office-only*, offender location and apprehension strategies; the other approach augments these office strategies with field investigation and surveillance techniques. After random assignment to treatment (combined office and field activities) and control (only office-based activities) groups, each

absconder was tracked during a three-month follow-up period
(beginning January 1, 1990). In addition to reviewing casefile
data on probation officer activities during a three-month
follow-up period, we collected data on the disposition of each
case that resulted in an apprehension. These data allow us to
assess the relative merits of both *office-only* and *combined
office/field* offender location and apprehension strategies, while
also examining the nature of the judicial response to
apprehended absconders in Maricopa County, Arizona.

Our findings suggest that early identification of
absconders by supervising probation officers, combined with
proactive (i.e., combined office and field investigations) offender
location and apprehension strategies, may result in higher
apprehension levels with no significant change in return to
prison/jail rates due to formal revocations. When viewed in this
context, a proactive, probation-based warrants unit appears to be
an effective strategy for locating and apprehending offenders
who abscond. However, our analysis of the absconder problem
in Maricopa County raises broader issues about (1) how
offenders are sentenced to probation; (2) when and why special
probation conditions are set; (3) whether probation agencies
should be in the offender location and apprehension business at
all; and (4) the relationship between technical violations and new
offense activities.[8]

## The Maricopa County's Probation Warrants Unit

### The Creation of the Warrants Unit

According to a recent review by del Carmen and Byrne
(1989), Arizona is one of only seventeen states that deploy
separate warrant/absconder units located administratively
within the adult probation department. The warrants unit
highlighted in this article began in 1987 after the presiding judge
in Maricopa County's Superior Court expressed dissatisfaction
with the existing procedures (i.e., the sheriff's office had the
warrants responsibility) for locating absconders and bringing

them before the court. The county sheriff's office did not generally give priority for probationer absconders unless the warrant involved a serious *new* crime. Absconders represented only a small percentage of all warrants received by the sheriff's office. Additionally, the sheriff's office only conducted a cursory search for absconding probationers; in fact, the average time on computer-aided address locations was six minutes (del Carmen and Byrne, 1989). Without significant increases in staff, the sheriff's office argued that they could do little about the problem of outstanding warrants for absconders from probation.

The initial response of the presiding judge to the inability of the sheriff's office to effectively respond to absconder warrants was to order probation to develop their own warrants unit. With probation having its own unit, the judge felt that the office would be more responsible to the absconder population. At the time the probation warrants unit was developed, about 13 percent (1,600) of the total probation population of 13,487 were classified as absconders. According to departmental policy:

> A probation absconder is defined by policy to be any probationer who fails to comply with the standard terms of probation by either failing to report as directed or by changing place of residence without notification. (Faust and Soto, 1990: 1)

By absconding, probationers were directly challenging the ability of the court to control offender behavior in the community. Moreover, the fact that there was a backlog of outstanding warrants could be viewed by the public (and probationers, specifically) as an indication that probation really involved a series of "empty threats" (Morris and Tonry, 1990). Probation, under this scenario, did not involve a sound strategy of offender control. The size of the absconder population was viewed by the presiding judge as undermining both the potential for general and specific deterrent effects of the probation sentence.

Before we describe the operation of this unit, it is important to consider the unique sociopolitical context in which the unit was created. First, the presiding judge identified the number of outstanding warrants for probationers as an issue deserving immediate attention. Importantly, he viewed the problem as an enforcement problem (i.e., the "locate and apprehend" issues) as well as a crime prevention problem (i.e., the potential for reducing the number of offenders who decide to abscond and the potential for reducing the number of probationers committing new crimes). Second, since the sheriff's office was unable to secure more county resources to serve warrants, it was decided to place the responsibility for this function in the probation department. This was possible because, unlike the majority of states, probation is viewed as a judicial function in Arizona. Third, the judge was able to reallocate existing probation resources and a few new positions to expand the unit to its current size, despite internal pressure to phase out the unit and return these probation officers to active caseload supervision. And finally, even though the development of the unit had more to do with pragmatism than any philosophical shift (e.g., from treatment to surveillance/control), the unit supervisor and division director now believe a strong argument can be made for the continuation and further expansion of a separate, probation-based unit.[9]

After reviewing the Maricopa County warrants unit, del Carmen and Byrne (1989: 8) offered the following statement of purpose:

> The deployment of a specialized unit represents the department's attempt to control all key aspects of community supervision, beginning at initial assessment and continuing through the end of the offender's probation period. Thus, the department's supervision role does not stop at the point a warrant is issued; it ends at the point that absconder status is removed and the probation period is over.

The warrants unit, therefore, allowed the probation agency the opportunity to handle probation cases from initiation to final disposition, whether that disposition involved a successful termination of the probation period or a revocation due to noncompliance with probation conditions, absconding, or arrest for a new criminal offense. It appears that the probationer warrants unit represents something other than a pragmatic, short-term response to a local problem. The chief probation officer responsible for designing and implementing the probation-based warrants unit has since resigned. Yet, the unit still functions and provides the probation agency with better control and management of its cases.

## A Description of the Warrants Unit

The original unit (in 1987) was comprised of two probation officers and two clerical staff. Since the fall of 1989, the unit has been staffed by six probation officers, two surveillance officers, and three clerical staff. The unit receives approximately 200 *new* warrants cases each month from the superior court, and, as of July 1990 the total caseload consists of more than 1,700 outstanding warrants. Faust and Soto (1990) identified the three basic functions of the unit:

> This team is responsible for locating probationers who are no longer reporting to their supervision officers as ordered. . . . In addition to absconder location responsibilities, the warrants unit also processes all out-of-state extraditions. . . . A third area of responsibility is the reviewing and purging of existing files. (pp. 1–2)

Although the focus of our experiment is the location and apprehension of absconders, one must recognize that the warrants unit has a broader range of responsibilities for the probation agency.

The offender location process, depicted in Figure 1, begins with a probationer who fails to report for supervision to the Maricopa County Adult Probation Department. In 1990, the average daily active population was 18,000 offenders who were under probation supervision ordered by the superior court; during that year, at least 10 percent of these offenders were officially classified as absconders (Faust and Soto, 1990). An unknown number of probationers may have also absconded, but the supervising probation officer decided *not* to file a formal "petition to revoke" with the court. Such discretionary decision making by line probation officers is important to consider, since it reveals that any estimates of changes (over time) in the *size* of the absconder population will be affected not only by the

**Figure 1: Key Stages in the Maricopa County Probation Department's Absconder Location and Apprehension Process**

Step 1: Offender fails to report for supervision[1]

↓

Step 2: Probation officers formally request that a default warrant be issued[2]

↓

Step 3: Sheriff's office receives warrant and forwards it to the Probation Unit[3]

↓

Step 4: Initial case file review

↓

| New residential address identified | Request visitor info. check | Supervising PO is contacted | Employer/ employment address identified | Associates address ID'd | Other address (e.g. favorite hangout) |

↓

Step 5: Field/Investigative Follow-Up

↓

| Public Utilities | Phone Company | M.V. Identi-fication | Interview Arresting Officer | Children's School | Family, relatives | DES | Other: VA Social Security State Revenue Drug Store |

↓

Step 6: Direct Location Verification Activities

↓

| P.O. drives by area | P.O. calls location | P.O. contacts Apartment Manager | P.O. tracks offenders in the field |

↓

Step 7: Apprehension Assistance?

↓

| On-site (at car) | No on-site assistance | On-site (arrest scene) |

↓

Step 8: Offender Apprehended?

↓

| Offender apprehended without dept. assistance | Location-only support by dept. | Offender still at large[4] | Apprehension Assistance by dept. |

1 Under current policy, P.O.'s with offenders on maderate and minimum risk/need supervision have up to 60 days to ask the Judge to issue a warrant, while P.O.'s with offenders on maximum supervision have up to 30 days.

2 In some instances, P.O.'s may not request that a default warrant be issued, even though it is clear that the offender has absconded.

3 The length of time may vary a bit from case to case, but the warrants unit receives most warrants within a few days of the date they were issued.

4 We estimate that about one in every three absconders will be "at large" at the end of our three-month follow-up period. Moreover, another third of the absconders will be apprehended without any assistance from the warrants unit.

*behavior* of the probationers (i.e., failure to report), but also by the *response* of line probation officers to that behavior.

The site of this experiment, Maricopa County, has policies defining the length of time that must elapse between when an offender fails to report for supervision and when the probation agent is required to issue a formal request for a petition to revoke probation. Interestingly, departmental policy has defined the acceptable "reporting window" in Maricopa County to vary by the offender's assigned risk classification level; for offenders in intensive or maximum supervision, the petition "must be filed within 30 days of when the officer first becomes aware of the problem; for moderate or minimum [supervision] cases, it must be filed within 60 days" (Faust and Soto, 1990: 2).

The purpose of this reporting policy is straightforward: "high risk" offenders who abscond should be viewed as priority cases for location and apprehension. However, this institution-alized delay in the notification process seems difficult to justify, since it effectively gives absconders up to a two-month grace period, even assuming perfect compliance by line staff. In fact, in this study we found that all of the absconders on intensive supervision were formally "petitioned" within the 30-day period, but only 44 percent of the maximum supervision cases were petitioned within 30 days, and only 60 percent of the absconding probationers on moderate or minimum supervision were petitioned within the 60-day deadline.

It seems logical to suggest that the warrants unit's ability to locate an absconder will be affected by the time elapsed between absconding and the initiation of the actual location search. There are many time factors involved: the "reporting window" between absconder failure to report and issue of formal petition to revoke; the time involved for the judiciary to respond to the revocation petition; the time for the sheriff's office to receive the default warrant and to process it; and, the time for the initial casefile review in the warrants unit (generally three to seven days). All of these time factors precede the actual "location and apprehension work" and somehow affect the likelihood of being located and subsequently apprehended. The minimum thirty-day "reporting window" can easily be translated into forty-five to fifty days from the time the absconder last reported to the probation office before the location activities actually begin. The warrants unit is, therefore, affected by these time factors—the experiment allows us to explore how time factors may affect the location and apprehension of absconders.

## The Location/Apprehension Process

This experiment allowed the warrants unit to examine the impact of different combinations of office and field strategies for locating and apprehending probation absconders. Typically, the *office* location process relies on the casefile for potential leads about the absconder. The probation officer reviews the initial casefile, including the arrest report. The review involves an examination of the possible addresses of the absconder such as a present or former residence, or the address of others closely associated with the offender (i.e., spouses, parents, siblings, relatives, close friends, other acquaintances, etc.). Employers, past or present, are also identified as possible information sources about the absconder's whereabouts. Other leads include favorite places the absconder prefers (i.e., bars, restaurants, crack houses, etc.).

The initial casefile review is generally followed by contact with other typical sources, including record checks with the motor vehicle associations, state revenue office, and social security offices. Telephone contact is generally made with utility offices (i.e., gas, electric, water, etc.), schools (of the absconder's children), veterans hospitals, drugstores, and public welfare agencies. Officers are also likely to contact the arresting officer(s) regarding particular information on an absconder.

In the experiment, probation officers were required to use field-based location techniques to augment the office-only efforts for the experimental group. Instead of relying on the casefile review and telephone, the probation officer made personal appearances to verify casefile information and to identify new "leads." The probation officer physically verified information in the field by going to the present or prior residence of the absconder, favorite "spots" or hangouts, etc. Officers also contacted preferred acquaintances or friends to develop new leads on the whereabouts of the absconder.

For the experimental category of combined *office/field* cases, the probation officer had the option of being involved in the apprehension of the absconder. On location, the probation officer could assist with the apprehension, although law enforcement agencies were primarily responsible for the arrest of the absconder. On-site apprehension activities consisted of assisting the law enforcement official with the arrest. In fact, the warrants unit cultivated and developed a special relationship with the police department. This relationship evolved over time but it has resulted in a mutual understanding of complimentary roles in the location and apprehension of absconders. In the *office only* cases (control group), probation officers were not involved in the apprehension of the absconder.

## Methods and Data: The Experiment

### The Random Assignment Process

Figure 2 presents an overview of the random assignment process used in this experiment. It also illustrates the attrition that occurred in the experiment. The random assignment of cases to experimental categories occurred from January through March 1990. During this time frame, the probation office received and the sheriff's office processed 544 absconder warrants. Of these 544 warrants, 505 were deemed eligible for random assignment. Cases were excluded from the experiment for a variety of natural reasons including the following: (1) the absconder was already pending extradition or had been arrested at the time the case was received by the unit; (2) the absconder was a companion of another offender already in the study; (3) the offender was viewed as a threat; and (4) the warrant was quashed.[10]

Of the 505 absconders in the experiment, ninety were removed after the random assignment procedure. The removals generally occurred because the absconder was arrested within one week and the officer had only completed an initial review of the case. (The initial review merely consists of reading the

casefile and making notes of possible sources to investigate.)
Other cases were removed because the warrant was "quashed"
or the supervisor felt that the case presented a threat to the
community and required immediate field response.[11]

Figure 2: An Overview of the Random Process Assignment with
Highlights of Key Attrition Points

|  |  | Number of Cases |
|---|---|---|
| Step 1: | Offender absconds | [unknown] |
| Step 2: | Probation officer requests warrant | 544 |
| Step 3: | Sheriff's office receives warrant | 544 |
| Step 4: | Unit supervisor identified those cases available for random assignment (Exclusions N=39) | 505* |
| Step 5: | Random assignment by data specialist; warrant cases are assigned to one of eight unit members | 505** |
| Step 6: | Cases are removed from study *after* random assignment to treatment and control groups (Removal N=90) | 415*** |
| Step 7: | Final study sample:            Field (205)   Office (210) | |

* Thirty-nine (39) absconders were excluded for the following reasons: (1) the
absconder was already pending extradition at the time the case was received by
the unit (N=25); (2) absconder was living/traveling with an offender already
assigned to the study (N=3); (3) absconder was arrested *before* the casefile arrived
at the unit (N=1); (4) data were missing on offender background characteristics
(N=5); (5) absconder viev ed as a threat to the community requiring "special"
attention (N=3); and (6) warrant subsequently quashed (N=1)
** The process involved assigning the absconder case to one member of the
warrants unit. Each member of the warrants unit handled both office-only and
office/field cases to reduce the possibility of an officer interaction effect on the
location strategy used on cases in the same experimental group.
*** The reason that the ninety cases were removed after random assignment was
that eighty-five of the cases were arrested with a new charge within the one-
week period from initial case review, and five cases were apprehended (without
new charges) within this same time frame. Essentially, the probation officer did
not have a chance to initiate any location activities before the absconder was
apprehended.

## Characteristics of Offenders in the Study

Table 1 provides a comparison of select characteristics of probationer absconders assigned to the *office-only* and *office/field* location strategies in the experiment. The *office-only* strategy is the control group (the typical process for locating absconders), while the *office/field* strategy is the experimental group (a combination of both office and field based strategies). As shown in this table, there are no statistically significant differences in the characteristics between the control and test groups, which suggests that the random assignment procedure was properly conducted.[12]

The absconders are generally on probation for felony offenses and with a mean sentence of eighteen months of probation. Nearly 85 percent of the offenders are convicted of either a substance abuse offense (41 percent) or a property offense (44 percent). The drug offenses consist of driving under the influence (35 percent), possession of controlled dangerous substances (35 percent), and sales of controlled dangerous substances (25 percent). Interestingly, a small percentage of the offenders (only 10 percent) were convicted of crimes against a person. The mean number of months on probation prior to absconding is 12.5, although nearly 30 percent of the probationers were on probation for less than three months prior to the date of absconding.[13] Basically, the data suggests that the sample is similar to other metropolitan probation agencies with probationers primarily convicted of property or drug offenses. The data also confirms the experience of many probation agencies that technical violations, including absconding behavior, is likely to occur early in the probation supervision period.

Table 1: A Comparison of Selected Case Characteristics for
Absconders by Location/Apprehension Strategy
(Office vs. Field)

| Selected Characteristics | Office (N=205) | Field (N=210) |
|---|---|---|
| Instant Offense Type: | | |
|    Drug/DWI | 40.0% | 41.0% |
|    Property | 44.9% | 43.8% |
|    Person | 14.6% | 14.3% |
|    Other | .5% | .9% |
| Average Time on Probation Prior | | |
|    to Violation:[1] | 13.3 Months | 12.2 Months |
| Risk/Supervision Level: | | |
|    ISP | 12.2% | 11.4% |
|    Maximum | 15.6% | 14.8% |
|    Moderate | 52.7% | 59.0% |
|    Minimum | 19.5% | 14.8% |
| Offender Background: | | |
|    Single | 78.0% | 76.7% |
|    Average age (Mean) | 28.6 Years | 28.9 Years |
|    Prior convictions in past | | |
|       five years | 6.6 | 6.7 |
| Specialization Patterns During | | |
| Criminal Career: | | |
|    Drug offender | 24.9% | 18.6% |
|    Property offender | 28.8% | 28.1% |
|    Person offender | 5.4% | 3.8% |
|    No discernable pattern | 38.0% | 46.7% |
| Risk Characteristics | | |
| (at initial assessment): | | |
|    Under age 18 at first arrest | 29.3% | 24.3% |
|    Unemployed | 21.0% | 20.0% |
|    With at least one prior | | |
|       probation/parole revocation | 60.5% | 63.8% |
|    Some college (or beyond) | 13.2% | 13.8% |

| Selected Characteristics | Office (N=205) | Field (N=210) |
|---|---|---|
| Viewed by probation officers as motivated to change | 18.0% | 22.9% |
| Need Characteristics | | |
| Stable family relationships | 40.5% | 36.2% |
| With no negative companions | 44.4% | 42.4% |
| With alcohol problem | 48.8% | 49.0% |
| With drug problem | 64.9% | 60.5% |
| Viewed as "high needs" | 29.3% | 36.2% |
| Prior probation/parole revocations | 29.3% | 22.9% |

1. Median time on probation was 8.2 months; 30 percent were on probation for less than three months.

The majority of the offenders in the study are male and single. The average age is twenty-nine years old with a range of eighteen to sixty-five years old. On average, these offenders had nearly seven prior convictions in the past five years. Nearly 60 percent had at least one prior probation/parole revocation and 11 percent had three or more prior convictions. Nearly 25 percent of the absconders had their first arrest prior to 18 years old and nearly one-fifth were unemployed at the time of being placed on probation. Approximately 30 percent have specialized as a property offender with nearly 42 percent having no particular criminal career pattern.[14]

The Maricopa County Probation Department uses a combination risk and needs screening instrument modelled after the National Institute of Correction's risk/needs instrument. The instrument provides a score that can be used to classify offenders into risk categories which is used operationally to place offenders into different levels of supervision.[15] More than half of the absconders are assigned a moderate risk classification while nearly 12 percent are in intensive supervision, and nearly 15 percent are on maximum supervision. Probation officers indicated that approximately 20 percent were motivated to change, with nearly 50 percent of the absconders having an alcohol problem, and nearly 60 percent of the absconders having a drug problem.

The characteristics of these absconders illustrate that the Maricopa County absconders, for the most part, are similar to other offenders on probation (Petersilia and Turner, 1990). On review, it does not appear that these general characteristics can account for the absconding behavior, nor affect the warrant unit's ability to locate absconders. In fact, the data does not provide any insight into the reasons for absconding.

# Findings

The experiment allowed us to answer three main questions about the effectiveness of field location and apprehension strategies: (1) What is the differential pattern of apprehending absconders using different location strategies? (2) Do field-based strategies allow for the more expeditious apprehension of absconders? and (3) What is the judicial response to the apprehension of absconders? The answers to these questions concern the ability of the warrants units to contribute to public safety and to provide more information about the relationship between technical violations and new offense activities.

We will begin by reviewing each of these questions separately. The first two questions will be answered by using data on the three-month follow-up from the experiment. The last question will examine the judicial responses (e.g., sentences for the absconders), which includes an additional three months of follow-up to allow for disposition.

## 1. What is the differential pattern of apprehending absconders between the experimental and control groups?

Table 2 illustrates the different patterns of apprehending absconders with the *office-only* and *office/field* location and apprehension strategies. Overall, the *office/field* strategies resulted in 61.4 percent of the absconders being located, apprehended, and arrested as compared to the *office-only* apprehension rate of

51.2 percent, which is statistically significant at the .05 level. Stated simply, the combination *office/field* based strategies resulted in locating more absconders than *office-only* strategy. The combination of *office/field* strategies was effective in leading to the location of more absconders, which ultimately resulted in more apprehension of the absconders.

It is generally believed that most absconders are located due to an arrest for a new criminal charge. In this experiment, it was possible to examine the relationship between location and apprehension of offenders and arrests for new criminal charges. Of the 415 absconders, 60 cases (14.5 percent) had new charges filed during the 3-month period of the experiment. During the experiment, 35, or nearly 50 percent, of the absconders with new charges were located and apprehended. As shown in Table 2, the *office/field* strategy is more likely to result in the location and apprehension of absconders without new criminal charge(s), either in the given jurisdiction or surrounding jurisdictions. Specifically, 46.2 percent of the absconders were arrested by *office/field* strategies without an arrest for a new criminal charge as compared to 36.6 percent of the absconders by *office-only* strategies. The ability to locate and apprehend offenders prior to the absconder's arrest for new criminal charges reflects the public safety function offered by the warrants unit.

As previously discussed, the warrants unit is not always involved in the location and apprehension of absconders. Without the assistance of the warrants unit, absconders can be located through naturally occurring events such as arrests for new charges, civil actions, or traffic citations. In fact, it is commonly believed that many absconders are typically located by traffic violations. In this experiment, 28 percent of absconders in the *office/field* experimental group and 20 percent of the *office-only* cases were apprehended as a direct result of the involvement of the warrants unit, which is statistically significant at the .05 level. Thus, the *office/field* strategies was directly responsible for the apprehension of more absconders than the *office-only* location procedures. The efforts of the warrants unit contributed to the location and apprehension of offenders without relying upon natural events of traffic citations, new arrests, etc.

Table 2: Percentage of Absconders Apprehended
by the Different Location Strategies

| | Type of Location Strategy | | |
|---|---|---|---|
| | Office | Field | |
| Location and Apprehension | (N=205) | (N=210) | Chi square |
| • Apprehended in county— No new crime | 36.6% | 46.2% | 3.94* |
| • Apprehended out county— Pending extradition | 5.4% | 4.3% | .26 |
| • Apprehended out county— No extradition | 0.5% | 2.9% | 2.20 |
| • Apprehended—New crime in county | 7.8% | 5.7% | .72 |
| • Apprehended—New crime out county—Pending extradition | 1.0% | 1.9% | .14 |
| • Apprehended—New crime out county—No extradition | 0.0% | .5% | .00 |
| Total Apprehensions | 51.2% | 61.4% | 4.39* |

* p <.05

The analysis of the location and apprehension patterns in the three-month follow-up studied revealed that the warrants unit is more likely to be successful in locating absconders in its own jurisdiction. It appears that it is easier to find absconders who have not relocated. With nearly 56 percent of the absconders in the study located, the majority of these offenders were located in the site of the experiment. Only 6 to 9 percent of the offenders were located outside of the given jurisdiction. It is not known whether the other absconders had relocated to another jurisdiction.

## 2. Do field location and apprehension strategies result in more expeditious apprehension of absconder?

Although *office/field* based strategies result in a greater percentage of all apprehensions, the question remains as to the timing of these apprehensions. Time to apprehension is important because it indicates the effectiveness of the warrants unit as both a prevention and enforcement tool. Time is an important ingredient in ensuring public safety by apprehending absconders prior to their involvement in criminal behavior. It is generally assumed that the sooner the absconder is "caught," the less likely the absconder will become involved in criminal activities.

In our study, we discovered that absconders charged with *new* offenses were likely to be apprehended early in the location process. Of the sixty absconders charged with new offenses, 22 absconders, or 36 percent, were apprehended in the first month the warrants unit had the case, two were apprehended in the second month, and five were apprehended in the third month. Thus, absconders who are charged with new crimes on violation are likely to be apprehended quickly. The warrants unit is therefore serving a preventive role by removing absconders that are known to be criminally active.

The study also revealed, as shown in Table 3, that the type of location strategy used did not make a difference in the timing of the apprehension of absconders. Both *office/field* and *office-only* strategies are equally likely to result in the same pattern of apprehending absconders; *office/field* strategies merely result in the apprehension of more absconders than *office-only* strategies. Table 3, however, does illustrate that more absconders are likely to be apprehended within the first thirty days of receiving the case. It appears that location and apprehension is easier during the early period before the case "ages." This has significant implications for departmental policies on timing of notification of a possible absconder case.

In fact, the experiment provided an opportunity to examine the "age" of the absconder case and the probability of apprehension. The agency's operational policies defined the possible time frames to report absconder behavior. Officers were required to report intensive and maximum supervision cases as absconders within thirty days of noting a problem (e.g., missed a scheduled appointment, etc.). In other cases, the probation officer had up to sixty days to classify the case as an absconder. This policy results in high-risk cases (i.e., intensive and maximum supervision cases) being flagged and the warrants unit being notified sooner of these cases than those on medium or minimum supervision. Overall, 62.7 percent of the absconders apprehended occurred in the first thirty days of the assignment of the case to the warrants unit. During the under 30-day time frame, 100 percent of the intensive supervision cases (N=49) were apprehended, 44.4 percent of the maximum supervision cases (N=28) were apprehended, 33.6 percent of the moderate cases (N=78) were apprehended, and 31 percent of the minimum cases (N=22) were apprehended.

Table 3: Percentage of Absconders Apprehended Within
Different Time Frames by Location Strategies

|  | Type of Strategy | |
|  | Office | Field |
| Time Frame to Location Apprehension | (N=205) | (N=210) |
| --- | --- | --- |
| Under 30 Days | 32.2% | 36.2% |
| 31–60 Days | 7.8% | 9.5% |
| 61–90 Days | 4.3% | 6.7% |
| Over 91 Days | 6.9% | 8.0% |
| % Total Apprehensions | 51.2% | 61.4%* |

* Using a chi-square test, p < .05.

The policy of earlier notification of intensive and maximum cases, therefore, appears to have a statistically significant difference in the apprehension potential of absconder cases (chi-square=5.02, p=.02). Intensive and maximum supervision cases are more likely to be quickly apprehended (within thirty days after initial review of the case) than the moderate and minimum supervision cases. Departmental policy dictates that the intensive and maximum supervision cases are required immediate notification of absconsion, whereas the other supervision cases have slightly more leeway. It appears that time at risk is an important variable in the location and apprehension of the absconders.

## 3. What is the judicial response to the apprehension of absconders?

In Table 4, we provide the responses of the judiciary to the location and apprehension of absconders. The data are not presented according to the location strategies used in this experiment (*office-only or office/field*) because there were no statistically significant differences between the experimental groups and the type of dispositions. It is not surprising that the judiciary did not respond to apprehended absconders based on the strategy used by the warrants unit to locate and apprehend the absconder. Since the experiment occurred within the probation agency (more specifically, the warrants unit), and the probation agency was the only agency affected by these strategies, it is very likely that the judiciary was not informed about the *office* and/or *field* strategies used to locate the absconder. In fact, the judiciary are primarily concerned with the service of the absconder warrants, not the means to serve the warrants.

Table 4, however, presents the data according to whether apprehended absconders were charged with new offenses or not charged with new offenses at the time of apprehension. The judiciary did not respond differently to absconders with charges for criminal offenses in the disposition of the apprehended offenders. In nearly 60 percent of the cases, the judges reinstated absconders to probation, regardless of the presence of new criminal charges. Absconders were predominately reinstated to standard probation (39.9 percent), although intensive supervision was ordered for some absconders (16.8 percent). Interestingly, absconders with new criminal charges were more likely to be reinstated to standard probation (47.9 percent) than probationers with no new criminal charges (34.5 percent). Intensive supervision was also ordered for 18.2 percent of the absconders that did not have new criminal charges as compared to 15.3 percent of the absconders with new criminal charges.

Table 4: Subsequent Dispositions for All Apprehended Offenders (Office and Field Combined) by Whether New Crime Charged at Apprehension

| Disposition | New Crime N (%) | No New Crime N (%) | Total N (%) |
|---|---|---|---|
| Revocation | 36 (36.7%) | 50 (45.5%) | 86 (41.3%) |
| Reinstated/Standard | 45 (47.9%) | 38 (34.5%) | 83 (39.9%) |
| Reinstated/Intensive | 15 (15.3%) | 20 (18.2%) | 35 (16.8%) |
| Terminated | 2 (2.0%) | 2 (1.8%) | 4 (1.9%) |
| Total | 98 (99.9%) | 110 (100%) | 208 (99.9%) |

Note: Twenty-six cases were pending extradition; for these cases, no data were available on either crime type or subsequent disposition. Analysis of dispositions for absconders apprehended via office and field techniques did not reveal any significant differences between the two groups.

In 41.3 percent of the apprehensions, the probation sentence was revoked and the offender received jail/prison time. Surprisingly, the judges appear to be more likely to revoke probation for those absconders that did not include new criminal charges. The mode sentence was for eighteen months in jail, although most of the offenders received an average of four months' credit for time served. The results from this experiment appear to confirm concerns about how the judiciary is responding to absconders on technical violations of probation. The judiciary appears to be constrained by limited options and alternatives for probationers with technical violations such as absconding. However, Maricopa County has recently developed a series of new intermediate sanctions which offer the judiciary some additional options for handling troublesome probationers.

## Implications and Future Directions

Absconders present the criminal justice system with many problems, especially probation agencies charged with the responsibility of supervising offenders in the community. The decision of the Maricopa County Adult Probation Department to proactively confront and address the issue of absconders, instead of relying on local law enforcement agencies, is the subject of this study. The Maricopa County Adult Probation Department developed an innovative approach to addressing the problem of absconders. The warrants unit is devoted to the location and apprehension of the absconder. While Maricopa County undertook this responsibility due to a lack of resources and commitment by law enforcement agencies for "probation's problem cases (absconders)," this study has revealed that the warrants unit has some distinct advantages to the probation agency. Yet these advantages have specific policy implications for the probation agency. First we will provide an overview of the advantages of the warrants unit. Then we will review specific policy implications of a probation-based warrants unit.

### *Advantages of a Warrants Unit*

For probation agencies, a warrants unit offers some unique advantages to fulfill the mission of the probation system. First and foremost, with the warrants unit, the probation agency has total responsibility for the probation case from initiation to closure. For the probation agency, this responsibility translates into more input into decisions about how to handle a case, especially decisions about policies and procedures for locating absconders. Ownership is important because it may provide the agency, and specific probation officers, with more incentive to "work with" the most difficult cases. As the agency expands its role, it is likely that the agency will develop better policies and procedures to address troublesome behavior such as absconding.

Second, the probation agency can develop, and employ, techniques to specifically handle absconders. These techniques will include the development of procedures for conducting "successful" field investigations as well as using proven location and apprehension strategies such as the combined *office/field* techniques used in Maricopa County. Probation officers will thus have an opportunity to develop new skills which can be used to fulfill the mission of the agency.

Finally, while the presence of a warrants unit expands the role and responsibilities of the probation agency, it also serves the goals of protecting the community and protecting the integrity of the probation system. The latter is especially important because the warrants unit provides the probation agency with timely and available resources to re-enforce one specific condition of probation which is the pinnacle of the probation system; the probationer must appear for scheduled appointments. With a warrants unit, probation agencies can serve as a deterrent against technical violations within the probation system. Timely apprehension of absconders will provide a safeguard that many probation agencies do not currently have.

## Appropriate Responses to Absconding Behavior

Absconding is just one form of technical violations from probation. As shown in this study, the probation and criminal justice system must develop strategies for addressing the problem of technical violators. In fact, different strategies and options are needed for the probation system and the judicial system to ensure that the goals of the sentence are being reinforced. The probation system needs clearly defined policies and procedures for both "defining" and targeting absconders. In Maricopa County, the policies depend on the risk classification system for probationers. Intensive supervision and maximum risk classifications had a thirty-day "reporting window" (thirty days from the last appointment) before the agent was required to issue a default report, whereas moderate and minimum cases had a sixty-day window. This study found that the less time at risk, the more likely the absconder will be located and apprehended. The results from this study can thus be used to redefine the absconder definition policy in Maricopa County, which should increase the agency's ability to apprehend more absconders.

The probation agency's policy on defining absconders can, therefore, be very important in facilitating the location and apprehension of absconders. With a smaller "reporting window," probation agencies may actually increase the number of absconders "found" prior to their involvement in new criminal activities, which serves to protect the community. Smaller "reporting windows" also have the advantage of reinforcing the integrity of the probation system. One of the concerns of the chief judge supporting the need for a probation-based warrants unit was the need for the probation system to be a deterrent for violators of probation conditions. Under the current system, the probation agency is usually not a deterrent; instead, it can be described as a "toothless club" (Morris and Tonry, 1990). As shown in this study, reducing the "reporting windows" provides a clear message to probationers that the agency does not tolerate missed appointments or absconsions.

This study also found that a combination of *field/office* efforts will yield the apprehension of more absconders. *Field/office* strategies resulted in the apprehension of significantly more absconders than *office-only* strategies, and fewer of these absconders were charged with new crimes at the time of arrest. The field strategies also sends a similar deterrent message as reducing the reporting windows; probationers are aware that the agency will not tolerate missing scheduled appointments (or other conditions). Otherwise, the probation office will come looking for the probationer. Probationers may respond differently if they know that the probation officer will come "knocking at their doors" or the "doors" of their relatives, friends, etc., and that the probation agency will initiate immediate actions.

While probation officers appear constrained by the system for addressing technical violators, judges also share this concern. In this study, judges did not appear to have or use options to address probationers who defy the conditions of community supervision. Nearly 58 percent of the apprehended absconders, with almost half of the absconders having charges for new criminal offenses, were reinstated to probation. Incarceration in jail or prison was only used as an option for 41 percent of the probationers. It appears that the judges did not feel that incarceration was always the most appropriate response for the violation of probation. The question remains as to what are the appropriate "responses" to violations, especially violations as fundamental to community corrections as failing to appear for scheduled appointments. In fact, the results of this study imply that as new intermediate sanctions are developed, especially those that rely on closer supervision and monitoring of the behavior and lifestyles of the probationer/parolee, the system should also develop strategies to address the offender's failure to comply with the stated conditions of probation. This is especially important in light of the repeated findings from studies of intensive supervision projects that the more closely the offender is supervised, the more likely the offender will not be able to meet the conditions of probation/parole (Byrne, 1990; Petersilia and Turner, 1990; Turner and Petersilia, 1991). The judges in Maricopa County clearly indicated that, while it is important to locate and apprehend absconders, they did not feel that incarceration was always an appropriate reaction to the failure to comply with the conditions of probation.

## Protecting the Community

The warrants unit both expands the role of the probation agency to addressing the problem of wayward probationers as well as enhancing the capability of the agency to protect the community. While the probation agency assumes responsibilities for cases from initiation to termination (successful or unsuccessful), the probation agency is also responsible for timely and appropriate responses to offenders that defy their court orders. This experiment revealed that, when a probation agency takes responsibility for locating and apprehending absconders, the community is well served. A combination of *field/office* strategies is likely to lead to an increase in the volume of apprehensions, many of which are not involved in new criminal activities. The warrants unit tended to find absconders prior to their involvement in criminal activities. Surprisingly, the reaction of the judiciary was not to incarcerate the absconders in jail/prison but rather to reinforce probation's need to maintain integrity in the system. Apprehending absconders thus serves the dual purpose of protecting the community from offenders that are violating conditions of release, as well as protecting the integrity of the probation system by providing a more immediate response to the absconding behavior.

## Probation as a Law Enforcement Agency

Warrants units within probation agencies are another example of the "muddling" of the role and responsibilities of probation agencies. From its inception, the probation system has worn the dual hat of "rehabilitation" and "law enforcement." If probation assumes responsibilities for locating absconders in the community, especially with the use of field investigative techniques, probation may begin to resemble law enforcement more than rehabilitation. The field techniques used in this experiment require the probation officer to investigate "leads" in the field in a manner similar to police officers. Development of a warrants unit, therefore, requires the probation agency to consider the implications of the probation agency assuming more law enforcement type functions. These implications are important for the direction and philosophy of individual probation agencies.

Location and apprehension field activities, such as the ones employed in the Maricopa County warrants unit, require the probation officer to participate in activities that may not be typical for a probation officer. These activities are associated with certain legal liabilities that must be considered before making a commitment for probation officers to perform these law enforcement activities. The liabilities include the potential for physical harm and danger, the need to equip probation officers with law enforcement tools (e.g., guns, bulletproof vests, etc.), and the appropriate training for serving in a quasi-law enforcement position. Probation agencies need to be aware of these liability concerns as they make decisions to assume additional responsibilities such as the service of absconder warrants.

## Conclusion

The findings from this experiment suggest that early identification of absconders by supervising probation officers, combined with proactive (i.e., combined office and field investigations) offender location and apprehension strategies, may result in higher apprehension levels. The increase in volume of apprehensions is not associated with any significant change in the return to prison/jail rates as a result of formal revocations. When viewed in this context, the proactive, probation-based warrants unit appears to be an effective strategy for locating and apprehending absconders, especially early in the absconding period. The results from this experiment have significant implications for probation agencies and community correctional programs—implications that require the agencies to reexamine their philosophies, roles, and responsibilities to the criminal justice system and the community. Additionally, the agency must also consider the liability implications of assuming more law enforcement-type functions.

Our analysis of the absconder problem in Maricopa County raises broader issues about sentencing practices and judicial responses to technical violators. These issues include the need to reexamine how offenders are sentenced to probation, why special probation conditions are set, when special conditions are set, and how the system should respond to violations. Each issue needs to be further researched. But, it is apparent from this study that technical violators are an increasing problem for the criminal justice system, especially in this current environment of "collateral penalties" (Dawson, 1990), which the system must be prepared to adequately address. The system needs options for handling violations to prevent the "toothless club" articulated by Morris and Tonry (1990). The options for violators must include alternatives to incarceration in jail/prison similar to the current efforts to define better intermediate sanctions which are directly tied to the goals of the sentence and the rationale behind the collateral penalties. The development of strategies to deal with the technical violators in community corrections will be a challenge for the system, especially the probation system. Yet in the long run these strategies will strengthen the system. Refined approaches and strategies may also result in probation reexamining and then redefining its priorities in handling offenders in the community.

## NOTES

1. See Byrne, Lurigio, and Baird (1989), or Byrne and Kelly (1989) for a discussion of the interaction between community and correctional control. Byrne and Kelly estimated that about half of all new prison admissions in 1989 were offenders on probation and parole who either were sent/returned to prison via a formal revocation hearing or who were reconvicted of a new offense while still under community supervision. Austin and Tillman (1988) estimated that between 30 and 50 percent of all new prison admissions are likely to be community supervision failures.

2. As of Dec. 31, 1979, there were 28,817 parolees or other conditional release violators (e.g., probationers and offenders on supervised mandatory release) returned to prison, representing 15.8 percent of all new admissions. By year-end 1988, the number had increased to 101,354, which represented 26.8 percent) of the 379,742 new admissions to prison in that year (a 68.4 percent increase). See the Bureau of Justice Statistics report, *Correctional Populations in the United States, 1988* (Table 5.10) for more detail.

3. See Dawson (1990: 3–4) for a more detailed review of the sample (N = 51,594) selection and methodological issues. According to his report, the use of multiple special conditions varied by most serious conviction offense type; burglars (52 percent) were most likely to receive restitution along with probation, drug traffickers (29 percent) were the most likely to get fined, and convicted rapists (47 percent) were the most likely to be given a mandatory treatment condition when placed on probation. The use of these conditions was much less likely in non-probation cases (18 percent of all offenders sentenced to prison/jail without a probation term). However, "offenders receiving split sentences and offenders receiving straight probation were equally likely to have a collateral penalty" (Dawson, 1990: 6).

4. Because of data limitations, it is difficult to assess changes in the rate of absconders and revocations over time. However, some

estimates of the changes in the size of the absconder and revocation populations are available from state-level annual probation reports (e.g., Wisconsin Department of Health and Social Services, 1989) and nationwide surveys of probation departments (e.g., Dawson, 1990; Bureau of Justice Statistics, 1990). We used these data to estimate the changes in the size of the current absconder population.

5.  Dawson (1990: 4) highlighted the results of a 1983 survey of 3,000 convicted state felons from sixteen different counties across the United States. The key findings on compliance with special conditions were as follows:

> (1) Treatment—23 percent of felony probationers were ordered to participate in a drug or alcohol treatment program; 38 percent of these probationers "were either making no progress or, more commonly, had failed to satisfy the order" (Dawson, 1990: 4).
> (2) Drug Testing—14 percent were ordered to submit to drug testing; of these, 31 percent were either making no progress or, more commonly, had failed to satisfy the order" (p. 4).
> (3) Community Service—9 percent were ordered to perform community service; of these, "37 percent were either making no progress or, more commonly, had failed to satisfy the order" (p. 4).
> (4) Fines—67 percent were ordered to make one or more type of financial payment; of these, "26 percent had paid nothing [and] the total amount of payment made represented 27 percent of the total amount assessed" (p. 4).

6.  It is difficult to provide an accurate assessment of the impact of probation failures on the prison population because of the manner in which state admission data are collected. For example, a recently released report from the National Corrections Reporting Program (Bureau of Justice Statistics, 1990: 10) indicated that their admissions survey identified only 3.2 percent of the offenders in prison as probation revocation cases. However, they emphasized that "this category may be underreported because many probation violators were reported as court commitments." A more accurate assessment of the size of the probation "violator" population is included in a recent Bureau of Justice Statistics report, *Felons Sentenced to Probation in State Courts—1986* (Dawson, 1990: 4).

7. For a recent review highlighting changes in justice system expenditures for probation, see Bureau of Justice Statistics (1990: 5, Table 6). Between 1977 and 1988, the percent of total state and local corrections expenditures for probation decreased from 17.6 percent to 11.1 percent; during this same period, the percent of total corrections expenditures for institutions increased from 74.4 percent to 84.9 percent of all correctional spending. A similar pattern is found for federal government corrections spending. In 1979, 58.5 percent of all federal government corrections spending went to institutions, as compared to 82.2 percent in 1988; during the same period, federal spending for probation, parole, and pardons dropped from 21.1 percent to 13.0 percent. See Michalowski and Pearson (1990) for an analysis of the "political economy" of our current corrections crisis and for an examination of changes in funding for institutional and community corrections between 1970 and 1980.

8. The topic of absconders has been largely ignored by researchers: we know little about why they abscond and how best to locate them. The focus of the research literature is on juvenile offenders who abscond from institutions (e.g., Thornton and Speirs, 1985). Although estimates of the size of the adult absconder population for individual states can be identified (e.g., New York Department of Correctional Services, 1989; Wisconsin Department of Health and Social Services, 1989), we know next to nothing about what states do about the problem. General assessments of possible judicial responses to absconders (including the use of intermediate sanctions) can be found in Byrne (1990), and Clear (1987). Del Carmen and Byrne (1989) report that in 1985, twenty-seven probation units in seventeen states had established their own warrants units, but more recent reviews of the use of probation-based warrants units have not been completed to date (4/15/91).

9. See Faust and Soto (1990) and del Carmen and Byrne (1989) for a more complete discussion of this point. Faust and Soto (1990: 16) report that the proportion of absconders to total probation caseload has declined from 13 percent (1987) to 10 percent (1990), a measure of improved compliance by probationers since the unit was initiated.

10. The procedures used in this random assignment process were designed to increase the number of eligible absconder cases and to reduce selection bias. The majority of the exclusions (twenty-six) were due to the absconder being located and arrested by law enforcement agencies, either in Maricopa County or other jurisdictions. As indicated earlier, there is a minimum delay of forty-five days from time to fail to appear for probation and time to begin work to locate an offender. It is

likely, and as demonstrated here, probable that some absconders would naturally be apprehended and arrested. This selection problem is unavoidable. Procedures were taken on-site to reduce any selection bias problem, but as expected, nearly 10 percent of the sample was excluded.

11.   Removal was often the result of the absconder being arrested within one week of initial review, the case quashed by the superior court, and the absconder being targeted as a threat to the community. Again, the removals offer a potential, but unavoidable, selection bias problem. However, as shown in Table 2, there are no statistically significant differences between the control and experimental groups.

12.   The absconders excluded from the experiment had similar characteristics as the absconders included in the experiment. This suggests that there is no bias presented by offenders excluded from the experiment.

13.   The median time on probation was 8.2 months for both groups, which is less than the mean of 12.5 months. The mean is affected by a small number of probationers who had been on probation for a period of time prior to absconding.

14.   Crime specialization refers to the type of criminal behavior that an offender is likely to commit. The coders reviewed the criminal histories of the absconders in this experiment and classified them according to the nature of their offense—property, drug offenses (including trafficking), and personal. The offenders with no pattern were classified as having no prior criminal career pattern.

15.   The risk/needs instrument used by Maricopa County has not been validated. The instrument is similar to the National Institute of Corrections (NIC) risk/needs instruments used by many probation/parole agencies to classify offenders. The agency is currently revising its risk/needs instrument to focus more on a needs assessment classification tool.

## REFERENCES

Austin, James, and Robert Tillman (1988). *Ranking the Nation's Most Punitive States*. San Francisco: National Council on Crime and Delinquency.

Bureau of Justice Statistics (1990). *Compendium of Federal Justice Statistics, 1986.* Washington, DC: National Institute of Justice (November).

—— (1990). *Correctional Populations in the United States, 1988.* Washington, DC: National Institute of Justice.

—— (1991). *National Update 1* (2). Washington, DC: National Institute of Justice (October).

Byrne, James M. (1986). "The Control Controversy: A Preliminary Examination of Intensive Supervision Programs in the United States." *Federal Probation* 50(2): 4–16.

—— (1990). "Future of Intensive Supervision Probation." *Crime and Delinquency* 36 (1): 6–39.

Byrne, James M., and April Pattavina (1991). "Split Sentencing and Other Forms of Intermediate Incarceration." In J. Byrne, A. Lurigio, and J. Petersilia (eds.), *Smart Sentencing: The Emergency of Intermediate Sanctions.* Newbury Park, CA: Sage.

Byrne, James, and Linda Kelly (1989). *Final Report to National Institute of Justice: An Evaluation of the Implementation and Impact of the Massachusetts Intensive Probation Supervision Program.* Lowell, MA: University of Lowell.

Byrne, James M., Arthur Lurigio, and Christopher Baird (1989). "The Effectiveness of the New Intensive Supervision Programs." *Research in Corrections* 2 (2): 1–48.

Clear, Todd (1987). "Helping, Punishing, and Controlling: The Use (and Misuse) of Conditions in Community Supervision." Paper presented at the annual meeting of the American Society of Criminology, Montreal, Canada.

—— (1989). "Statistical Prediction in Corrections." *Research in Corrections* 1 (1): 1–40.

Clear, Todd, and George Cole (1990). *American Corrections.* Pacific Grove, CA: Brooks/Cole.

Dawson, John (1990). *Felony Probation in State Courts.* Washington, DC: National Institute of Justice.

del Carmen, Rolando V., and James M. Byrne (1989). "An Assessment of the Maricopa County Probation Department's Warrants/Absconders Unit: A Technical Assistance Report to the Maricopa County Probation Department." Unpublished report.

Dillingham, Steve (1990). *National Corrections Reporting Program, 1985.* Washington, DC: National Institute of Justice.

Faust, Dot, and Marty Soto (1990). *The Probation-Based Absconder/Warrants Unit in Maricopa County*. Maricopa County, AZ: Adult Probation Department.

Jankowski, Louis (1990). *Probation and Parole, 1989*. Washington, DC: Bureau of Justice Statistics (October).

Langan, Patrick A., and John Dawson (1990). *Felony Sentences in State Courts, 1988*. Washington, DC: Bureau of Justice Assistance (December).

Michalowski, Raymond, and Michael A. Pearson (1990). "Punishment and Social Structure at the State Level: A Cross-Sectional Comparison of 1970 and 1980." *Journal of Research in Crime and Delinquency* 27(1): 52–78.

Morris, Norval, and Michael Tonry (1990). *Between Prison and Probation: Intermediate Punishments in a Rational Sentencing System*. New York: Oxford University Press.

New York Department of Correctional Services (1989). Unpublished report on offender flow. Albany, NY.

Petersilia, Joan, and Susan Turner (1990). *Intensive Supervision for High-Risk Probationers*. Santa Monica, CA: Rand Corporation.

Taxman, Faye S. (1990). "Drunk Driving: The Use of Education and Treatment as a Condition of Probation and Its Impact on Recidivism." Paper presented at the annual meeting of the American Society of Criminology, Baltimore, MD (November).

Thornton, David, and Sheila Speirs (1985). "Predicting Absconding from Young Offender Institutions." In David P. Farrington and Roger Tarling (eds.), *Predictions in Corrections* Albany, NY: State University of New York Press.

Turner, Susan, and Joan Petersilia (1991). "Focusing on High Risk Parolees: An Experiment to Reduce Commitments to the Texas Department of Corrections." Paper presented at the annual meeting of the American Society of Criminology, San Francisco, CA (November).

U.S. Department of Justice (1991). *Correctional Populations in the United States, 1988*. Washington, DC: Bureau of Justice Assistance.

Wisconsin Department of Health and Social Services (1989). "Offender Movement in the System." Unpublished report.

# CHAPTER TEN

# Reintegrating the Criminal Offender Through Community-Based Vocational Networks

## *Thomas C. Tomlinson*

This chapter describes the strategies used to implement community vocational networks for offenders. These strategies are based on the experiences of four such networks in Illinois that were part of a pilot project sponsored by the Illinois State Board of Education/Department of Adult, Vocational, and Technical Education (ISBE/DAVTE). The projects were funded from July 1988 to July 1991, though they were still ongoing in early 1992.

## The Community Vocational Network Concept

A community vocational network is made up essentially of people concerned with high recidivism rates of offenders and with making the local community a better place for all to live. These concerned people come from the criminal justice and education systems, social service agencies, and from the general citizenry.

The basic goal of such networks is to help offenders reintegrate into the community. This is done by providing training, education, and jobs to those offenders who qualify and make it through the program established by each network. To reach the goal of reintegration, certain basic mechanisms and connections must be in place in the community. These mechanisms and connections are the basis of the network. Criminal justice personnel must first determine which offenders will profit from such assistance. For diversion and probation bound offenders, the criminal justice personnel includes the prosecutor, judges, and probation officers. For the "parolee," the personnel includes the department of corrections, prisoner review board, and parole officers.

Once it is determined that an offender can be helped, other agencies are asked to provide essential services to the offender. Usually these services are provided by educational agencies, but also include addiction recovery services, family services, and other assistance. An offender cannot, and will not, obtain education/training if there is a substance abuse problem, a family problem, or if they cannot find adequate food, shelter, and clothing.

Once these problems have been identified and solved, the offender is expected to obtain the needed education/training for a job that requires his/her skills. He/she is also expected to acquire basic job hunting skills, such as interviewing, resume writing, etc., as well as to improve their self-concept. Community colleges provide most of the education and training services to offenders, from adult basic education (ABE) through advanced college courses. They also provide basic programs and courses on assessment of career interests, job application, and job-keeping skills. Some community colleges have developed special courses for offenders in the network programs.

The community colleges also provide all of the basic assessments of skills and attitudes so the offenders can be properly placed. In doing all of these things, community colleges have become a most integral part of the networks.

After education/training is completed, the offender is expected to find a job. Some networks have helped directly in this process by contacting employers and providing help of volunteers to the offender in his/her job search activities. Other networks work closely with Job Training Partnership Act (JPTA) and the Illinois Job Service. Many offenders have already found jobs, while many others are still participating in their educational programs. Given the short time the networks have been in operation, the number of offenders in secure, permanent jobs is expected to increase steadily.

These networks have the advantage of using existing resources and people. Little new money is required and the increase in services to offenders is great. Most people assume that these services are available to offenders without any intervention from a network program. This is not the case. Most criminal justice, educational, and community service agencies do not usually communicate, and thus do not know or understand the services or procedures of agencies other than their own. When the networks began, the probation officers seldom knew what the community did; the educational agencies knew little about court services; service agencies knew little of the court or probation.

With little knowledge and communication, offenders were not afforded all services available, nor were they helped to improve themselves. The networks have reduced these problems greatly. Now agency people call other agency people. Bureaucratic barriers are reduced, time is saved, the appropriate placements are made, and the offender is better assisted and more likely to reintegrate. This new "network" spills over into the general community as well and helps many other types of clients who are not offenders.

## Who Are the Clients?

Research has shown that many offenders are high-risk people with little education, poor job skills, and low self-confidence who are unemployed or underemployed. The networks are set up to help this type of offender solve these problems in order to become a productive member of society.

The four network projects were distributed throughout the state to see how strategies worked in different service environments and social contexts. Two projects are in northern Illinois. One of these is in a Chicago suburb, the other is in a semi-rural area with a large state university nearby. A third project is located in a rural area of western Illinois, also with a large state university nearby. A fourth project is in an extremely low income, highly rural area in southern Illinois.

Clients vary among the projects. The two northern Illinois projects service parolees and probationers, both before and after release from the county jail. The southern Illinois project services only returning offenders under mandatory supervised release (parole) from the department of corrections, while the western Illinois project services mainly probationers and clients diverted from the courts. Clients therefore differ as to type of crime committed. Among the parolees, the crimes committed include armed robbery, drug offenses, kidnapping, burglary, arson, and breaking and entering. Among probationers and divertees, crimes include DUI, theft, forgeries, bad checks, repeated drunk and disorderly, and other lesser felonies. Clients' ages average in the mid- to late twenties across all projects, although the range is eighteen to seventy. In the rural areas, most clients are white (75 percent), while the suburban clientele is half white and half minority. Most clients served are male, but the western Illinois and suburban Chicago projects have a significant number of females.

By design, and in line with the purposes of the projects, clients selected have some significant personal or social problems (though they were thought to be good risks for the program). Among the most prominent problems are the following:

1. Personality Problems
   a. Negative attitude toward people and the future
   b. Little self-control
   c. Lack of motivation
   d. Low self-esteem
   e. Little respect for others
   f. Poor interpersonai skills
   g. No trust in societal institutions or strangers
   h. Belief in American dream
2. Education and Preparation
   a. High school dropout
   b. No marketable skills
   c. Lack of practical knowledge to improve their situation

3. Social Background
   a. Family income at or below poverty level
   b. Absence of the family unit (divorce, death of a parent, illegitimate child)
   c. Negative relationships (parent attitude, abused childhood)
   d. Anomic living conditions
   e. Family turmoil from infancy
   f. Few possessions—not even houses or cars
4. Physical/Emotional
   a. Fear of failure
   b. Chemical dependency
   c. Strong desire for instant success without the required effort
   d. Influenced by peer pressure
5. Jobs
   a. Unemployed and no experience holding a secure, permanent job; semiskilled or unskilled temporary jobs for the most part
   b. Often no unemployment insurance

## Why Create Vocational Networks?

There are many reasons to create a vocational network. The main goal of each project has been the rehabilitation and reintegration of offenders. If that goal is accomplished, there will be less recidivism, less crime, and therefore fewer victims.

Generally, community-based vocational network programs provide many benefits for both communities and businesses. Based on studies of similar projects across the country and the experience of the projects in Illinois, the following benefits have been identified:

## Benefits for the Community

1. Vocational training and placement programs for offenders have reduced recidivism from 65 to 11 percent in Illinois communities.
2. Programs cost very little. For every dollar spent on job training for offenders, nearly six tax dollars are saved for use elsewhere in the community.
3. Vocational training and employment widen the tax base because employed offenders are taxpaying citizens instead of welfare recipients.
4. Vocational training and subsequent employment services for offenders promote success in probation and parole. There are very few revocations.
5. Vocational training and employment foster self-esteem, help offenders support their families, and provide income to pay victim compensation in some cases.
6. The networks have brought together agencies and individuals that hitherto had not worked together. Specifically, they have helped integrate the court and probation agencies with community service and educational agencies. This integration has provided better services for clients and for the community as a whole, and it has helped the court better understand the community these agencies serve.
7. The networks provide a way to concentrate services in rural communities where service provision is usually underfunded and scattered.

## Benefits for Business

1. Tax incentives to hire network participants can amount up to 50 percent reimbursement per offender.
2. Network screening of potential employees on the basis of risk, needs, and employability provides better employees and saves screening costs for the employer.

3. Training reimbursements for hiring and training offenders can often be provided to employers of network clients.
4. Free bonding insurance can often be provided to businesses hiring offenders.
5. Many large companies have successfully hired offenders and have experienced increased productivity.

## Benefits for the State

1. Vocational network programs reduce the state's overcrowded prison system by keeping offenders out of prison.
2. The crime rate could be reduced.
3. The projects make good use of state resources for offenders and provide the state with a beneficial return on use of those resources.
4. Tax increases for prison construction are avoided. Tax dollars are saved and the tax base is widened.

During the last decade, the Illinois prison population has grown at an alarming rate; there are currently almost 40,000 inmates behind bars. In fiscal year 1990 alone, the state's prison population grew 20 percent, surpassing the growth rate of all other states. Annual housing costs alone have increased to almost $20,000 per inmate. This would be the same as buying each inmate a new car or providing each inmate with tuition, room, and board for four years at a state university. In addition to the cost of annually housing each inmate, construction costs have risen to more than $50,000 per prison cell. For example, it costs more than $50 million to build a 750-bed prison. That same $50-million facility requires at least $15 million annually just to house the inmates (IDOC, 1991). Unfortunately, these facts have not received the full attention of government officials and private citizens. If the community could provide services and assistance through a vocational network, and if the positive impact can be widely known, many positive results can be achieved with relatively fewer resources than currently utilized.

# Community Needs and Offender Needs Justify the Establishment of Networks

One may reasonably ask why a network should be formed when most of the needed services already exist. One also may ask why so many offenders have need for such services in the first place. The answer to the second question will help answer the first.

It is not coincidence that poor and poorly skilled people break the law. The frustrations of poverty and low wages, coupled with the inability to get and keep a job, can promote both property and violent crime. Add a lack of self-confidence and self-worth to this frustration, and the stage is set for many crimes. If individuals are unable to provide proper food, clothing, and shelter for their families; if they see no avenues for escape; or if the community looks down on them, they may well try to solve their problems by theft or by drug abuse. Moreover, the frustrations of such a life can produce various forms of violent crime.

While these conditions are not excuses for criminality, they do allow us to see that there are somewhat indeterminate causes for this behavior. If these causes were eliminated, then the criminal behavior would be reduced. Providing skills through vocational training and a job enhances self-confidence and self-worth and thus reduces the social causes which lead to crime.

Unfortunately, many community agencies and citizens do not see that social problems helped produce the crime. The crime identifies the offender to the public and brings condemnation. The public label offenders as "bad" and therefore not in need of services. Admittedly, it would be much better if the social problems were identified and solved before criminal behavior resulted. However, this is not how our society currently works. We would rather identify offenders by their crimes, define them as "bad," and offer little help.

The community networks were developed to address this problem. The networks grew out of common concerns bearing on offenders. Participants joined once they were made aware of the problems facing offenders and of the possible benefits of such an alliance. Once members (and potential members) understood the common needs of offenders, they saw the need for a common solution; a solution that was to be multilevel and multi-agency. It then became apparent that common needs required common links among agencies and others within the community. No one agency could handle offender problems, but many could. The problem was that no formal or informal linkages had ever existed, as noted previously. In short, without common knowledge concerning offenders and without common linkages among all key agencies, offenders were not getting the services they needed. It was only after the networks became operational that offenders received needed services and job placements.

## What Activities Can a Network Accomplish?

The vocational networks all evolved to provide similar assistance to offenders. Both probationers and parolees have the same needs, which require similar services to help them find secure, permanent jobs and to deter them from crime. Survival needs rank high. These include housing, food, clothing, and medical assistance. The networks began early to assist in finding these services for offenders. This was done because it was soon realized that if offenders' basic survival needs were not met, they had no incentive to train for new skills or attend drug treatment programs.

The next level of offender needs pertains to coping skills. Many offenders need psychological or marital counseling, or drug and alcohol treatment programs. The third level of need is the occupational skills. It manifests itself in the needs for job training, educational advancement, and finally, job placement.

If the networks are to satisfy these needs, they require a full complement of agencies. These agencies should provide for survival needs, coping needs, and employment needs in that order. Survival needs are met by such agencies as the Salvation Army, Department of Rehabilitation Services (DORS), Department of Public Aid, regional councils, township supervisors, local hospitals, and churches. The coping needs are met by DORS staff, local drug treatment facilities, hospital psychiatric units, university clinics, and by volunteer counselors and ministers.

The occupational skills needs are met by local community colleges, universities, and high schools. The community colleges provide the most services to meet these needs. Offenders with these needs require assessment, basic skills training, self-esteem enhancement, value clarification, and skills in planning and decision making as they relate to life goals. They also need training in specific technical skills and in job search strategies. Community colleges supply courses or tutorials to serve most of these occupational needs, from literacy training, to adult basic education, to adult secondary education, to developmental skills education, and to vocational skills training.

Job search skills and assistance are provided by JTPA, the Department of Employment Security, Job Service, private temporary services, and network members themselves. The great amount of attention paid to offenders' needs usually results in secure, permanent full-time job placement for offenders.

Thus, the goals and needs of offenders can be met by existing agencies in the community. These agencies, because they are providing for different levels of needs, must be linked in the network. Yet the network must be held together as well. Each network needs a central coordinator to maintain communications among agencies and provide referrals for offenders. Clients need one place to call to find the necessary information about the agencies. The coordinator provides this service, but also works to maintain the network. He or she does this by keeping in touch with all agencies, both formally and informally, and by holding meetings of network members (usually quarterly). Common interests need a common focus, which the network coordinator provides.

## How Are the Networks Developed?

The ISBE/DAVTE plan called for the establishment of "community networks" to help offenders obtain training and employment without the creation of new community resources. It did not lay out any further guidelines.

Community vocational networks for offenders did not exist in any Illinois community prior to these pilot programs. They must be initiated, developed, and nurtured. The methods to do this become evident from review of the four pilot programs. What follows are the strategies that proved successful for all four. Review of project initiation and development shows that these strategies were developed independently by all projects, yet they are remarkably similar. These do not exhaust the possibilities, but they do provide general guidance for forming a vocational network. Other strategies could be adopted. In fact, a consistent finding across projects is that project initiators must improvise strategies as they deal with the specific problems and people in their communities.

Strategy 1: Assume No Communication or Coordinated Activities for Offenders Exist in the Community.

The first problem encountered in all projects was the almost total lack of communication among social service, educational, and criminal justice agencies, as noted before. Linkages among agencies, even those providing similar services, were almost nonexistent. Furthermore, since the agencies did not know what services others provided or how the clients interacted with multiple agencies, needs assessments and service provisions for offenders were almost nil. Given that community resource brokerage has been a goal of community corrections for twenty years, this pervasive lack of knowledge across all projects was quite surprising. In this type of situation, any increase in "networking" and services provided should have positive results for offender assistance and for recidivism reduction. Therefore, a good first strategy is to assume no coordinated effort exists in a community.

Strategy 2: Obtain Support from Key People in the Criminal Justice System and in the Community.

Since no community had a network and communication was minimal, each project coordinator independently decided to obtain initial support from key people in his or her project county. Identifying these key people was relatively easy, given the goals of the project. They had to be people who were influential in either criminal justice or education in the community. It was thought that if these people could be brought on board, it would legitimize the project and encourage more people to participate. In addition, it would be impossible to have a network at all unless these key people participated. In each case, these people included the state's attorney, the county sheriff, the adult probation department, the parole department, the local school district, and the local community college district. Each network coordinator approached key people in slightly different ways.

In one project, the coordinator sent letters to these people and then scheduled a face-to-face meeting with each of them. During these meetings, the project was explained and its goals described. Without exception, these people said they would participate in the program. After the interviews were completed, a meeting of the initial network was scheduled and invitations were sent to these people. Acceptance of the invitation was seen as increased commitment on their part. Staff from social service agencies were invited to participate later.

The coordinator of another project approached the task differently. Personal interviews were arranged and conducted with all criminal justice agencies in the region. Appointments were established with all agencies, and interviews were conducted. During these interviews, the goals of the project were explained and reactions were solicited. Individuals from these agencies were positive about the project and gave constructive feedback to the coordinator. The coordinator then established personal contact with educational and service agencies in the region. Interviews were used to determine the availability and interest of these key people and to establish a need for a joint meeting with the criminal justice agencies. This meeting centered on a discussion of regional needs and the activities required to meet them. Thus, interviews were conducted with community college representatives, and with individuals from Job Service, JTPA, the educational service center, the department of public aid, and vocational rehabilitation. These people showed a high interest and began to see their agencies as necessary and useful components of the project.

In the third network, the coordinator obtained support from key people by making phone calls to all appropriate social service and law enforcement personnel. The coordinator explained the project and solicited support. The phone calls were followed by an invitation to a luncheon. Many agencies showed genuine interest in the project, but the luncheon was not well attended by some segments of the service community.

Based in a community college, the fourth project coordinator contacted potential participants and invited them to a meeting to organize the network. Much informal discussion occurred between the coordinator and potential participants before the invitations were mailed. This communication was probably done more informally than in the other projects because the college already had ongoing relationships with many agencies.

Thus, in most projects, potential participants were contacted on an individual basis and their opinions were sought, the project goals were explained, and formal commitments were solicited. Without exception, this personal contact paid off, since formal commitments were obtained from most parties. An obvious additional strategy, therefore, is to begin such projects as much as possible with personal contacts.

Strategy 3: Hold Meetings with Key People to Form a Network Early.

Coordinators from all projects eventually held meetings. The key people attended these meetings and discussed furtherance of the networks. Because of prior personal contacts and commitments, they came to these meetings with some knowledge of the projects and with a common goal in mind. Therefore, the meetings were usually productive and advanced the goals of the projects.

The meetings were necessary to implement the networks. By definition, a network needs to communicate, and these meetings produced that communication. People began to realize what other agencies did and how each could affect offender clients. They began to see the interconnectedness of the social, educational, and criminal justice support systems in their communities. This understanding would ultimately lead to the joint production of goals and practices commensurate with project needs. These meetings were held either monthly or quarterly. More frequent meetings were not looked at positively by participants for two reasons. First, most of these people felt they spent too much time in meetings. Second, an eventual consensus had to develop over time. People needed time to think, discuss with others, figure out "community politics," and do some "private networking." The strategy seemed to work across all projects.

Project coordinators approached the meetings differently. Invitations to the first meeting of one project were only sent to the criminal justice and educational personnel originally contacted. They came to discuss openly community and offender needs and their roles in providing those needs within the network. Many good initial ideas came from the meeting, and all participants agreed to meet again shortly thereafter to further plans.

In another project, the luncheon meeting mentioned earlier was attended by a number of criminal justice and social service agency personnel. Notably absent was the county sheriff, who never did participate. During the meeting, goals and benefits of the project were explained by the state's attorney and a representative from Job Service. Agency personnel responded positively, and the stage was set for the provision of network services.

The third project coordinator also held a breakfast meeting for business and industry leaders at which officials from several agencies, including Job Service, gave presentations and discussed benefits to employers. This meeting did not yield much business participation in the network.

Meetings were also conducted in the southern Illinois project. Individuals who had been personally contacted by the coordinator were invited, and most came. The meetings were used to develop interagency awareness of the basic objectives of the network and to use those present as a sounding board for "community needs assessment." These activities were successful.

Given the unique focus on parolees of the southern Illinois program, another activity of that network for criminal offenders was to meet with the state department of corrections. This meeting was held to arrange a working profile from which release notices and file information could be obtained on those offenders who would be released from state facilities.

The network coordinator met with the case manager coordinator for the department of corrections and cleared an avenue of information release on offenders. Ongoing contact with the department of corrections cleared a working procedure for notice of release dates of offenders and for access to records. This procedure enabled the network coordinator to prepare assistance for offenders prior to their return to the region.

To communicate the progress of the network, a second meeting was convened. Seventy-six percent of the major agency contacts made earlier by the program coordinator were represented at this meeting. During the informal meeting, participants expressed a renewal of the goals of the program, reiterated their support for the program, and expressed their willingness to be "working partners" in continuing program efforts.

The Chicago suburban community college project also began holding meetings quite early in the process. The participants at the first meeting were from among all agencies personally contacted earlier. The participants included public schools, court services, and probation/parole personnel. Committee members became acquainted with each other and heard presentations on the results of research on vocational education and offenders.

A second meeting of this network was held shortly after the first. The sheriff's office was now included among the participants. This meeting highlighted presentations by agency personnel concerning the availability of vocational education opportunities through their agencies. Agencies included work release, the private industry council, court services, department of corrections, and the area vocational center. The participants of the meeting determined that many needed services were offered by these agencies but that they were not coordinated or well-known by potential clients. These individuals also decided that needs assessments and provisions for assistance were immediate priorities.

Strategy 4: Assess Offender, Community, and Agency Needs.

One conclusion that was independently arrived at after each network's initial meetings was that needs assessments had to be done. These assessments were to be of offender needs and risks, as well as community and agency needs. Each network collected data for these assessments. Most of the data gathered from agencies and offenders related to demographic characteristics of offenders. However, some networks surveyed offenders in more depth to find out about their problems and attitudes. This data revealed the characteristics and needs of offenders described earlier in this chapter.

The western Illinois network staff delved much more deeply into assessment than the others. They assessed offender needs and attitudes, community needs and attitudes, and business resources and attitudes. The results of the assessments proved extremely useful in initiating and maintaining the project. While it is not the purpose of this chapter to report all such research results, it may be useful to highlight some important findings.

The project staff conducted four surveys/interviews. The first interview was with the key people in criminal justice and educational agencies. These interviews included many questions about offenders and how the respondents saw themselves in relation to offenders. The interviews were timed not only to gather needed information, but also to further "break the ice" with key people. Generally, the interviews showed that the respondents saw the need for vocational education and jobs for offenders. While most respondents did not know about available services, all agreed that they would welcome participation in the network. Also, when asked questions concerning their attitudes toward offenders, these people surprisingly were much less punitive than the general citizenry. They were less likely to say everyone belongs in jail and more likely to see the need for education and jobs as means of rehabilitation and reintegration. They also believed many services were lacking in the community. This last perception proved false, however, once the assessments of the community were made.

A second set of interviews was done with probationers who were on the caseload of the county probation officers. These provided insights into the offenders' needs and perceptions. The results paralleled the findings of the other networks and were reported earlier in this chapter.

A third set of data was gathered from a questionnaire sent to a representative sample of county residents. The return rate for these surveys was 35 percent, which is about normal for this type of research. The findings, however, proved useful in attempts to organize and maintain the network. Some of these findings are important to consider for purposes of initiating the network in other communities.

The respondents to this survey favored vocational training and placement for offenders, but did not want to pay for it, especially if the offenders were drug users. Citizens who said offenders should be helped thought vocational education was a proper way to do it. However, these citizens were strongly divided as to how they viewed the offenders in general. Most of them thought that offenders should receive relatively harsh punishment so they would be deterred from further crime. In fact, many thought that punishment should occur whether it deters or not. A smaller percentage of citizens agreed that rehabilitation/reintegration was desirable for offenders. Also, it was not surprising that a significant number of citizens thought that delivery of vocational/rehabilitative services would be hindered by a lack of money and high public resistance, as well as by a lack of cooperation on the part of the offenders and by rivalries between service agencies.

These citizens, given their general views, also felt that only criminal justice agencies should initiate such services to keep offenders in line and promote community protection. In their view, educational agencies should not initiate programs for offenders. However, this is incongruous since most services the offenders need come from the educational institutions. A final insight into the public mind about offenders comes from asking citizens what jobs offenders should be trained for. A clear majority felt that offenders should be trained and placed only in nonprofessional and nonclerical jobs. These are the less productive jobs in modern society and do not provide a great deal of self-esteem or job security. Finally, the survey showed citizens to be fearful of offenders in general, but willing to work with them in a job setting. Thus, the citizenry shows itself to stereotype offenders greatly and to misunderstand the goals of corrections in general and of community corrections in particular.

A fourth survey was also conducted to assess the attitudes of business people and their willingness to help in the network project. Some important findings from this survey may be useful to planners of new networks. Like the community survey, this study of businesses explored attitudes regarding a number of relevant issues.

While the number of responses from businesses was not sufficient to present detailed findings, a number of summary observations can be made regarding views of smaller businesses within this rural county:

1. a majority of responding businesses favor both training and placement for criminal offenders;
2. most businesses do not favor financial aid to criminal offenders to pursue vocational training;
3. more than three-fourths of businesses oppose increased tax support for offender vocational services;
4. most business leaders favor deterrence and punishment and due process and rehabilitation as a combined direction for community corrections;
5. most respondent businesses feel that financial funding, public resistance, and the offender's lack of cooperation would be obstacles to successful vocational programming for criminal offenders;
6. a majority of responding businesses favor involvement of the courts, vocational agencies, probation, and law enforcement as the initiators and planners of vocational services;
7. most businesses indicate that they would not mind hiring or working with criminal offenders (the group least accepted was drug offenders);

8. many of the businesses specify those job areas for which they would hire an offender (i.e., almost all businesses favor hiring offenders to perform service and laborer jobs).

The knowledge accumulated through these surveys was of great help in initiating a network. The general attitude of the community is important because community support is essential for network development. The network must rely on community resources and cooperation. Thus, ways need to be found to encourage community participation while at the same time giving factual information and breaking stereotypes. Support for programs increases dramatically when citizens know the facts.

The same is true for business leaders. Their participation increases when they know the truth about offenders and the program and when stereotypes are broken. Thus, another strategy is needed.

Srategy 5: Do Everything Possible to Make the Project Known to the Community.

The extreme stereotyping produced by lack of factual information is a major barrier to network building. The stereotypes found in the surveys in western Illinois were also found in the other three communities. As noted before, personal one-on-one contact with citizens and agencies is the best way to get out the facts and encourage participation. However, this is not entirely feasible or practical in larger communities.

Initially, a major channel of information dispersal to the larger community was the news media in each community. Every network project relied on newspaper articles and, in some cases, local television news programs. Some of these media stories were purely informational, while others asked for help with the projects. It is good advice only to contact the media when there is something positive to report since most people will interpret anything negative they hear through their stereotypes. It is also good advice to be prepared for bad media coverage if an offender in the program does commit a new crime. These failure stories can do much harm even though most offenders in the program are doing very well.

Another way to gain positive attention is by use of the community surveys. It was found that when people received personalized mailings, many remembered the program, even if they did not return the questionnaire. Further informational mailings also generated community support. Several projects initiated a newsletter for mail distribution to selected citizens as well as agency and business officials. The newsletter proved useful in keeping the project in public view and in disseminating positive information to the community.

Additional strategies must be applied to obtain business participation in providing jobs. Business officials were not willing to discuss hiring until much of the network was in place. They needed to see a purpose and to know that the key people and the community were behind the project. They still had concerns about hiring offenders, but usually these fears were reduced by showing them results of other similar projects that were successful.

Strategy 6: Fit Community Services with Community and Offender Needs.

After needs assessments are completed, the next step is to identify the community resources already available to the network for use in helping offenders meet their needs. After these resources are identified, work can begin on "networking" them into a useable flow for offenders. Usually, this exercise will show that the community has more resources than previously thought. This realization will help put the project in perspective and make it seem much more possible to accomplish.

The identifying of services could start with the criminal justice agencies. Since sheriffs usually run county jails, the sheriff's office is a good place to begin. The jails should be checked to see if they have vocational training programs, GED and Adult Basic Education (ABE) programs, life survival skills, and pre-employment classes. While these classes are usually offered by community colleges, some are offered by the high schools. The larger jails in the most populated areas of the state are most likely to have such programs. Rural jails do not have the tax or population base to offer such programs. It should be noted that the jails are an important focal point for the networks since they house not only people awaiting trial, but also offenders convicted of relatively minor offenses who will eventually be released into the community. Some of these people, who are jailed periodically, usually have jobs. Therefore, offenders can be offered advanced job services if they have a job or basic services if they do not work.

Another agency whose services need to be identified is the private industry council (PIC). This agency will often provide funds for vocational education and remedial courses. To offset the employers' costs, PIC also may negotiate with employers for placement and on-the-job training pay for offenders. PIC also can provide job search assistance and may provide or pay for assessments. JTPA can also provide many of these services if the offender fits their criteria for program enrollment.

Court services is another agency that can either provide or broker services. In larger communities, probation officers are assigned to broker services for offenders and to monitor their progress. Local high schools and area vocational centers also provide many services. Many vocational education courses are offered through these agencies. They are especially indispensable when the network tries to provide services to younger offenders.

As noted before, the resources the community colleges can bring to the network are great, and they should be specifically identified. The community colleges can provide tutoring, literacy training, GED preparation, ABE, adult secondary education (ASE), developmental courses, and vocational courses. For residents of the college districts, the literacy, ABE, and ASE courses are usually free, while often the higher level courses can be taken for reduced cost. This is a big help to unemployed or underemployed offenders and may act as an incentive for their participation.

Another set of services are those that can be provided by drug and alcohol abuse programs. The programs may be stand-alone or attached to other agencies such as hospitals. The services are invaluable since many offenders have substance abuse problems which need to be solved before they enroll in vocational education programs. Some of these services can be provided through the network at reduced or no cost to the offender.

Other services that need to be identified include housing, food, clothing, and medical services. Agencies such as the Salvation Army, public aid, township supervisors, and local churches should be contacted.

Strategy 7: Allow the Network to Develop on Its Own Terms.

As each project got underway, the coordinators did not dictate the form or content of the network. They offered direction, but if the people did not want to follow that direction, the issue was not pursued. The network participants are volunteers whose goodwill and cooperation must be reinforced. These people face many problems in their work. They each have individual bureaucratic and "political" problems to deal with. The network operation must be allowed to develop from these exigencies as they are worked out in the communicative setting of the network. Given this, and the varying social context of each community, no single best way to organize the specific components of the network emerges. However, broad parameters can be identified.

## Components of a Successful Network

While the individual agencies and people involved in each pilot network differed somewhat, the basic components were remarkably similar, considering they were arrived at independently. The consensus reached by network participants always, at some point, included the realization that a full complement of social services was needed for the offender-client. The conclusion reached by these practitioners was the same as that reached by empirical studies. Fortunately, this conclusion came about relatively early in network development, and time was not wasted. Thus, each network incorporated many social service agencies as basic components.

The results of Strategies 1–7 were networks that were functional, but still emerging and developing. As time went on, each network grew in number of participants as successes were achieved, and word spread about the project goals. Most of the additional people were from social service agencies, but some new criminal justice personnel also agreed to participate. By the end of the three-year period of the pilot study, three of the four networks had the full complement of community people needed for ongoing network activities.

While each network obviously has some different agencies performing the tasks, similar functions are accomplished in all projects. For example, in the IDOC parolee project, it is IDOC that decides on parole and community supervision, not the state's attorney who recommends probation. It is also the parole officer, not the probation officer, who supervises the client. Also, some clients volunteer while others are in the program under court order. While it is too early to assess fully the differences, it now seems that volunteer clients have a better record of accomplishment than the non-volunteers. Social service agencies also differ by network as does the means of "offender assistance." However, other components are common to all networks. It is to these common components that we turn our attention.

A unique feature of this project is the business contacts' subcommittee. This group of people has canvassed the major employers in the county by conducting personal interviews and asking for employers' commitments to hire offenders who finish the program. At the onset of the project, each employer was sent a letter and information about the network. The positive aspects were spelled out both for the community and the employer. After that, an interview was scheduled so that face-to-face discussion could occur. Later, a follow-up letter was sent. Approximately a year later, all major employers were again interviewed. These tactics produced some commitments and kept potential employers informed. The services of JTPA were also used for clients who qualified for them.

The other networks also developed a network that was similar to the western Illinois Network in terms of agencies involved, flow of clients, and services provided. The suburban Chicago network focused mainly on jailed clients and their needs before release. In addition, the program was targeted toward inmates on work release and halfway house residents. The most unique aspect of this project was the offering of a career enhancement course. Because of poor attendance at such courses for general community-based offenders, the network tried to offer it while clients were still under detention so their attention was more easily obtained. The program is the result of a two-year collaborative effort by the Lake County Vocational Networking Committee. The committee represents the College of Lake County, Halfway House, Sheriff's Office Jail Division, Lake County Sheriff's Work Release Program, Private Industry Council of Lake County, Lake County Area Vocational Center, Court Services Division, Adult Services, and Lake County Regional Vocational System.

Offenders who have been sentenced by judges and who will be released less than a month after completing the course are eligible for this program. They must have probation as part of their sentence. This is done to permit a follow-up study to see if education will reduce their jail return rate. To date, more than thirty men and women between the ages of eighteen and sixty-two, single, married, or single parents whose educational levels range from seventh grade to a year or two of college, have participated in this program.

The main objective of the career enhancement course is to provide clients with the tools they will need to secure employment and rebuild their lives after their release. The course is targeted toward a group that has many of the needs considered before that are due to unemployment or underemployment.

The course consists of 24 hours of classroom instruction, including career planning, goal setting, resume preparation, job hunting techniques, interviewing skills, and appropriate job attitudes. Besides skill development, the course provides assistance in changing attitudes and developing a positive image. For example, at the beginning of the course, many students make little eye contact with others and have little trust in the content and concept of the course. By the end of the course, these traits usually disappear and self-confidence increases significantly.

One important part of the course is role play in which students learn about themselves, speak about their experiences, discover their hidden talents, and learn how to answer job interview questions honestly about their jail term. This gives the students the opportunity to work constructively on their problems. The result is that they develop positive attitudes, raise their self-esteem, and improve self-confidence.

At the completion of the course, students not only earn a certificate from the college but also have a career plan, which includes an official resume developed by them. They also have a better sense of direction. Assistance is also given when offenders need identification for employment, for example, when applying for duplicate Social Security cards or birth certificates. In addition, information is provided on food, housing, and temporary jobs available immediately upon release.

After the course is completed and the inmates are released, their progress is monitored and documented by their probation officers for a year. Approximately ten students will first be selected for complete vocational testing through area vocational centers. Some will then receive one tuition-free course at the college to enhance their employability skills in a specific area.

Approximately seventy-five men and women will benefit from this program during the initial year of full implementation. All agencies involved are committed to the future of this program and will seek support from the community by asking small businesses and large corporations to join in this positive venture. Students' reactions to the course are also very positive.

## Common Network Elements and Commentary on Strategies

The descriptions just given illustrate the nature of the networks in some detail. However, many of the common aspects of these four projects can be formulated into strategies for maintenance and further development of the networks.

Strategy 8: Promote Communication Between Probation/Parole
Officers and Network Participants.

The role of the probation/parole officers is vitally
important to each project. They assess and provide supervision
plans, as well as the supervision itself. They also should be
community resource brokers; however, in most cases, current
officers did not see themselves as initially fulfilling that role.
Gradually, all accepted the brokerage role as the "networking"
continued. The strategy is to keep them communicating, so they
can see the connections with other agencies. These officers now
make referrals and help offender volunteers in routine fashion.

Strategy 9: Allow the Network to Find Its Own Best Methods of
Assessment.

Assessments must be performed before clients can be
provided with educational and job search help. Vocational
testing is usually provided by the community colleges at no cost
to clients. In some cases, JTPA can provide such assessments.
Initially, in most projects, these two agencies did not know that
their assessments overlapped and that clients were being tested
twice. Networking at meetings revealed these problems, and
they were subsequently solved. In addition, drug and family
assessments are done in most of the projects. Each project
worked out different ways and used different agencies to do this,
but usually some social agency in the community has the
resources and expertise to do this. The strategy is to let the
network find its own people for such assessments.

These assessments must be conducted in order to place
clients in subsequent stages of the program. Vocational/
educational assessments help place offenders in the appropriate
training. Classes must be properly chosen for clients. Clients in
the wrong class may not be willing to follow through and as a
result, may drop out. Drug/family assessments identify
problems that must be solved before offenders can properly
obtain training and jobs. Because substance abuse and family
problems should be solved before vocational training begins,
social service agencies in the network should have these clients
referred to them.

Strategy 10: Continue to Allow the Network to Develop as It Sees Fit: Promote Communication.

Social service agencies vary by project, but most initially included representatives from public health, public aid, job service, child care resources, employment security programs, group assistance programs, shelter and clothing provision programs, and counseling programs. Most of these agencies or their personnel have now become part of the network, thus providing needed services to clients. This expansion of the original network was not predicted, but has proven useful. By allowing the networks to grow on their own as the needs of the community and clients dictate, more positive outcomes are produced. This is particularly true when we note more interagency communication regarding services available to offenders and more freedom to refer offenders among the agencies. Thus, the lack of coordination and communication among agencies has been greatly reduced while service provision has greatly increased.

Strategy 11: Incorporate the Educational Institutions into the Networks Early.

Educational institutions play a crucial role in such projects. In Illinois, the community colleges are the main provider of vocational education, basic life skills courses, and literacy training. The entire population of the state has access to these institutions, and many basic courses are available without charge. In the early stages of all four projects, these institutions saw themselves as key players. Personnel in community college adult education departments did not need to be persuaded to join the network. Rather, they wanted to know how they fit into the networks and how their services could be most useful. State universities were helpful in providing services when the community colleges could not. Local school districts were not as cooperative in providing services to juvenile offenders, however. Their most often used tactic was to refer such juveniles to the community colleges. The basic strategy here is to incorporate the educational institutions into the networks very early in the process.

Strategy 12: Continue to Cultivate Employer Contacts Personally.

Obtaining business support for these networks has been the most problematic aspect of the process. Businesses, especially retail, are understandably uncertain and somewhat fearful of hiring offenders. All projects have attempted to incorporate business people, chambers of commerce, and similar organizations. None has been able to get them to participate fully in the network. Two different approaches to businesses have been tried. In one, luncheons or dinners were organized specifically for business people. Attendance was usually poor, with those attending usually not wanting further participation in the network. The second approach involved personal visits by network staff to each employer. Those visited were usually personnel directors. In these one-on-one discussions, their personal questions and biases were more easily addressed and their cooperation more readily obtained. This may be because they did not want the other businesses, or the general public, to know they were willing to hire offenders.

The projects that used this personal approach found that repeated follow-up phone calls and mailings, providing new information and encouragement for their support, helped keep employer interest and commitment at a higher level. One major incentive for employers that was found during the meetings was the assessments of offenders. Employers were much more likely to hire offenders who had been thoroughly assessed. They were "safer" to hire, and it cost employers less than doing their own assessments. Also, economic and tax incentives made employers more receptive to hiring offenders.

In addition, all projects used JTPA agencies in their communities. Initially, JTPA offices were unwilling to participate in the projects. Some were even hostile, thinking the projects were encroaching on their agency territory. Great amounts of "networking" by project staff and other network members usually brought JTPA into the fold. It must be noted that JTPA can only help certain offenders find certain jobs as defined by federal law. Therefore, independently cultivating employer contacts must be a continuous ongoing effort for network projects.

Strategy 13: Continuously Recruit, Train, and Use Volunteers.

Another component of most networks is the citizen volunteer. Much of the necessary day-to-day work can be done by concerned volunteers. The use of volunteers varies among the projects. However, there are certain areas where their help is invaluable. We will use the example of the western Illinois project described previously to illustrate how citizen volunteers help with network goals.

Volunteers for the western Illinois project were organized by a group called the "offender assistance subcommittee." This group was originally made up of several network members interested in directly helping the offenders. They took it upon themselves to recruit and organize citizens from the community. Many of these volunteers came from the churches, but others came from the ranks of senior citizens and college students.

Volunteers provide personal assistance to offenders. Such assistance includes helping them fill out forms and applications, instructing them on how to dress for an interview, helping them register for classes, helping them find needed social services, and providing transportation to classes and appointments. These services are valuable because they help offenders overcome barriers to their participation in the program. By helping these people over barriers they have never before crossed, volunteers are providing them with new experiences and greater chances of making it. These new experiences, plus the personal attention given to offenders by volunteers, also serve to promote a more positive self-concept in offenders. Overall, volunteers help offenders complete vocational training and obtain a job.

Volunteers, to be most useful, must be continually coordinated. In the western Illinois case, the chair of the offender assistance subcommittee serves as coordinator. In other networks, the general project coordinator serves in this role. A central part of the coordination is keeping open the lines of communication between all parties. There is a great potential for miscommunication in projects such as these, and it must be kept at a minimum, given the fears and stereotypes among business people and members of the community.

In sum, each of the major components discussed above seems necessary for a successful network. Equivalent groups that can perform the same functions are necessary.

## Persistent Problems and Some Suggestions for Solutions

Similar problems have emerged in all four projects. Five persistent ones that must be dealt with involve communication, coordination, bureaucracy, money, and business support.

### *Communication*

Communication problems are inevitable when so many different agencies and people are involved in such a project. Often these problems stem from lack of knowledge or of expectations. Agencies work under different bureaucratic guidelines and mandates, depending especially on their funding source. These guidelines do not usually mesh. For example, the community colleges are told not to give assessment reports to anyone but the client. The probation officers, however, need such reports; indeed, they are mandated to obtain them. Each group cannot understand the other's requests. There is a communication breakdown. In such cases, the role of the project coordinator becomes very important. As an outsider to both organizations who uses one-to-one persuasion, he or she can bring about mutual understanding and solve such problems in an amicable manner. Periodic meetings of the network members also help break down such barriers.

### *Coordination*

As every network evolved, the problem of coordination became more acute. The opening and maintaining of the necessary lines of communication described earlier take much time and effort. This is because many agency officials are overworked (especially criminal justice agencies) and do not have the time to communicate fully with officials from other agencies. It is also because all agency officials easily lose sight of network goals when their major concern is their own agency's goals. These agency goals are not always compatible with the network's goals. Network goals are secondary to agency goals for these people, and personnel will act in accordance with the goals of higher priority.

Thus, there is need for a full-time coordinator (or office of coordination) to keep the network going. This coordinator must be a *prime mover* within the network. He or she must work to keep information flowing and agencies interested. He or she also must work with the community and its leaders to portray a positive image to the community and to keep lines of communication open. The coordinator must build working relationships with key agencies such as Department of Commerce (DOC) (for parolees) and court services (for probation). It also seems to work best if the coordinator is the main referral source for the offender. One central source of information and help is more readily used by clients. Clients who feel hassled by the great number of agencies with which they must deal will not usually finish vocational training. Finally, central coordination is required to direct volunteers as they are assigned to and work with clients. In this regard, all networks have found that a common needs assessment/intake form and common legal releases need to be used, so the information is known to all and the client is not lost in the paperwork.

Another aspect of effective coordination involves the network structure itself. As the network grows and matures, operating procedures and the role of each member should be formalized. In every community, people move away and others arrive. The network structure must not be dependent on an individual or on personalities, but on positions and the functions performed by people in those positions. The network also must be very clear as to its goals and structures.

At the very least, a network must have three goals: (1) to place offenders in vocational training, (2) to place offenders in jobs, and (3) to maintain and increase community support for the network and its clients. These goals must be clearly stated and stated often. The network committee members must ensure that network goals are being met. To do this, they should suggest modifications of current operating procedures, advise other members on policy, do ongoing assessments of the program and its clients and, most importantly, find areas of need and the resources to meet those needs.

Individual network committee members can do many things to promote network services and to enhance the network's impact. They can act as liaisons with businesses and the community. In so doing, they help offenders find job placements and obtain employers' commitments to provide jobs. In addition, individual network members can advocate network goals to the community, help offenders find educational opportunities, help guide offenders through the process, and even train offenders in their areas of expertise or in basic life skills.

The network committee should meet at least once a quarter. At that meeting, major problems can be discussed, as well as new directions for providing offender assistance. Care must be taken to make the meetings informative and useful, or attendance will eventually decline. These meetings are important because they keep the communication flow going so fewer problems occur.

Another aspect of network committee structure has to do with division of labor. Not all members do the same things well. Individuals must be allowed to do what they do best in order to get business done and to make them want to keep their membership. Probably the best way to make certain that the work gets done by the people best equipped to do it is to appoint subcommittees. These subcommittees should be developed along the lines of a functional division of labor. Perhaps subcommittees in the following areas would work: offender assistance, business contacts, advocacy, and assessment. Of course, members of all subcommittees should continue to recruit newly interested community members into the program. Up to a point, more members on the committee and its subcommittees provide better service because of the diverse knowledge required to run the network. Also, there are more people to do the needed work, which relieves the burdens on all.

## Bureaucracy

The bureaucratic problems involve what could be called "bureaucratic incompetence," red tape, and record keeping. State and local agencies often reveal a lack of knowledge and understanding. Many of the officials are not trained in areas concerning criminal offenders, or, because of their civil service status, do not care to help with any more than minimal effort. Therefore, work for the project that should require little time and effort becomes cumbersome. It may become so much so that clients give up.

The "red tape" problem comes from the innumerable forms that must be filled out for every agency. This process is an obstacle to even the most knowledgeable volunteer and can divert and intimidate an offender. Bureaucratic record keeping also poses problems because of attempts to keep data private. For instance, under new rules, the DOC will no longer provide project personnel with records of released inmates. This means the service providers are working "blind" when trying to plan for the parolee. Solutions for these problems will not come without changes in state law.

## Money

Another problem, money, is one that no project has yet completely solved. Sources of money to provide training and other offender assistance must be found. This money is also to be used for classes, food, shelter, and transportation. Money is also needed for a full-time coordinator. The networks have been fortunate in securing funds on an informal and temporary basis, but permanent sources, either public or private, must be found. Perhaps arrangements to share costs can be made with local governments. Perhaps private foundations will fund pilot programs. The amount of money needed is much less than what is needed to keep a client in prison.

## Business Support

The lack of support from businesses has been the greatest problem facing the networks. Businesses supply the jobs for the clients; they must be won over. Without repeating what previously was said about businesses, every network must work constantly to cultivate business support. Some employers will help early in the process. If these employers hire clients who "make it," these success stories should be told to other employers. Successful job placement will convince other businesses to join the network. The result has often been demonstrated in other projects of this kind throughout the country.

## Assessing Network Outcomes

It is not the purpose of this chapter to detail assessment techniques. However, certain aspects of assessment are obvious to those who have worked with the networks over time.

The most important outcomes of the networks are successful clients. However, there are several different ways to define success. One way is to find out how many offenders complete their supervision plan. This may show motivation to stay with the program. Another way is to measure who enters training or education courses. This will measure how clients are proceeding but will not show if they attained final job goals. Still another way is to measure who is able to find and/or retain employment. This is an important measure since it assesses the accomplishment of one major goal of the network. The type of job obtained and the length of time it is held are both important to measure. Another important measure is recidivism. How many of the offenders successfully leaving the program do not return to crime? There are many problems in measuring recidivism, and the interested reader is referred to any good criminology text.

One final aspect of assessment is to measure the client's individual attitudes and motivation. This can be done by constructing questionnaires which use various attitudinal scales.

The client's traits could be measured before beginning the network program and again after completion of training and job search. Any movement toward increased motivation and positive attitude would show the positive impact of network programs.

Finally, the number of clients utilizing the program is a good assessment measure. Currently, the western and southern Illinois networks each have about twenty clients. About seventy-five clients are using the suburban network, while about forty offenders are in the northern Illinois network. Most of these offenders have completed courses and are looking for jobs. Since most offenders who have completed the program in the past have found jobs, these individuals should find them as well. These numbers show that, so far, the networks have achieved success.

Thus, these network programs can and do work. They help reintegrate offenders and can reduce prison crowding. Lowered crime, more employment and productivity, and cooperation among agencies are all positive aspects of the projects that can affect everyone in the community.

# REFERENCES

Abadinski, H. (1987). *Probation and Parole: Theory and Practice.* Englewood Cliffs, NJ: Prentice Hall.

Bartollas, C. (1985). *Correctional Treatment.* Englewood Cliffs, NJ: Prentice Hall.

Bureau of Justice Statistics (1989). *Special Report: Recidivism of Prisoners Released in 1983.* Washington, DC: Author.

Byrne, J.M. (1989). "Reintegrating the Concept of Community into Community-Based Corrections." *Crime and Delinquency* 35 (3): 471–499.

Carter, R.M., and L.T. Wilkins (eds.). (1976). *Probation, Parole, and Community Corrections.* New York: John Wiley and Sons.

Chiricos, T. (1987). "Rates of Crime and Unemployment: An Analysis of Aggregate Research Evidence." *Social Problems* 34 (2): 187–212.

Clear, T.R., and G.F. Cole (1986). *American Corrections.* Monterey, CA: Brooks/Cole.

Cole, G.F. (1986). *The American System of Criminal Justice.* Monterey, CA: Brooks/Cole.

Cromwell, P.F., Jr., G. Killinger, H.B. Kerper, and C.D. Walker (1985). *Probation and Parole in the Criminal Justice System.* St. Paul, MN: West Publishing.

Cross-Drew, C. (1984). *Project Jericho Evaluation Report.* Sacramento, CA: California Youth Authority.

Crow, I., P. Richardson, C. Reddington, and F. Simon (1989). *Unemployment, Crime, and Offenders.* New York: Routledge.

Cullen, F.T., and K. Gilbert (1982). *Reaffirming Rehabilitation.* Cincinnati, OH: Anderson.

Currie, E. (1983). "Fighting Crime." In J.J. Sullivan and J.L. Victor (eds.), *Criminal Justice 83/84—Annual Editions* (pp. 102–103). Guilford, CT: Duskin Publishing.

Dollar, E.M. (1988). "Keeping Them from Coming Back to Prison: In Oklahoma." *Vocational Education Journal* 39 (1): 29–33.

Duffee, D.E., and K.N. Wright (1990). "Reintegration Policy in Practice: Transition Programs in the 1970s." In D. Duffee and E.F. McGarrell (eds.), *Community Corrections: A Community Field Approach* (pp. 185–216). Cincinnati, OH: Anderson.

Gendreau, P., and R.R. Ross (1987). "Revivication of Rehabilitation: Evidence from the 1980s." *Justice Quarterly* 4 (3): 349–407.

Glaser, D. (1964). *The Effectiveness of a Prison and Parole System.* Indianapolis, IN: Bobbs-Merrill.

Hassell, L.W. (1988). "Keeping Them from Coming Back to Prison: In Arkansas." *Vocational Education Journal* 39 (1): 28–33.

Illinois Criminal Justice Information Authority (ICJIA) (1985). *Research Bulletin: Repeat Offenders in Illinois.* Chicago: Author (November).

——— (1989). *Trends and Issues 89: Criminal and Juvenile Justice in Illinois.* Chicago: Author.

Illinois Department of Corrections (IDOC) (1991). *Insight into Corrections (1990 Annual Report).* Springfield: Author.

Killinger, G.G., and P.F Cromwell, Jr. (1978). *Corrections in the Community: Alternatives to imprisonment.* St. Paul, MN: West Publishing.

Lauerman, C. (1987). "The Safer Way Out." *The Chicago Tribune Sunday Magazine*, pp. 10–16, 26, 27 (8/2).

Lichtman C.M., and S.M. Smock (1981). "The Effects of Social Services on Probationer Recidivism: A Field Experiment." *Journal of Crime and Delinquency* 18: 81–99.

McCarthy, B., and B.J. McCarthy (1984). *Community-Based Corrections*. Belmont, CA: Brooks/Cole.

Martinson, R. (1974). "What Works: Questions and Answers About Prison Reform." *Public Interest* 35: 22–54.

Menard, S., and H. Covey (1983). "Community Alternatives and Rearrests in Colorado." *Criminal Justice and Behavior* 10 (1): 93–108.

Miller, M.J. (1976). "Vocational Training in Prison: Some Social Policy Implications." In D.M. Peterson and C. W. Thomas (eds.), *Corrections: Problems and Prospects* (pp. 136–144). Englewood Cliffs, NJ: Prentice Hall (Reprinted from *Federal Probation*, September, 1972, 36: 19–21).

National Advisory Commission on Criminal Justice Standards and Goals (NACCJSG). (1973). *Corrections*. Washington, DC: U.S. Government Printing Office.

Smith, R.R. (1984). "Reported Ex-Offender Counseling, Services, and Rehabilitation." *Journal of Offender Counseling Services and Rehabilitation* 8 (4): 300–312.

Smykla, J.O. (1981). *Community-Based Corrections: Principles and Practices*. New York: Macmillan.

Switzer, M.E., and A.P. Roberts (eds.). (1973). *Vocational Rehabilitation and Corrections: Readings in Prison Education*. Springfield, IL: Thomas.

# CHAPTER ELEVEN

# The Probation Mentor Home Program: An Evaluation

## Chinita A. Heard

An increasing number of troubled youths is appearing before Allen Superior Court's Family Relations Division in Fort Wayne, Indiana. This increase has resulted in accelerating costs of out-of-county placement for troubled youths. Placement costs reached an alarming $1.5 million in 1987 and nearly $2 million in 1988 (Charles, 1988; *Probation Mentor Home Program Policy and Procedure Manual*, 1989). In a local study, Charles (1988) found that Allen County youths who are court-ordered into out-of-county placement can be better served by utilizing vocational, educational, and other treatment services within the local community.

Faced with enormous budgetary constraints coupled with the need for community-based alternatives for troubled youths, officials at Allen County Juvenile Probation Department had previously implemented an electronic monitoring program in 1987 (Charles, 1989). The Probation Mentor Home was established in 1989 (*Probation Mentor Home Program Policy and Procedure Manual*, 1989; Heard, 1990).

The program, which is the focus of this chapter, is designed for nonviolent youths who are between the ages of ten and seventeen. Youths targeted for the program include those who are currently institutionalized, recently adjudicated, and at risk of residential treatment as a result of delinquency problems. This community-based therapeutic approach is designed to place troubled youths in a structured, stable foster home environment for six months with a goal to reintegrate them into their original homes. This process will be accomplished by providing therapeutic intervention strategies which are designed to promote stabilization for the youths and natural parents (*Probation Mentor Home Program Policy and Procedure Manual,* 1989).

This evaluation is designed to assess the process and outcome of the mentor home program within Allen Superior Court's Juvenile Probation Department. Emphasis is placed on the following: (1) compliance with program criteria and procedures specified in the *Probation Mentor Home Program Policy and Procedure Manual* (1989); (2) demographic characteristics of mentor parents and court-ordered youths; (3) treatment (behavior and resource) outcome; and (4) cost effectiveness. Findings generated from this evaluation process may be helpful in the justification for program operation in the future.

# Background

The Probation Mentor Home Advisory Committee, which includes juvenile probation officials, developed the *Probation Mentor Home Program Policy and Procedure Manual* in 1989. A number of events have transpired since that time. For instance, on January 8, 1990, a press conference was held and the Probation Mentor Home Program was officially introduced to the general public. Thereafter, official implementation began with aggressive mentor home recruitment strategies such as public service announcements on television, speaking engagements, posters, pamphlets, and word of mouth. Almost three-quarters of the people who initially inquired about the program mentioned that they saw the television public service announcement (Heard, 1991). It was not until June 8, 1990, that seven mentor homes were licensed for placement. Also, the first youth was placed in June. By July 1990, four youths had been court-ordered for placement (Heard, 1990). Mentor parents were selected after the completion of home studies, psychological evaluations, and background checks. Youths were selected based on the recommendations of the Juvenile Probation Placement Board and the judge.

During March 1991, findings from the preliminary evaluation of the mentor home program were presented by Heard (1991) at the Academy of Criminal Justice Sciences conference in Nashville, Tennessee. Results from this initial evaluation revealed that since initial placement in June of 1990, a total of eighteen youths had been court-ordered into mentor homes. Of these, 44 percent (eight) had been removed, and 56 percent (ten) were still in mentor homes. Among the eight who did not complete the program, in six cases the placement board did not recommend these youths for mentor home placement. Judicial discretion overruled the placement board's recommendation. Of these six cases, five youths who were originally placed in mentor homes were later committed to Indiana Boys' or Girls' School, which was the placement board's original recommendation. Additionally, out of seventeen charges, ten offenses were committed by only three juveniles. More than half of the offenses were committed by repeat offenders who did not complete the program. On the other hand, none of the youths who were still in placement had committed three or more offenses. Heard concluded that program operation has progressed without major difficulties; however, it was simply too early to make an objective assessment of overall program effectiveness, especially since no youths had completed the program. It has been over three years since the first youth was placed (June 1990) in the mentor home. At this time, another evaluation of program outcome will be conducted.

# Methods

Probation mentor home records maintained at the Allen County Juvenile Probation Department were utilized in this evaluation process. A data collection instrument was designed by the evaluator to collect information on the following: program criteria, goals and objectives, mentor parents, court-ordered youths, treatment outcome, and cost effectiveness. Mentor home staff collected necessary data for this evaluation. Also, mentor home staff were interviewed to clarify data on mentor parents, youths, and natural parents. The mentor home staff have frequent contact with all participants. The evaluation period was between June 1990 and April 1992. During this period, eighteen youths had completed the program, sixteen were removed, and eight are still in the program.

# Findings

*Criteria Evaluation Outcome:* First, the Mentor Home Advisory Committee specified the targeted age group of youths to be between ten and seventeen (*Probation Mentor Home Program Policy and Procedure Manual,* 1989). It was found that the age of the youngest youth who participated in the program was eleven, while the oldest was age seventeen. This finding shows compliance with the age criteria originally specified. Second, it was established that violent and sex offenders would not be suitable for the program. It was found that among the thirty-four youths who participated in this program, there were 120 total charges for prior offenses. More than 5 percent of the charges involved a few repeat offenders. The most prevalent offenses were status offenses (runaway) and property offenses (theft). Twelve of the charges were for violent offenses (battery and robbery). Violent offenses represent 10 percent of all the charges. Overall, these findings appear to show 90 percent compliance with the criteria of nonviolent youthful offenders.

*Goals and Objectives Evaluation Outcome:* First, a goal of a six-month placement time period was examined. A few exceptions have been made for adjustment time and school considerations. To date, these exceptions are designed to enhance the placement outcome by allowing for a smoother stabilization process, especially since some youths may need a longer adjustment period. Second, the goal to reduce reliance on out-of-county placement by attempting to increase the usage of mentor home placement was examined. It was found that in 1991, there were two fewer juveniles ordered placed into residential placement facilities than were ordered in 1990. Third, the goal to increase the number of transfers out of institutions was examined. For institutional placements such as Indiana Boys' and Girls' School, no reduction in length of stay has been found. In the near future, however, it is expected that a significant reduction in the population at Indiana Boys' School will take place, especially since the institution is under a court order to reduce the population to 250 by 1993. By May 1992, approximately sixty nonviolent youths ages sixteen and seventeen were to be transferred to the newly established Fort Wayne Youth Achievement Center. Consequently, this reduction, which is desperately needed, is not attributed to increased usage of the mentor home program. Status offenders appear to be heavily targeted for mentor home placement.

*Description of Mentor Parents:* There are nine mentor homes currently participating in the program. In five of these homes, slightly more than half (56 percent)of the mentor parents who were approved for this program were already experienced in working with troubled youths. Additionally, all mentor parents continue to participate in four hours of training per month. This training is sponsored by Allen Superior Court's Family Relations Division.

The demographic characteristics of mentor parents show that marital status includes 67 percent (six) married, 22 percent (two) divorced, and 11 percent (one) widowed. The sex of mentor parents includes 60 percent (nine) females and 40 percent (six) males. Single parents were not ruled out of the selection process. Early on, it was established that a stable therapeutic home environment is the primary focus of placement, regardless of gender or marital status of mentor parents. In regard to the race of mentor parents, there are twice as many white mentor parents (76 percent [ten]) than African-American mentor parents (33 percent [five]).

The need for additional African-American mentor homes was discussed in a November 1991, article by Janet Collins, a staff writer for *Frost Illustrated*. In this article, the Fields family encouraged other African-American families to become involved in the program. It was discovered, however, that of the African Americans interviewed, there was a reluctance to take in troubled youths, mainly because of the multitude of social and economic problems that these families are already confronting

(Collins, 1991). Since this publication, there has not been a significant increase in the number of African-American mentor parents.

*Description of Youth:* Out of thirty-six youths court-ordered into the program, data were available on a total of thirty-four troubled youths because two youths did not work out during the preplacement period. Among these, 53 percent (eighteen) have completed the program, while 47 percent (sixteen) have been removed from the program. Among those removed, six were committed to either the Indiana Boys' or Girls' School, and four were ordered into residential treatment facilities. In most of these cases, despite the placement board's recommendation, however, these youths were still court-ordered into the mentor home. This finding suggests that original recommendations by the place-ment board should be followed. Violations of these recommend-ations weaken the success rate of the mentor home program.

The demographic characteristics of youths who completed the program and those who were removed from the program were examined (Table 1).

For those who have completed the program, 11 percent (two) were age twelve or younger, 50 percent (nine) were ages thirteen and fourteen, and 39 percent (seven) were ages fifteen and sixteen. For those who were removed from the program, 6 percent (one) were age twelve and under, 38 percent (six) were ages thirteen and fourteen, and 56 percent (nine) were ages fifteen through seventeen. These findings suggest that younger youths are more likely to have successful experiences while in the mentor home. For those who completed the program, 67 percent (twelve) were males and 33 percent (six) were females. Among those who were removed from the program, 44 percent (seven) were males and 56 percent (nine) were females. For race, 50 percent (nine) of the youths who completed the program were white, while 44 percent (eight) were African American, and 6 percent (one) were of another. For those who were removed from the program, however, 69 percent (eleven) were white, 25 percent (four) were African Americans, and 6 percent (one) were of another race.

### Table 1: Demographic Characteristics of Participants, Probation Mentor Home Program

|  | Completed Program | | Removed from Program | |
|---|---|---|---|---|
| **Age** | | | | |
| 12 or younger | 11% | (2) | 6% | (1) |
| 13–14 | 50% | (9) | 38% | (6) |
| 15–16 | 39% | (7) | 56% | (9) |
| Total | 100% | (18) | 100% | (16) |
| **Sex** | | | | |
| Males | 67% | (12) | 44% | (7) |
| Females | 33% | (6) | 56% | (9) |
| Total | 100% | (18) | 100% | (16) |
| **Race** | | | | |
| African-American | 44% | (8) | 25% | (4) |
| White | 50% | (9) | 69% | (11) |
| Other | 6% | (1) | 6% | (1) |
| Total | 100% | (18) | 100% | (16) |

Prior to placement, a total of eighty-six offenses was committed by the eighteen youths who have experienced success in a mentor home. A total of thirty-four offenses was committed by the sixteen youths who did not complete the program. The majority of these youths were repeat offenders; however, for those youths who completed the program, almost half of the prior offenses were status offenses. For example, 41 percent were status offenses (thirty-three runaway and eight truancy), 38 percent were property offenses, 9 percent were violent offenses (seven for battery, one for robbery), 2 percent were drug and alcohol offenses, and 2 percent were other offenses. Clearly, a 91 percent compliance rate with the selection criteria of nonviolent offenders is found. On the other hand, prior offenses committed by those who were removed from the program include 32 percent status offenses (ten runaway and one truancy), 50 percent property offenses, 12 percent violent (four battery) offenses, 3 percent were drug offenses, and 3 percent were other offenses. These findings show an 88 percent compliance rate with the nonviolent selection criteria. A higher rate of compliance was found among those cases in which successful experiences have been demonstrated.

*Behavioral Outcome of Youths:* As expected, some of the youths have returned to their homes, while a few others have committed new offenses or have violated the technical terms of the mentor home program. Mentor parents appear to be consistent, provide positive verbal feedback, are interested in the juveniles' concerns and opinions, and are able to hold youths responsible for their actions. Among the recognized problems, mentor parents state that youths experience difficulties with school adjustment, temper control, and impulsiveness. Some youths have verbalized improvements in the areas of family and peer relationships due to tendencies to be better able to make appropriate decisions, reduce impulsiveness, and to better express their feelings, while others simply did not want to be in the program. Overall, those youths and natural parents who experienced success with mentor home placement were open to support from mentor parents and program staff. These youths conformed to policies of the mentor home program and did not appear to be significantly increasing serious delinquent involvement.

The most common offenses committed while in or after completion of the mentor home program appear to be runaway, truancy, and technical probation violations. The most serious offense committed while in the mentor home program was the theft of one mentor family's automobile, which resulted in an automobile accident that destroyed it. In summary, youths who failed to complete the program tended to experience behavioral problems in school, ran away from mentor homes, and expressed their refusal to conform to the rules of the mentor home program. These individuals stayed in the mentor home an average of three months.

*Resource Evaluation Outcome:* An assessment of the availability of community resources is necessary to determine program effectiveness. Probation officials were asked whether community resources were available to allow the program to work successfully. It was found that counseling (family and individual) and school resources were available and were utilized by the youths and natural parents. It was suggested that mentor youths and natural parents are more likely to need resources related to temper control, substance abuse, loss issues, sexuality (including more resources for pregnant teenagers), and decision-making skills. These needs could be better met if adequate resources are available to provide these services.

*Cost Evaluation:* A primary goal of the development of this program was to reduce the cost of placement. Compared to an average per diem of $96.75 for residential treatment placement, the per diem is $25 for placement in a mentor home. The mentor home program appears to be cost effective during the period from October 1, 1990, through February 29, 1992. For mentor home placement, the expenditure was $125,900 for thirty-six youths with an average expense per youth of $3,497.22. Residential treatment expenditures were significantly higher than mentor home placement expenditures. Residential treatment expenditures were $664,828.65 for forty-two youths, an average expense of $15,829.25 per youth (Table 2). Although there were six additional youths in residential treatment (forty-two) than ordered to mentor home placement (thirty-six), residential treatment costs five times more than mentor home placement. The average expense per youth was four times higher for youths in residential treatment.

Table 2: Cost Analysis, October 1, 1990, to February 29, 1992

| Type of Placement | Expenditure | N (Average Expense per Youth) |
|---|---|---|
| Mentor Home | $125,900 | 36 ( $3,497.22) |
| Residential Treatment | $664,828.65 | 42 ($15,829.25) |

The outcome of this evaluation produced findings that demonstrate overall compliance with program criteria, goals, and objectives. First, the findings show compliance with the age criteria specified in the *Probation Mentor Home Program Policy and Procedure Manual*. Second, a 90 percent compliance with the criteria of nonviolent youthful offenders was established. Third, a few exceptions were made for the six-month placement period due to adjustment time and school considerations. Fourth, no major reduction in reliance on out-of-county placement was noticed. Only two fewer juveniles were ordered placed into residential placement facilities in 1991 than were ordered in 1990. Fifth, no major transfers out of institutions such as Indiana Boys' and Girls' School occurred due to implementation of the mentor home program, mainly because youths with only status offenses are not sent to these institutions, but are at risk of institutionalization if their behavior progresses. However, the transferal of about sixty nonviolent youths from Indiana Boys' School to the newly established Fort Wayne Youth Achievement Center is expected to reduce the Indiana Boys' School population.

An assessment of demographic characteristics of mentor parents and youth was conducted. For instance, mentor parents were likely to be married, female, and white. There were twice as many white mentor parents than African-American parents. Additional African-American mentor parents are needed. For youths, successful experiences were likely to involve younger male youths. A higher percentage of females were removed from mentor homes. White youths were twice as likely to be removed from mentor homes. A significant number of prior offenses involved status offenses such as runaway and truancy.

When considering the cost savings to Allen County taxpayers, so far this program appears to have met primary objectives without seriously compromising public safety. Overall, there appears to be a fifty-fifty chance that a youth will complete the mentor home program. However, the long-term outcome is yet to be determined.

## REFERENCES

Charles, Michael T. (1988). *Allen County Juvenile Probation Placement Services: The Costs and the Benefits*, pp. 1–22. Report submitted to Allen Superior Court, Family Relations Division (Juvenile Probation Department), Fort Wayne, IN.

—— (1989). "The Development of a Juvenile Electronic Monitoring Program." *Federal Probation* VII: 3–11.

Collins, Janet (1991). "Fields Family Shares Home, Lifestyle with Troubled Youth." *Frost Illustrated* 23 (47): 11.

Heard, Chinita A. (1990). "The Preliminary Development of the Probation Mentor Home Program: A Community-Based Model." *Federal Probation* 54 (4): 51–56.

———— (1991). "A Preliminary Evaluation of the Probation Mentor Home Program: A Community-Based Approach." Presented at the Annual Meeting of the Academy of Criminal Justice Sciences, Nashville, TN (March).

*Probation Mentor Home Policy and Procedure Manual* (1989). Allen Superior Court, Family Relations Division (Juvenile Probation Department), Fort Wayne, IN.

# CHAPTER TWELVE

# Diversion Center Operations: An Assessment of Staffing Needs

## Damon D. Camp

Over the past decade, considerable attention has been given to various alternatives to incarceration and their role in decreasing prison overcrowding. Sanctions which provide more structure than traditional probation but require less physical and fiscal investments have received the most attention. Alternatives such as shock incarceration, intensive probation supervision, and diversion center programming have generated a great deal of interest. These programs have become popular with legislators and the public alike, and as a result they are being used on a wider basis. While there are some questions as to the effectiveness and the efficacy of these sentencing options, there seems to be little doubt that they will continue as primary alternatives to incarceration. The escalating use of such programming poses certain management problems to correctional administrators, particularly in the area of program staffing. In this research effort, diversion center operations were examined in order to ascertain staffing patterns and needs.

As one of the fastest-growing alternatives in Georgia, diversion centers provide judges with a cross between traditional probation and incarceration. Offenders are placed on probation but also sentenced by the court to a 120-day term in one of the state's eighteen non-secure diversion centers. While there, probationers are required to work in the community and reside at the center. They are also charged with certain other responsibilities such as community service, care and upkeep of the center, and participation in programs such as Alcoholics Anonymous. Successful completion results in a transfer to regular or intensive probation. Those who do not successfully complete the program are subject to probation revocation.

From an early start as "adjustment" or "restitution" centers in the mid-1970s, these correctional facilities have grown to number more than twenty in 1990. Organizationally they represent somewhat of an oddity in the correctional system. Unlike their institutional counterparts, they are non-secure, offender-oriented facilities designed to provide probationers with a structured living environment. However, as an institution they pose traditional supervision problems which accompany residency (such as food, safety, discipline, and the like): problems with which probation management and line personnel are typically unfamiliar. Georgia's response to this dilemma was to create a hybrid institution which drew on the personnel and knowledge from both camps: institutions and probation. Although this marriage of concepts appears to be organizationally sound, little has been done to assess its results. This research effort is an attempt to fill that gap. Specifically, the research focused on the various activities of center personnel in order to identify administrative problems and potential training needs.

The research involved encompassed both qualitative and quantitative methodologies. Interviews were conducted with job incumbents, and based on these interviews, a job analysis questionnaire was developed. Survey instruments were distributed to the total known population and anonymous returns were analyzed. The results of both types of analysis support the notion that diversion center personnel are a diverse group with a wide range of education and experience. The job analysis indicated that most incumbents are involved in the general monitoring and documenting of resident movement, but tend to become involved in counseling-related activities as well.

## Review of the Literature

The literature concerning the alternatives to incarceration is replete with works which advocate their use and evaluate their effectiveness. In the early 1970s, Claude Pepper (1972), then the chairman of the U.S. House Select Committee on Crime, discussed a wide range of community-based programs and called for their use in dealing with what he termed the "prison crisis" in the United States. Some eight years later, Blackmore (1980) examined the research in the field and noted that few evaluative studies had been made in the rapidly growing field. However, by the late 1980s, such research was being conducted and knowledge about correctional alternatives was being expanded.

The history of diversion centers can be traced to the efforts of the British. The Elliot House was established in 1970 as a diversion center in Birmingham, England. Originally created as a "therapeutic community," the probation hostel was approved by the Home Office for young adult offenders with long criminal histories. When the house was evaluated in 1975, it sported a 58 percent success rate (Haydon, 1976).

Milstead (1973) reviewed community treatment centers (halfway houses) in the United States and recommended that structural program objectives be utilized to establish programs to divert people from prison. Such programs were founded and many were based on a philosophy examined by Benoit (1976). In his review of diversion in Massachusetts, Benoit discussed a variety of justifications for diversion centers including utilizing them as a means of correcting offenders. However, he also cited potential problems with creating programs to divert offenders from the justice system simply to avoid the labeling effect.

Recently, research efforts have focused on program participant selection. For example, Bonta and Motiuk (1987) examined offender classification in Canada and found that predictive instruments are available that increase the likelihood of appropriate placement.

Some of the first diversion centers were established in the Midwest. One of these was Portland House in Minnesota, which was modeled after the Probation Offenders Rehabilitation and

Treatment (PORT) project (Minnesota Governor's Commission on Crime Prevention and Control, 1974). Carlson and Eskridge (1976) reviewed a similar program in Ohio. Like the Minnesota commission, they found that the center generally met the intended goals but that residents had consistently higher rates of alcohol, drug, and mental health related problems than did a control group under study. An Ohio center, Cope House, was evaluated by Donnelly and Forschner (1984). According to the authors, 65 percent of the residents of this coeducational facility, which served parolees as well as probationers, were considered "successful."

The state of Georgia has traditionally utilized this sentencing alternative either formally or informally. Self (1982) reviewed sentencing practices in the state and found that between 1978 and 1981, there had been a general decrease in the use of probation, a reduction of the utilization of split sentencing, and an increase in the percentage of nonviolent offenders being sentenced to prisons. Self went further in suggesting that state tax dollars could be saved and prison population rates could be lowered by using incarceration alternatives along with intensive probation supervision.

Shortly thereafter, Georgia embarked on a venture that has become a model in the field of alternatives to institutionalization. A heightened emphasis was placed on diversion and several new centers were established. However, these efforts represented, for the most part, "ground-breaking" enterprises and little was known about the most effective way of administering services to probationers involved in these alternatives. The literature provides little assistance. For diversion programs, almost no assessments of staff needs exist, aside from general reviews of staff activities such as Milstead (1973) and the Minnesota Governor's Commission on Crime Prevention and Control (1974). The assessment undertaken here is an attempt to specifically address this problem.

# Methodology

The nature of the research involved in this project necessitated the utilization of both qualitative and quantitative methodologies. The primary objective was to discover the general activities of the principal staff members involved with the supervision of probationers sentenced to diversion centers.

In order to ferret out these general activities, a broad understanding of general operations was needed. As such, a series of structured interviews was conducted with individuals currently holding positions to be analyzed. Interviews were conducted in accordance with accepted qualitative practice (Gael, 1983) with the staff of six diversion centers. They focused on typical activities, overall duties, perceived training needs, and general problems associated with various jobs. Based on these interviews, a survey instrument was developed. The questionnaire included, as a major section, a job or task analysis where respondents were presented an array of tasks which were related to a specific job classification.

Developing an instrument was particularly challenging in that each center employed some fifteen to twenty people in nine different positions. While diversity from center to center was not overwhelming, major differences did exist due to the age, condition, and location of centers. However, in most centers, a majority of staff members did a portion of almost everyone else's job at one time or another. As a result, a broad job analysis was developed.

To accomplish this, each center in the state was asked to provide the research team with a list of the most important jobs for three separate positions. Center superintendents were asked to request job incumbents to specify ten major jobs performed frequently and ten performed infrequently in their respective positions. Seventeen of the eighteen centers responded. Based on their responses a broad job analysis was constructed.

The research team utilized these responses to develop a listing of five jobs for each position (ten for correctional officer) and four general jobs which crossed three or more positions. These fifty-nine jobs, along with a brief demographic listing, were reviewed by state correctional staff and the survey was revised to include sixty-one jobs. Respondents were asked to rate each case in three ways. First, how often the task was performed by them: never or seldom, monthly, weekly, or daily. Second, how important the task was to the diversion center. Finally, how important it was that employees be trained in the task. These two categories also had a four point answering scale: not important, somewhat important, important, and highly important.

## Qualitative Results

This research effort provided a unique opportunity to review diversion centers in detail. As a result of a number of hours of structured interviewing, many pages of field notes, and a review of several documents, a qualitative picture emerged. The following summary represents the views of the research team based on this review and is thus subjective in nature. It depicts findings as well as impressions and, taken with the quantitative results, should provide assistance in understanding the activities and needs of the staff involved in the program.

The first diversion center, initially called a restitution and adjustment center, was established in Rome, Georgia, in 1974 with the aid of Law Enforcement Assistance Administration (LEAA) funding. The program, which housed both parole and probation offenders in its early stages, grew to include four restitution and adjustment centers in Rome, Macon, Albany, and Cobb by 1977. When LEAA support ended in 1975, the state found funding to continue and expand the program to include eight centers by 1979. Parole was removed from its scope of services in 1978. In the early 1980s, the centers began to expand in their new primary role of providing offenders a diversion from prison. Currently, there are more than twenty diversion centers (DCs) in Georgia, with two centers in the planning stages (Georgia Department of Corrections, 1989).

These centers provide probationers with a "halfway in" status of confinement. Offenders are sentenced to a center for a specific term, generally around 120 days, but must be accepted by the superintendent. They live at the center, are required to work in the community, and pay room and board. Once they have completed their term, or in some cases earlier if judged honor residents by the staff, offenders are returned to their own community to serve the remainder of their sentence on probation (Georgia Department of Corrections, 1989).

Interviews with the staff of six different centers were conducted. These centers, which represent one-third of those operating in the state at the time, were located in the north, central, and southern sections of the state. In each center, the superintendent was interviewed and in most cases, the facility was toured and interviews with other staff were conducted.

All six centers appeared to be operating in concert with one another and with state goals and objectives. Each was authorized the same basic staff positions but the actual number of employees varied according to unfilled vacancies, authorized bed space, and special needs. For example, one center was coeducational and, therefore, was allocated additional correctional officers. Another had its meals catered by an adjacent correctional institution and thus had no food service workers on site.

The standard found for personnel was one superintendent, senior counselor, probationer officer, correctional sergeant, accounting clerk, bookkeeper, and senior secretary. In addition, most centers had at least two counselor ORs (offender rehabilitation), four correctional officers (COs), and two food service workers.

Generally speaking, each of these positions has assigned specific duties which were considered primarily the responsibilities of job incumbents. However, in virtually every center, a wide range of overlap existed where duties normally associated with one job were performed by someone else on a temporary basis. For example, in most centers, all professional staff were subject to "pulling" duty as a correctional officer, particularly during weekends and at night. In one center, even the accounting clerk was reported to have substituted for correctional officers. The individual involved had experience in the field, was considered qualified, and volunteered for such duty. In addition, when food service workers were not present—

during weekends, holidays, or days off—correctional officers or their substitutes were involved in meal preparation.

The duties of other staff members transcended traditional working hours as well: Resident checks had to be collected, accounts monitored, and court orders processed. When the individuals primarily responsible for such activities were absent, others assumed those duties.

In several centers a variety of tasks appeared to be virtually everyone's job. For example, while employment placement assistance might rest primarily with counselors, everyone, including clerical staff and correctional officers, assisted residents in securing work. Also, counseling, particularly crisis-intervention assistance, appeared to be something that was provided by a wide range of staff members. Not only did counselors and probation officers assist residents in this regard, but also correctional officers and other staff provided counseling to residents.

While most centers appeared to be similar in this sharing of responsibilities, a number of major differences surfaced on other fronts. First, centers varied in physical age and construction. These variances made for significant differences in operations. When a center was physically old and outdated, a considerable amount of staff time and energy was spent on maintaining the facility. In several centers, this significant problem dominated virtually everyone's concern and a number of individuals' time. Location and physical layout also presented problems for several centers and often dictated activities: Proximity to public transportation seemed to free up some staff time, while being located near several establishments which dispensed alcohol appeared to increase surveillance and monitoring requirements.

There were also several "philosophical" differences that appeared to surface. Some centers stressed treatment programs; others did not. Such programs were conducted in some cases by in-house staff, whereas in other centers they were contracted out. Policies on resident transportation varied as well. Some centers provided, or assisted in providing, transportation; others did not. Employment patterns differed between institutions. In some cases employment was readily available and in others it was not.

Finally, there was some variation in the orientation of the centers. They ranged from a tightly run, highly disciplined regimen to a more informal, loosely run atmosphere. All these differences, while not necessarily documented in the quantitative research, reflect divergent approaches to the same general goals and objectives.

# Quantitative Results

All personnel working at diversion centers across the state were asked to complete a two-part questionnaire. The first portion concerned respondent characteristics. The second contained a sixty-one item job analysis. The results are reported by area in the following sections.

## *Respondent Characteristics*

Of the 207 individuals responding, the largest number (70) reported their position as correctional officer or sergeant (Table 1). Based on estimates of currently filled positions, counselor ORs and food service workers/supervisors responded at the lowest rate (approximately 60 percent), whereas senior secretaries returned surveys at the highest rate—at or near 100 percent. The average age was almost 30 and more than 40 percent indicated that they were at least forty years of age. Just under 55 percent reported being male, and around 56 percent indicated that their race was caucasian. About two-thirds reported being married.

As to their experience, some 40 percent indicated less than five years in the correctional field and around 60 percent reported fewer than five years in diversion centers (DCs). About 25 percent indicated that they had worked in DCs less than a year. Almost half stated that they worked primarily on the day shift.

Table 1: Diversion Center Respondents by Position

| Position | N | % |
|---|---|---|
| Superintendent | 13 | 6.3 |
| Probation Officer | 15 | 7.2 |
| Food Service Worker | 13 | 6.3 |
| Business Manager | 16 | 7.7 |
| Senior Counselor | 14 | 6.8 |
| Correctional Sergeant | 14 | 6.8 |
| Senior Secretary | 18 | 8.7 |
| Food Service Supervisor | 9 | 4.3 |
| Counselor OR | 20 | 9.7 |
| Correctional Officer | 56 | 27.1 |
| Accounting Clerk | 13 | 6.3 |
| Missing/Not Reported | 6 | 2.9 |
| Total | 207 | 100.1 |

Note: Percentages may not total 100% due to rounding.

Education among center staff varied greatly. According to Table 2, more than 70 percent had done at least some college work. Around 35 percent had college degrees and more than 16 percent had at least a master's degree. Only one indicated less than a high school degree or its equivalent.

Table 2: Diversion Center Personnel Education Level

| Level of Education | N | % |
|---|---|---|
| Less than High School | 1 | 0.5 |
| High School or GED | 58 | 29.4 |
| Some College | 67 | 34.0 |
| Four-Year Degree | 20 | 10.2 |
| College Degree Plus | 19 | 9.6 |
| Master's | 32 | 16.2 |
| Total | 197 | 99.9 |

Note: Percentages may not total 100% due to rounding.

## Job Analysis

The complete results of the job analysis portion of the diversion center survey are provided in the Appendix. Task/Job item 61, *Maintain logs, documentation*, surfaced as the most frequently performed. Of the 202 individuals responding to this item, 158, or 78.2 percent, indicated that they performed this task daily, and only 20, or 9.9 percent, reported never doing it. This task was rated highest overall, garnered the third highest task importance rating, and had one of the highest training importance marks. Task/Job item 2, *Monitor resident movement and activity*, also drew high ratings. It was rated second in overall frequency, first as to task importance, and second in training importance.

Table 3 provides a listing, in descending order, of the ten highest scoring tasks and, in ascending order, the bottom ten when overall means are compared. As indicated, these jobs cover a wide range of duties and positions. Most relate to direct resident contact but several do not. All have importance ratings above 2.00 (important), but only four are reported as being performed on a weekly (2.00) or more frequent basis. The bottom ten rated tasks appear to be related to support services. For example, the lowest rated job was Task 41, *Monitor contacts with local vendors*. This item had a very low (but not the lowest) frequency rate and quite low importance ratings. Other tasks, however, related to residents directly (Q 44 and Q 50) or dealt with a normal duty of most supervisors (e.g., Q 27, *Conduct staff meetings*).

The task listing was purposely randomized in order to reduce the chance that respondents would be influenced unduly by jobs organized according to position classification. A reordering of tasks provides some insight into how Center personnel view various jobs by subject matter category. Table 4 provides such a listing for two areas: security and treatment.

Table 3: Top/Bottom Ten Rated Diversion Center Jobs (Means)

| Q# | | Frequency | Task Importance | Training Importance | Mean of Means* |
|----|---|-----------|-----------------|---------------------|----------------|
| **Top Ten** | | | | | |
| 61 | Maintain logs, documentation | 2.55 | 2.60 | 2.44 | 2.53 |
| 2 | Monitor resident movement | 2.31 | 2.70 | 2.50 | 2.50 |
| 20 | Monitor/document behavior | 2.07 | 2.56 | 2.51 | 2.38 |
| 19 | Counsel with individual residents | 2.02 | 2.52 | 2.45 | 2.33 |
| 13 | Secure buildings and grounds | 1.72 | 2.60 | 2.45 | 2.26 |
| 38 | Write disciplinary/incident reports | 1.78 | 2.44 | 2.36 | 2.19 |
| 30 | Interview/orient new residents | 1.69 | 2.43 | 2.30 | 2.14 |
| 14 | Write center-related reports | 1.80 | 2.35 | 2.25 | 2.13 |
| 10 | Receive/collect resident checks | 1.67 | 2.54 | 2.15 | 2.12 |
| 34 | Inspect center for cleanliness, Order, etc. | 1.83 | 2.33 | 2.07 | 2.08 |
| **Bottom Ten** | | | | | |
| 41 | Monitor contacts w/local vendors | 0.41 | 1.61 | 1.49 | 1.17 |
| 27 | Conduct staff meetings | 0.44 | 1.80 | 1.64 | 1.29 |
| 37 | Order food and supplies | 0.33 | 1.88 | 1.76 | 1.32 |
| 4 | Purchase materials/supplies for center and residents | 0.64 | 1.94 | 1.74 | 1.44 |
| 17 | Pay invoices/bills for center | 0.47 | 1.96 | 1.89 | 1.44 |
| 50 | Transport residents | 1.03 | 1.75 | 1.59 | 1.46 |
| 44 | Supervise activities related to visitation | 0.84 | 1.99 | 1.80 | 1.54 |
| 29 | Maintain personnel files | 0.77 | 2.00 | 1.83 | 1.54 |
| 53 | Temporarily assume duties of superintendent | 0.48 | 2.08 | 2.08 | 1.55 |
| 24 | Type reports and other materials | 1.04 | 1.89 | 1.75 | 1.56 |

* Mean ratings are based on the following: Never or Seldom Performed/Not Important = 0, Performed Monthly/Somewhat Important = 1, Performed Weekly/Important = 2, Performed Daily/Highly Important = 3. Mean of Means represents an average score of Frequency Mean + Task Importance Mean + Training Importance Mean + 3.

Table 4: Security and Treatment-Related Jobs

| Q# | Tasks | Task Frequency | Task Importance | Importance | Mean of Means* |
|----|-------|---------------|----------------|-----------|-----------|
| *Security Related Tasks* | | | | | |
| 2 | Monitor resident movement and activity | 2.31 | 2.70 | 2.50 | 2.50 |
| 7 | Conduct searches | 1.30 | 2.41 | 2.32 | 2.01 |
| 13 | Secure buildings and ground | 1.78 | 2.60 | 2.45 | 2.26 |
| 20 | Monitor/document resident behavior | 2.07 | 2.56 | 2.51 | 2.38 |
| 22 | Collect urine samples/administer alcolyzer test | 1.18 | 2.32 | 2.20 | 1.90 |
| 44 | Supervise activities related to visitation | 0.84 | 1.99 | 1.80 | 1.54 |
| *Treatment Related Tasks* | | | | | |
| 5 | Coordinate/supervise treatment programs | 0.96 | 2.19 | 2.19 | 1.78 |
| 6 | Develop treatment plans | 0.71 | 2.17 | 2.16 | 1.68 |
| 19 | Counsel with individual residents | 2.02 | 2.52 | 2.45 | 2.33 |
| 26 | Provide crisis-intervention counseling | 1.22 | 2.35 | 2.37 | 1.98 |
| 31 | Participate in group counseling/classes or treatment activities | 0.77 | 2.00 | 2.03 | 1.60 |
| 43 | Refer residents to outside services | 1.06 | 2.02 | 1.84 | 1.64 |

* Mean ratings are based on the following: Never or Seldom Performed/Not Important = 0, Performed Monthly/Somewhat Important = 1, Performed Weekly/Important = 2, Performed Daily/Highly Important = 3. Mean of Means represents an average score of Frequency Mean + Task Importance Mean + Training Importance Mean + 3.

Of the six security-related tasks, all but two (Q 22 and 44) produced average ratings (mean of means) above 2.00. Treatment tasks, on the other hand, had only one such rating, Q 9, *Counsel with individual residents*. Security tasks also were reported as being performed more frequently than those related to treatment. In Table 5, tasks have been reordered by position and reported scores have been averaged. Little can be learned from many frequency of performance scores due to the wide variation in participation by position: More than fifty correctional officers (COs) participated whereas fewer than fifteen responded from four other positions. However, several inferences can be made. On average, the positions of probation officer, counselor OR, correctional officer, accounting clerk, correctional sergeant, and senior secretary have duties that are more frequently performed than do the positions of superintendent, food service worker, business manager, and senior counselor. It is interesting to note that the positions of correctional officer and senior secretary have identical high frequency means, yet quite diverse participation rates. This indicates that the tasks related to both positions are performed by a fairly large number of personnel within the center. This would be expected of CO tasks because job incumbents constituted more than one-quarter of all respondents, but not so for secretaries who comprised fewer than 9 percent of the sample.

Table 5: Mean* Scores by Position

| Position (Q #s) | Frequency Mean | Importance Mean | Training Mean | Percent Participating |
|---|---|---|---|---|
| Superintendent (Q#s 3, 15, 27, 40 & 51) | 0.76 | 2.07 | 1.98 | 6.3% |
| Probation officer (Q#s 8, 20, 32, 45 & 55) | 1.18 | 2.21 | 2.10 | 7.2% |
| Food service worker/supervisor (Q#s 12, 25, 37, 49 & 59) | 0.92 | 2.00 | 1.81 | 10.6% |
| Counselor OR (Q#s 6, 19, 31, 43 & 54) | 1.17 | 2.21 | 2.11 | 9.7% |
| Correctional officer (Q#s 2, 7, 13, 16, 22, 28, 34, 38, 44 & 50) | 1.51 | 2.30 | 2.14 | 27.1% |
| Accounting clerk (Q#s 10, 23, 35, 47 & 57) | 1.22 | 2.21 | 1.96 | 6.3% |
| Business manager (Q#s 4, 17, 29, 41 & 52) | 0.61 | 1.93 | 1.80 | 7.7% |
| Senior counselor (Q#s 5, 18, 30, 42 & 53) | 0.93 | 2.26 | 2.18 | 6.8% |
| Correctional sergeant (Q#s 9, 21, 33, 46 & 56) | 1.28 | 2.12 | 1.84 | 6.8% |
| Senior secretary (Q#s 11, 24, 36, 48 & 58) | 1.51 | 2.00 | 1.81 | 8.7% |
| General duties (Q#s 1, 14, 26, 39, 60 & 61) | 1.39 | 2.29 | 2.19 | NA |

* Means were calculated by averaging frequency and importance ratings reported in all questions in each position category.

Importance means also varied, with tasks relating to the position of correctional officer topping the list at 2.30. Training importance means showed a similar pattern. Here, however, tasks related to the senior counselor position garnered the highest marks. While these figures are subject to much criticism due to the compounded nature of their composition, this final example is worthy of close examination. Fewer than 7 percent of the respondents were senior counselors and most of their tasks garnered low frequency rates: 0.96, 1.14, 1.69, 0.40, and 0.48. Yet all of their general and training importance ratings were above 2.00. This indicates that these tasks are not frequently performed but are considered highly important by a wide range of center employees. No other position garnered such marks.

# Conclusion

The personnel working at diversion centers (DCs) across the state represent a diverse group of individuals who share a number of common jobs. By and large they are a heterogeneous group with varied educational, career, and personal backgrounds. Many have been working in these centers for only a short period of time: 25 percent of the 200-plus respondents have a year or less DC experience. However, the results of the interviews as well as the quantitative research seem to indicate a commonality of purpose despite this diversity in background.

The results of the survey clearly indicate that almost everyone is involved with security-related duties normally associated with the position of correctional officer. For example, the second-ranked task (Q 2) concerned the *monitoring of resident movement and activity*. More than 70 percent of the respondents indicated they "monitored" residents daily and less than 20 percent stated that they never performed this task, an interesting finding considering that more than one-third of the respondents held clerical or service/support positions.

In addition, a number of specialized tasks seemed to be shared as well. For example, Q 10, *Receive/collect resident pay/checks*, is normally associated with only one or two positions within the center and these positions accounted for less than 15 percent of the sample population. However, just under 70 percent of the respondents indicated performing this task at least monthly and almost 35 percent responded that they made collections daily. Likewise, the dispensing of monies to residents was shared by most staff. Almost 60 percent indicated performing this task at least monthly and more than 50 percent responded that they did so weekly or more often.

On the other hand, some tasks which were thought to be prevalent, based on interviews, did not surface in the survey as being frequently performed. For example, Task/Q 12, *Prepare and serve food*, produced a very low frequency mean because almost 70 percent of the respondents indicated that they never performed the task. Overall, most tasks were performed by many more individuals than would have been predicted based on job description/classification alone. Duties are widely shared by a number of different individuals at various levels. The qualitative research indicates that they do so willingly and for the most part even cheerfully. There seems to exist a real feeling of comraderie and a team spirit appears to be present. However, irrespective of the apparent positive attitude, there are certain training as well as administrative implications which should be addressed.

Both the qualitative and survey research points to a dire need for cross-training: Almost everyone needs to be cross-trained in a number of tasks which appear to be performed frequently by a number of people. In addition to those previously mentioned, a number of tasks are performed on at least a monthly basis by 60 percent or more of the respondents. These tasks include activities such as writing reports (Q 14, 83 percent), supervising work details (Q 16, 62 percent), counseling (Q 19, 75 percent), interviewing residents (Q 30, 78 percent), inspecting the center (Q 34, 68 percent), functioning as a receptionist for visitors (Q 36, 63 percent), writing disciplinary reports (Q 38, 71 percent), functioning as a telephone receptionist (Q 48, 66 percent), maintaining center-related files (Q 58, 69 percent), and maintaining logs/documentation (Q 61, 90 percent).

In addition to this general cross-training, specific skills-related training could prove helpful. Because so many individuals are involved in security-related duties, a "crash course" on monitoring resident activities and other essentials might provide a number of those who do not have security-oriented backgrounds with a much needed foundation. Also, the evidence indicates that a considerable amount of counseling takes place. Three-fourths of all respondents indicated that they counseled residents at least weekly and 70 percent stated they did so on at least a weekly basis. More than half of all employees provide counselling *daily* to residents. Clearly, training in this area would be beneficial.

Finally, center personnel might find training in two other areas helpful. Because more than 80 percent write reports at least monthly and over 70 percent write disciplinary/incidence reports, skills training in this area should be delivered. Most respondents agreed that training in these two tasks was important, rating them between 2.25 and 2.40 on a 3-point scale. Also, due to the degree and amount of contact between staff and the residents, specialized interpersonal management training might be beneficial as well.

As to administrative/organizational concerns, the implications are less clear. Certain micro-level matters could be easy to rectify. Cross-training might be instituted to alleviate certain concerns in center operations, and procedures could be specified to deal with others. For example, because a wide range of personnel is involved in the receipt and disbursement of resident monies, clear policies and accounting procedures ought to be present. Other more global issues are less easily addressed.

Clearly, the general activities of most center personnel do not match their job descriptions: The data repeatedly emphasized that many duties are shared. This not only violates sound management principles, it also presents a host of problems for state administrators, particularly in a merit system.

When an individual is hired for (or promoted to) a job, there should be a clear understanding of what is expected. Regardless of the management theory, from classical to situational, employee responsibilities must be clear. Workers must know what is officially expected of them, and they must be capable of controlling the outcome of their activities. If an employee is going to be held accountable for a job and evaluated on the basis of job performance, then that individual must be *the* person responsible for doing that job. Such is not the case in diversion centers.

Bureaucratic problems for the merit system exist as well. Qualifications and pay should be directly job-related. In a state merit system, job classifications specify duties and pay grades and are grounded in a hierarchy of responsibilities. However, persons hired for diversion center positions become involved in a wide range of work, some of which is above their classified responsibility, and some of which is below. They are neither trained nor paid for much of what they do; clearly an administrative problem.

Two basic, equally distasteful, alternatives exist. First, management could "crack down" on center administrators and require that employees fulfill their job requirements and only those duties. This approach would not only jeopardize the excellent reputation that diversion centers have, but also would be contrary to most modern management approaches. In all six centers reviewed in the qualitative phase of this research, there was a high degree of comraderie and a group approach was apparent. This "team spirit" is quite likely the result of shared responsibilities and may very well account for center successes. Taking away the flexibility of current practices and replacing it with bureaucratic rigidity could seriously jeopardize center operations. It would also be contrary to modern management and production concepts which laud individual initiative and scorn control for control sake (Peters and Waterman, 1982).

The second alternative, redesign job classifications, is equally problematic. There are obviously headaches associated with designing a new and generally unique set of positions and establishing pay scales for a divergent group of jobs. There are also problems with the "soundness" of such a move. Diversion centers, like other minimum security correctional facilities, present a unique blend of treatment and custody. Unlike their institutional counterparts where treatment is often used to temper custody, the reverse is the case with diversion centers. In diversion centers (unlike prisons), security is a by-product of a scheme designed to foster success in the community. The purpose of the diversion center is to provide offenders with a structured environment in which custody is used as a tool, not as a major goal in and unto itself. However, the diversion center is nonetheless a correctional facility with specific security and treatment needs. Trained correctional officers capable of maintaining order and discipline are an integral part of center operations just as are food service workers, counselors, and the like. Reordering responsibilities could upset the delicate balance that seems to exist.

Perhaps the most appropriate way to deal with this dilemma is to do little more than a fine tuning and recognize the diversion center as an entity which should be allowed to operate somewhat independently. This appears to have been the case in Georgia and may well be the reason behind the team spirit which seems to exist and the clear sharing of responsibilities. Obviously, more research in this area is needed. Further information is needed on the attitudes of center employees on shared duties and on the impact this concept has on offender success rates. This is particularly critical as the diversion center and other like alternatives assume an increasing share of the burden of criminal sanctioning.

# REFERENCES

Benoit, P.K. (1976). "Pre-Court Diversionary Programs in Massachusetts: 'Diversion' and Its Relationship to Probation." *International Journal of Offender Therapy and Comparative Criminology* 20 (1): 48–52.

Blackmore, J. (1980). "Community Corrections." *Corrections Magazine* (October): 4–14.

Bonta, J., and L.L. Motiuk (1987). "The Diversion of Incarcerated Offenders to Correctional Halfway Houses." *Journal of Research in Crime and Delinquency* 24 (4): 302–323.

Camp, D. (1988). *Georgia Probation Officer Task Analysis: Final Report.* Atlanta: Department of Criminal Justice, Georgia State University.

Carlson, E.W., and C.W. Eskridge (1976). *Alvis House Probationary Diversion Program—A Second Year Report* (NCJRS Publication No. 053535). Washington, DC: National Institute of Justice.

Donnelly, P.G., and B. Forschner (1984). "Client Success or Failure in a Halfway House." *Federal Probation* 48 (3): 38–44.

Gael, S. (1983). *Job Analysis: A Guide to Assessing Work Activities*. San Francisco, CA: Jossey-Bass, Inc.

Georgia Department of Corrections (1989). *Georgia's Diversion Program*. Atlanta: Author.

Haydon, D. (1976). "A Therapeutic Community in Birmingham (England)." *International Journal of Offender Therapy and Comparative Criminology* 20 (3): 263–271.

Milstead, R.J. (1973). *Use of an Objectives Hierarchy in Planning, Operating, and Evaluating Halfway House Programs* (NCJRS Publication No. 028239). Washington, DC: National Institute of Justice.

Minnesota Governor's Commission on Crime Prevention and Control (1974). *PORT (Probation Offenders Rehabilitation and Treatment). ALPHA—A Preliminary Evaluation Report* (NCJRS Publication No. 016592). Washington, DC: National Institute of Justice.

Pepper, C. (1972). "Prisons in Turmoil." *Federal Probation* 36 (4): 1–11.

Peters, T.J., and R.H. Waterman (1982). *In Search of Excellence*. New York: Harper and Row.

Self, J. (1982). *Population Management Strategies—A Review of Sentencing Practices and Options* (NCJRS Publication No. 088662). Washington, DC: National Institute of Justice.

# Appendix
## SAI Task Analysis Summary of Means

| Q# | Task | Frequency | Task Importance | Training Importance | Mean of Means* |
|----|------|-----------|-----------------|---------------------|----------------|
| 1. | Evaluate/supervise employees and their activities | 1.24 | 2.13 | 2.16 | 1.84 |
| 2. | Monitor resident movement and activity | 2.31 | 2.70 | 2.50 | 2.50 |
| 3. | Prepare/administer/develop center budget | 0.46 | 2.11 | 2.10 | 1.56 |
| 4. | Purchase materials/supplies for center and residents | 0.64 | 1.94 | 1.74 | 1.44 |
| 5. | Coordinate/supervise treatment programs | 0.96 | 2.19 | 2.19 | 1.78 |
| 6. | Develop treatment plans | 0.71 | 2.17 | 2.16 | 1.68 |
| 7. | Conduct searches | 1.30 | 2.41 | 2.32 | 2.01 |
| 8. | Interview/screen potential residents | 0.78 | 2.21 | 2.11 | 1.70 |
| 9. | Develop schedules/rosters | 1.09 | 1.94 | 1.80 | 1.61 |
| 10. | Receive/collect resident pay/checks | 1.67 | 2.54 | 2.15 | 2.12 |
| 11. | Prepare/type correspondence | 1.29 | 2.00 | 1.85 | 1.71 |
| 12. | Prepare and serve food | 0.82 | 2.10 | 2.02 | 1.65 |
| 13. | Secure buildings and grounds | 1.72 | 2.60 | 2.45 | 2.26 |
| 14. | Write center-related reports | 1.80 | 2.35 | 2.25 | 2.13 |
| 15. | Act as a liaison with courts, prosecution, law enforcement, etc. | 1.11 | 2.26 | 2.25 | 1.87 |
| 16. | Supervise center work details | 1.61 | 2.18 | 2.05 | 1.95 |
| 17. | Pay invoices/bills for center or residents | 0.47 | 1.96 | 1.89 | 1.44 |
| 18. | Supervise disciplinary process/chair disciplinary committee | 1.14 | 2.24 | 2.07 | 1.82 |
| 19. | Counsel with individual residents | 2.02 | 2.52 | 2.45 | 2.33 |
| 20. | Monitor/document resident behavior | 2.07 | 2.56 | 2.51 | 2.38 |
| 21. | Supervise/coordinate center maintenance and repairs | 1.43 | 2.11 | 1.98 | 1.84 |
| 22. | Collect urine samples/administer alcolyzor tests | 1.18 | 2.32 | 2.20 | 1.90 |
| 23. | Maintain/monitor resident accounts | 1.00 | 2.13 | 2.02 | 1.72 |
| 24. | Type reports and other materials | 1.04 | 1.89 | 1.75 | 1.56 |
| 25. | Supervise residents in kitchen/dining area | 1.36 | 2.04 | 1.87 | 1.76 |
| 26. | Provide crisis intervention counseling | 1.22 | 2.35 | 2.37 | 1.98 |
| 27. | Conduct staff meetings | 0.44 | 1.80 | 1.64 | 1.29 |
| 28. | Dispense medicine | 1.50 | 2.24 | 2.06 | 1.93 |
| 29. | Maintain personnel files on center staff | 0.79 | 2.00 | 1.83 | 1.54 |
| 30. | Interview/orient new residents | 1.69 | 2.43 | 2.30 | 2.14 |

| Q# | Task | Frequency | Task Importance | Training Importance | Mean of Means* |
|----|------|-----------|-----------------|---------------------|----------------|
| 31. | Participate in group counseling/classes or treatment activities | 0.77 | 2.00 | 2.03 | 1.60 |
| 32. | Prepare court-related documents | 0.97 | 2.13 | 2.13 | 1.74 |
| 33. | Oversee inventory of center equipment/ tools/supplies | 1.24 | 2.03 | 1.87 | 1.71 |
| 34. | Inspect center for cleanliness, order, etc. | 1.83 | 2.33 | 2.07 | 2.08 |
| 35. | Deposit collected monies | 1.07 | 2.28 | 1.90 | 1.75 |
| 36. | Function as receptionist for visitors/ incoming persons | 1.57 | 1.88 | 1.69 | 1.71 |
| 37. | Order food and supplies | 0.33 | 1.88 | 1.76 | 1.32 |
| 38. | Write disciplinary/incident reports | 1.78 | 2.44 | 2.36 | 2.19 |
| 39. | Testify in court and at hearing | 0.55 | 2.33 | 2.29 | 1.72 |
| 40. | Promote the center through public relations activities in the community | 0.87 | 2.03 | 1.91 | 1.60 |
| 41. | Monitor contracts with local vendors | 0.41 | 1.61 | 1.49 | 1.17 |
| 42. | Train new staff members | 0.40 | 2.36 | 2.28 | 1.68 |
| 43. | Refer residents to services outside of the center | 1.06 | 2.02 | 1.84 | 1.64 |
| 44. | Supervise activities related to visitation | 0.84 | 1.99 | 1.80 | 1.54 |
| 45. | Monitor fee/fine payments | 0.93 | 2.16 | 1.95 | 1.68 |
| 46. | Monitor/control compliance with fire and safety standards | 1.30 | 2.37 | 2.30 | 1.99 |
| 47. | Dispense monies to residents | 1.19 | 2.08 | 1.87 | 1.71 |
| 48. | Function as telephone receptionist | 1.78 | 1.97 | 1.70 | 1.82 |
| 49. | Monitor freezer/refrigerator temperature | 1.17 | 1.91 | 1.62 | 1.57 |
| 50. | Transport residents | 1.03 | 1.75 | 1.59 | 1.46 |
| 51. | Participate in center policy establishment/ revision | 0.85 | 2.14 | 1.97 | 1.65 |
| 52. | Maintain financial records | 0.75 | 2.16 | 2.03 | 1.65 |
| 53. | Temporarily assume duties of superintendent | 0.48 | 2.08 | 2.08 | 1.55 |
| 54. | Assist residents in finding employment | 1.31 | 2.32 | 2.07 | 1.90 |
| 55. | Supervise/monitor community service program | 1.17 | 1.98 | 1.81 | 1.65 |
| 56. | Investigate disciplinary events | 1.35 | 2.16 | 2.06 | 1.86 |
| 57. | Provide financial counseling to residents | 1.15 | 2.00 | 1.84 | 1.66 |
| 58. | Maintain center-related files | 1.86 | 2.24 | 2.04 | 2.05 |
| 59. | Clean kitchen and equipment | 0.92 | 2.06 | 1.78 | 1.59 |
| 60. | Perform duties in "on-call" capacity | 0.96 | 1.97 | 1.79 | 1.57 |
| 61. | Maintain logs, documentation | 2.55 | 2.60 | 2.44 | 2.53 |

* Mean ratings are based on the following: Never or Seldom Performed/Not Important = 0, Performed Monthly/Somewhat Important = 1, Performed Weekly/Important = 2, Performed Daily/Highly Important = 3. Mean of Means represents an average score of Frequency Mean + Task Importance Mean + Training Importance Mean ÷ 3.

# Contributors

**J. Arthur Beyer** is an assistant professor in the department of political science/law enforcement at Mankato State University. Professor Beyer has extensive experience in law enforcement and institutional and community corrections. He has a B.A. in correctional counseling and an M.A. in public administration from Boise State University and is currently completing his Ph.D. in justice administration and applied policy studies at Washington State University. He has authored two chapters on inmate classification and assessment processes and has co-authored several articles on juvenile delinquency.

**Anthony A. Braga** is a doctoral candidate at the School of Criminal Justice and member of the research staff at the Center for Crime Prevention Studies at Rutgers University. He received his B.S. in criminal justice from the University of Massachusetts at Lowell. His research interests include drug policy, policing, and the use of intermediate sanctions.

**James M. Byrne** is a professor of criminal justice at the University of Massachusetts at Lowell. Byrne has served as the principal investigator for a number of evaluations in the field of community corrections, including a nationwide review of the effectiveness of intermediate sanctions, the Massachusetts intensive supervision program, a classification system assessing gender bias, and a field experiment on the most effective strategy for the location and apprehension of probationers. He is the co-editor of *Smart Sentencing: The Emergence of Intermediate Sanctions* and *The Social Ecology of Crime.*

**Damon D. Camp** is an associate professor and former chair of the department of criminal justice at Georgia State University.

He has a master's degree in urban life from Georgia State and a Ph.D. in government from the Claremont Graduate School. An active member of the Academy of Criminal Justice Sciences, he is also past president of the Southern Criminal Justice Association. His research interests include alternatives to incarceration, the entrapment defense, anti-hate crime legislation, and civil liability in the field of law enforcement training.

**Todd R. Clear** is professor and faculty chair in the School of Criminal Justice at Rutgers University. His B.A. (sociology and social work) is from Anderson College, and he has an M.A. and Ph.D. in criminal justice from the University of Albany. He is the author of numerous publications regarding correctional policy, penal philosophy, non-incarcerative correctional programs, and innovations in corrections. Among his recent books are *Controlling the Offender in the Community, American Corrections,* and *The Pre-Sentence Investigation Report.* He has worked in more than thirty states and three countries, designing and evaluating offender management programs. In 1986, he received the Cincinnati Award of the American Probation and Parole Association for his research on supervision technologies. His current research includes intermediate sanctions policy, religion in prison, and the concept of penal reform.

**Christine Curtis** is the assistant director of criminal justice research for the San Diego Association of Governments (SANDAG). While at SANDAG, she has been a principal investigator on projects addressing a wide range of issues, including youth gangs, serious juvenile offenders, enforcement of drug laws, crime prevention, and intermediate sanctions such as intensive probation and electronic monitoring of offenders. She is currently the principal investigator on three NIJ-funded evaluations and manages SANDAG's regional criminal justice clearinghouse project which provides crime and justice information to elected officials through compilation of data and special studies. She is actively involved in several professional organizations and is current president of the Association for Criminal Justice Research (California) and is the vice president and program chair for the Western Society of Criminology.

**Charles B. Fields** is an associate professor in the department of political science/criminal justice at Appalachian State University. He has a B.A. and M.A. in political science from Appalachian State University and received his Ph.D. in criminal justice from Sam Houston State University in 1984. His most recent articles/reviews have appeared in the *Journal of Criminal Justice, Criminal Justice Policy Review, Quarterly Journal of Ideology,* and the *Journal of Criminal Law and Criminology,* among others. He is the current president of the Southern Criminal Justice Association and is Region Two trustee on the executive board of the Academy of Criminal Justice Sciences.

**Jill A. Gordon** is currently a doctoral student in criminal justice at the University of Cincinnati. She received a B.S. from Bowling Green State University and an M.S. from the University of Cincinnati. Her research interest is in the area of correctional policy.

**Chinita A. Heard** is a visiting assistant professor in the criminology and criminal justice program at the University of Texas at Arlington. She is currently on leave from the School of Public and Environmental Affairs at Indiana University at Fort Wayne. She is a 1993 Alabama State University "Alumni of Distinction" honoree. An active member of the Academy of Criminal Justice Sciences and the American Society of Criminology. Heard's most recent publications are in the *Journal of Criminal Justice Education, Criminal Justice Review,* and the *Journal of Research on Minority Affairs*. Her research interests are juvenile delinquency, institutional and community-based corrections, mentoring, criminal justice education, and minorities and crime. She received a Ph.D. in criminology from Florida State University in 1988.

**Darlanne Hoctor** is an associate research analyst for the San Diego Association of Governments (SANDAG) Criminal Justice Research Division. Her research interests include the criminal justice response to crime, the effects of police strategies, jail overcrowding, intensive probation supervision, and gang involvement in criminal and drug activity. Currently, she is evaluating an intensive drug treatment program for probationers and victim assistance programs in San Diego County, both funded by the National Institute of Justice.

**G. Mark Jones** is an assistant professor at East Carolina University. He has published in *Federal Probation, The International Journal of Offender Therapy and Comparative Criminology,* and the *Journal of Contemporary Criminal Justice.* His research interests include the diversionary impact of intermediate sanctions. He is currently conducting an evaluation of a new probation program in Harris County, Texas.

**Edward J. Latessa** is professor and head of the department of criminal justice at the University of Cincinnati. He received his Ph.D. from Ohio State University in 1979. He has written extensively in the area of intensive supervision and correctional treatment and is the co-author of three books: *Probation and Parole in America, Introduction to Criminal Justice,* and *Statistical Applications in Criminal Justice.* Latessa is a past president of the Academy of Criminal Justice Sciences.

**Sue Mahan** is associate professor of criminal justice at the University of Central Florida and coordinator of the criminal justice program at the Daytona Beach campus of U.C.F. She has authored or co-authored two books and several articles and reviews and is active in the Academy of Criminal Justice Sciences, the American Society of Criminology, and the Southern Criminal Justice Association. Her research interests include women and crime, penology and corrections, and applied social psychology. Mahan was the recipient of a Kellogg Foundation fellowship in international development (1991–93) for leadership activities in cross-cultural projects. She received a Ph.D. in sociology from the University of Missouri at Columbia in 1979.

**Lori Leigh Osta** received a B.A. from the University of Central Florida and is currently a graduate student in public administration.

**Susan Pennell** has been the director of the Criminal Justice Research Division of the San Diego Association of Governments (SANDAG) since 1980. During her tenure at SANDAG, she has completed the following projects: Needs Assessment of Substance Abuse (San Diego County), The Impact of

Undocumented Persons on the Criminal Justice System in San Diego and El Paso, and Nationwide Study of the Guardian Angels—Community Crime Prevention. Currently, she is conducting several NIJ-funded projects, including an impact assessment of a multi-jurisdictional task force designed to reduce gang-related activity, an evaluation of a drug treatment program for probationers in intensive supervision, and an assessment of the costs and consequences of drug control strategies. Her areas of expertise include drugs and crime, gangs and the justice/community response, crime statistics, program evaluation, and survey design. She is also the manager of the Drug Use Forecasting (DUF) program in San Diego.

**Sudipto Roy** is currently assistant professor in the School of Public and Environmental Affairs at Indiana University Northwest. He received a Ph.D. in 1991 from Western Michigan University. Roy's primary research interests include juvenile restitution, victim-offender reconciliation programs, and electronic monitoring.

**Faye S. Taxman** is a principal associate with the Institute for Law and Justice in Alexandria, Virginia. Taxman has conducted numerous studies and evaluations of community correctional programs, including a pre-trial release program, a substance abuse program operating in a local jail, a diversion program for drug users, and a field experiment on the most effective strategy for the location and apprehension of probationers. She recently developed a series of materials on intermediate sanctions, systems, and programs for the National Institute of Justice. Previously, she was responsible for criminal justice planning and research for a local government, where she coordinated the implementation of several new intermediate sanction initiatives.

**Thomas C. Tomlinson** is an associate professor and former director of the graduate program in law enforcement administration at Western Illinois University. He is the author of *Reintegrating the Criminal Offender Through Community-Based Vocational Networks: Strategies from Four Projects*.

**Gennaro F. Vito** is a professor in the School of Justice Administration at the University of Louisville. He holds a Ph.D.

in public policy and management from Ohio State University. The co-author of five textbooks and several articles on program evaluation in criminal justice, Vito was named the 1991 Outstanding Educator by the Southern Criminal Justice Association. In addition to drug treatment in community corrections, his present research interests include policy analysis of capital punishment.

**Terry L. Wells** is a doctoral fellow at the George J. Beto Criminal Justice Center at Sam Houston State University. His research interests include community-based correctional programs and he is currently involved in studying attitudes and orientations of halfway house counselors. He has a B.S. in criminal justice and an M.P.A. from Appalachian State University.